Between
Two Evils

Between Two Evils

*The World War II Memoir
of a Girl in Occupied Warsaw
and a Nazi Labor Camp*

Lucyna B. Radlo

McFarland & Company, Inc., Publishers
Jefferson, North Carolina, and London

LIBRARY OF CONGRESS CATALOGUING-IN-PUBLICATION DATA

Radlo, Lucyna B., 1931–
    Between two evils : the World War II memoir of a girl in
occupied Warsaw and a Nazi labor camp / Lucyna B. Radlo.
        p.   cm.
    Includes index.

    ISBN 978-0-7864-4032-0
    softcover : 50# alkaline paper ∞

    1. Radlo, Lucyna B., 1931– —Childhood and youth.
2. Girls—Poland—Biography.   3. World War, 1939–1945—
Personal narratives, Polish.   4. Poland—History—Occupation,
1939–1945—Biography.   5. World War, 1939–1945—Poland—
Warsaw.   6. Concentration camps—Poland.   7. World War,
1939–1945—Refugees.   8. Brest (Belarus)—Biography.
9. Polish Americans—Biography.   10. Immigrants—United
States—Biography.   I. Title.
D811.5.R23   2009
940.53'161—dc22   2008044268
[B]

British Library cataloguing data are available

Cover photograph: Lucyna Radlo's first communion portrait after
the ceremony at St. Alexander Church on Three Crosses Square,
Warsaw, 7 June 1941

Manufactured in the United States of America

*McFarland & Company, Inc., Publishers
  Box 611, Jefferson, North Carolina 28640
  www.mcfarlandpub.com*

In writing my life story there were many bitter and tragic moments that simply had to be told, no matter how painful, but one of the enjoyable aspects of writing this memoir was the reliving of good times spent with my family and many friends. A great many individuals, to whom I am exceedingly grateful, inspired me to write these reflections and recollections, but most of all I wish to express my appreciation to my dearest ones: my beautiful and courageous mother, my never-to-be-forgotten late father, my caring and so very patient husband, and my loving children, who through all these years were willing to listen to the bits and pieces of the story of my life.

Table of Contents

Preface   1

1. War: Choosing Between Two Evils   3
2. Flashbacks   7
   Life at Krasnyy Dvor   10
   1914–1918   13
   Vyazma   14
   Return to Brest   16
   Life in Brest, 1921   18
   1931–1936   30
   Brest, 1936–1939   36
   Brest, 1939, on the Eve of World War II   50
3. Occupied Warsaw   52
4. Coping with Daily Life   66
5. Father Dies in Auschwitz   75
6. My Father, Feliks Stanislaw Kucharski   88
7. *Handel* (Black Marketing)   94
8. Warsaw Uprising, August 1, 1944   104
9. Forced Labor Camp   111
10. Kleine Maria Zell, Austria   120
11. Flight from the Soviets   123
12. Via Oxcart to Regensburg   133
13. Back to School   137
14. *Obshchina*   140

15. "Save Me, Tante Luzie!"   143

16. Live Fish and Dead Bones   150

17. "Quanta la Gusta"   156

18. A Girl's Best Friend   164

19. America Bound!   175

20. Nazareth   182

21. Little Russia, New Jersey   185

22. Work in the City   193

23. 1528 Second Avenue, New York City   198

24. Getting to Know the Radlos   206

25. Elizabeth Kucharska, My Mother   227

26. Married Life Begins   240

*Appendix: Who's Who in the Extended Romenko-
    Kovenko Family*   253

Index   255

Preface

Several different factors contributed to my writing this account of my childhood in Poland. I had always felt compelled to tell my story—the story of a war-torn childhood, a family displaced, forced labor, and the worst, the death of my beloved father in Auschwitz. When it came up in conversation with friends, or even with casual acquaintances, my story always surprised. This was mostly due, I think, to the contrast the traumatic war years had with the comfortable, cosmopolitan adult life I was now living. Americans, especially those who hadn't seen the war firsthand, had a hard time reconciling my care-free present with stories of running from the Soviets, hiding from Nazis, driving through battle-worn countries by ox-cart, or dealing on the black market. At times I myself had trouble believing my own memories. Returning to Warsaw some 40 years after the end of the war only added to the strange sense of unreality, for the city, nearly destroyed by the Nazis, had been entirely rebuilt by the Soviets and only a few memorable places remained.

Writing was a way of unburdening my soul as well as confirming my past. But there was another factor. My daughter gave me genealogical software and encouraged me to construct my family tree. After the Iron Curtain fell, I was able to retrieve genealogical information about my Russian and Polish relatives. But seeing the family tree with only the minimal facts—names, dates, perhaps a photo or two pertaining to each relative—left me dissatisfied. I wanted to fill them out. I'm fortunate to have been blessed with a very vivid visual memory, especially for minute, mundane details. If I experienced it, I remember it. But what of those I never knew? Coincidentally, at this time, my mother, 92 years old at the time, moved to live near me in California. I began to use our daily visits to collect all the missing information she could remember. From notes jotted on odd pieces of paper, I began to construct a family story encompassing my own.

This is the story of average people beset by the ravaging forces of political history. I was eight years old in 1939 when Nazi Germany invaded Poland and the Soviet Union occupied Brest, my mother's hometown. My immediate family had escaped the Soviets by exchanging homes with a family in

1

Warsaw, but this saving arrangement resulted in my father's arrest on charges of "aiding a Jew." I grew up in an atmosphere of uncertainty and fear, even as my resourceful relatives and neighbors attempted to find ways of living life as if normal. Again and again, however, there was disruption and loss. Recounting this odyssey, I was amazed at the resilience of my family and the very human ability to recover, even cheerfully, from misfortune.

1

War: Choosing
Between Two Evils

In a small way I first became a victim of World War II before it even started: in the spring of 1939 the inhabitants of the Polish city of Brzesc, including my parents, were so preoccupied with anxieties about and preparations for an impending war with Germany no one noticed that the sixteenth of May was my eighth birthday. A state of panic was beginning to develop in the city, with families stocking up on food and first-aid supplies, gathering family documents and photographs, clearing their basements for eventual use as bomb shelters, and digging foxholes in the open areas next to their dwellings. The city authorities also ordered proper bomb shelters to be built and the public was told to be on the alert for air raids. The military were more apparent than usual and civilian men were being drafted. My uncle, Misha Shlykov, who was in the reserve, had to leave for training with his reserve unit, where he became chief of food procurement. Zhorzh Vakul'chik, husband of Mother's sister Olga, was drafted into the army, but my father, who had invalid status because of wounds sustained in World War I, was excused from the draft, as was my uncle Nikolay Padukow, because he had only a part of one lung left after having had tuberculosis.

On the 1st of September 1939, at 4:45 A.M., Nazi Germany attacked Poland on land, at sea, and from the air. Brzesc (formerly, as well as after the war, known as Brest), an important railroad junction, was bombed from the air that same day, as were other cities in Poland. Sirens screamed loud and long. First we heard the bombs exploding and then we began hearing antiaircraft artillery firing nonstop. And there was some rifle fire, presumably firing at low-flying aircraft, but only now and then. Mother and I were the very first to run outside to the previously dug shelter (foxhole) that was more like an open grave site, except longer and just as deep, if not deeper. We jumped into it and pressed our bodies against its walls. The bombardment was so frightening and the rush to safety so hectic that Father, who was running behind us, was knocked down in the corridor of our apartment building. Neighbors, seeing him lying flat on the floor, quickly lay down beside him, thinking that was precisely the thing to do. Father shouted to them to get up and run for shelter. The chaos was such that no one knew what to do. Soon things became quiet; the bombing had been precise and quick. Mother and I tried to get out of our foxhole, but climbing out was impossible. Finally, Father came to our rescue. We later learned that one of the first bombs that fell on Brest fell on our "100,000 zloty house," a small commercial building that my parents had bought with lottery winnings, after I had helped select the winning numbers. The location of the building was to blame, it being right next to the railroad station, a prime target. Padukow's hotel, which was almost next door, did not sustain any damage. Fortunately, our property was empty of occupants, since they had all managed to find shelter away from the building. No one was killed or injured, but there was just a pile of rubble left. After the war, when we had resettled in the U.S., we made enquiries of the Belarussian government concerning restitution of the site where the building had stood at ulitsa Stetskevicha 4 in Brest and received the reply that the property had been nationalized by Soviet authorities in 1940 and that we now had no valid claim of ownership.

Now that the war was in full progress, the Nazis began taking one town after another. On September 26, 1939, Nazi-occupied Poland was renamed the General Government (*Generalna Gubernia*) of Occupied Poland, which became an administrative area not incorporated into Greater Germany, with *Obergruppenfuhrer* Hans Frank as General Governor. Quite a few of my parents' military friends perished in action in the early days of the war. On the very first day of the bombing in Brest, Father's friend, Major Zygmunt Rosinski, a battalion commander, while in a bunker, took off his helmet because of the very hot and humid weather and a piece of shrapnel hit his head, killing him instantly. His widow, "Dusia," *née* Tloczko, who was one of Mother's closest friends, and her daughter Krystyna later relocated to Warsaw. To survive, Dusia with two other friends opened a little eatery, whereas Krystyna was arrested and killed by the Germans. Dusia's mother, Janina Tloczko, or her sister, I don't recall which, had been a geography teacher at the *Gimnazjum im. Traugutta* in Brest.

The hospitals were quickly filled with wounded officers, soldiers, and civilians. Shlykov, serving at the rear of the fighting forces, was relatively safe and sound, and he was well fed, since much of the food for the front came through his command. However, his stay with his unit was cut short due to the fact that his wife Sonya could not cope alone with the huge responsibility of running their meat products business. She obtained permission for Misha to return home to continue to run their business so as to help assure a supply of meat for the civilian population. Poland was now being attacked from two sides: the Germans were taking over the western parts, while the Bolsheviks were approaching Brest from the East. My grandfather urged my parents, as a precaution, to leave the city and go into hiding on the outskirts of town. A Jewish acquaintance brought his wagon and took us to a nearby village, where the Padukows had a *dacha*. The horse-driven carriage, with us on it, crossed through the river, since the bridges had been bombed out and this was the only way to get to some areas. We stayed with the Padukows long enough to regain our composure and try to decide what to do next. At one point we felt it would be fairly safe for us to return to our apartment, if only for a short time. Upon arrival, my parents discovered that in our absence our housekeeper together with her boyfriend, who was a policeman, had robbed us of many things of substantial value. She was ordered by my parents to bring everything back or they would take court action against her. Actually, there probably was very little, if anything, that could have been done to make her bring the stolen goods back. But she became frightened and brought back what she and her friend had taken. Shortly after our return, Mr. Fuksman, our Jewish landlord, told us that he was concerned about the safety of his brother, who was living in German-occupied Warsaw. (Abram Fuksman, who lived at Hoza 19 in Warsaw, was co-owner of the Kresy Export Association of Agricultural Products.) Fuksman felt that in choosing whether to be under the Nazis or the approaching Russians, of the two evils, the Bolsheviks were considered to be less ominous for Jews than were the Nazis. Therefore, he suggested that we exchange apartments with his brother. We would leave our furniture in the apartment in Brest for his brother, and in like manner the brother would leave his Warsaw apartment fully furnished for us to move into. We, that is, my parents, were faced with the task of making a similar choice between two evils. Father was a native-born Pole and Roman Catholic, but Mother was a Russian brought up in the Orthodox Russian faith and all relatives on her side were White (i.e., anti–Soviet) Russians, most of whom were wary of remaining in Brest for fear of being subjected to arrests and persecutions, fears that, as it turned out, were well founded. My parents agonized for some time as to what decision to make, but finally decided to agree to Fuksman's offer and to move to Warsaw. We later had many occasions to doubt the wisdom of our choice, in view of what happened to Mother and myself and, in particular, to Father.

We immediately began looking for some way to travel to Warsaw. Normal means of transportation were not available because of the war, and we did not have an automobile at our disposal. We learned that Father's friend, Roman Rajpold, a well-known former cavalry officer who was the owner of a grain mill and a bakery, fearing for his own life, also wanted to leave Brest for the area west of the Bug River, which was occupied by Germans. Roman's wife decided to stay behind with their son, to watch over their enterprises. Having a wagon and horses, Roman suggested we join him for the journey west. And so, once more we were packed onto a wagon and started moving toward Warsaw. At the border, on the middle of the bridge between Brest and the Polish town of Terespol, we were met by my grandfather (Mother's father), who came with Mother's sister Olga and her son Yuriy ("Yura") to say good-bye. My parents offered to take Yura with us, and Olga at first agreed, but when the time came to part she changed her mind. She was pregnant with her second son Michael, and not knowing her husband's whereabouts, she could not let Yura go. And so we parted from her and my grandfather. It was very painful for me to see this brave, strong man cry. I never saw him again.

Nazi troops occupied Brest on September 15, 1939, and two days later the Germans agreed to pull back to the border separating Brest from occupied Poland, in accordance with the secret Ribbentrop-Molotov agreement between Germany and the Soviet Union, and a few days later Soviet troops occupied Brest.

2

Flashbacks

When we set out on our journey (our escape, really) from Brest (*Brzesc*) to Warsaw, I was only eight years old and barely understood what was happening, but I nevertheless felt strong and confused emotions, mostly of fear, sadness, and loss. I was shattered by the not clearly understood need to part, perhaps forever, with the many remarkable individuals I had learned to know and love on my mother's side of our extended family, who had remained in Brest, and my father's stepfather, who remained in Lodz and was the only member of the extended family remaining on my father's side. He died shortly after the war began. Many of the members of this extended family, as it turned out, played key roles in Mother's and my subsequent journey through the hell of World War II. (To help you understand the relationships of the many persons, I have attached an appendix listing their names and connections to each other.) In addition to my own recollections, I gathered much of the historical data on these people and places mostly from my mother and her two sisters, Aniuta and Sonya.

My great grandfather, Anton Romenko-Kovenko, together with his wife Tatyana and their four children, sometime in the 1880s came from Wielun' to manage a huge estate on the outskirts of Brest. Several years later, the owners decided to sell the property and offered it to Anton. Having a substantial amount of savings, Anton bought the property, which included houses, land, cattle, and farming equipment. Wielun's Bank was used to make the sale and transfer of the estate, which later became known as (in Russian) *Krasnyy Dvor* (*Czerwony Dwor* in Polish), which in English can be translated as Red Manor or Red Court. This area just outside Brest should not be confused with the town near Kaunas in Lithuania known as Raudonvaris, which translates to *Czerwony Dwor* in Polish. The confusion is chiefly due to the fact that the location in Raudonvaris was the site of a palatial estate that had been inherited in the early 19th century by a member of the Polish nobility, Count Benedykt Henryk Tyszkiewicz. During World War I the Tyszkiewicz estate was occupied by German forces and later in the war captured and demolished by troops of the Lithuanian army. In a fine display of parental generosity, once his children became of age, Anton gave portions of his estate to each of his sons. His daughter Sophia Antonovna Romenko-Kovenko got no part of Krasnyy Dvor but received a four-family house in the city of Brest, where she took up residence with her husband Jan and their three children, Mariya, Anton, and Yelena.

Anton's son, my grandfather, eventually (in about 1936), like his father, gave to his children when they reached maturity portions of the inheritance he had received. His daughter, Anna Nikitichna Padukow, kept the land she received and together with her husband, Nikolay Nikiforovich Padukow, built a house on the land and planted a vast orchard. Mariya Nikitichna Romenko-Kovenko divided land she had received from her father together with a small

portion of land at Wielun' she had received from her mother, Anastasiya Semenovna Janchuk Romenko-Kovenko, between her two daughters Nina Ivanovna Boguta Babich and Lidiya Ivanovna Boguta Prolisko. Mother, Yelizaveta Nikitichna Romenko-Kovenko (Kucharska, after she married), sold her share, receiving a down payment from the buyer, but because of World War II the bulk of the purchase price was never paid off. Pyotr Nikitich Romenko-Kovenko died before the division of the estate, as did Yelena Nikitichna Romenko-Kovenko Deviatnikova. Sofiya Nikitichna Romenko-Kovenko Shlykov retained her share, as did Olga Nikitichna Romenko-Kovenko Vakul'chik. The original homestead (*usad'ba*) consisting of a house and an unknown number of hectares of land, including barns and other structures, Nikita kept for himself, intending to turn the estate over later to his son Sergey. Bricks from a local brick plant were used to form the surface of the long road leading to the house. The sides of the

That's me, 5 years old, on the shoulder of my uncle, Mikhail Shlykov, at his dacha on the Muchawiec River, summer 1936.

Seated, left to right, Nikita Romenko (my maternal grandfather), Arkady Padukow (cousin), Nikifor Padukow (Arkady's grandfather); standing, Nikolay Padukow and Anna Padukow (Arkady's father and mother). About 1915.

road were lined with very tall, stately poplar trees. During World War II Nikita was forced to abandon the estate when it was taken over by the Soviet government, issuing Nikita a token "reimbursement" of 10,000 rubles. As a result of this action, Sergey was deprived of his future inheritance. Anton's other son, Nikolay, eventually gave the portion of Anton's estate he had received to one of his sons, Luka Nikolayevich Romenko-Kovenko, who later graduated from the Moscow Institute and became a forester. To his daughters Sofiya, Anna, and Yevgeniya, Nikolay gave houses, and his second son Vasiliy received the financing of higher education in Moscow. Anton's third son, Prokop Antonovich Romenko-Kovenko, sold his part of Anton's gift of land under loan agreements (*pod weksle*), as he needed to buy machinery and equipment for a newly opened business, but as he was often away from the property building roads (among them the main Warsaw-Moscow road), someone stole the loan documents and he never received the money he was owed. Prokop suspected, of all people, his good friend Nazarewicz. Prokop later moved to Wielun', where he bought property and where his wife also inherited some property from her parents. Until the time Prokop left for Wielun', all three brothers lived within a stone's throw of each other.

Life at Krasnyy Dvor

After my grandfather Nikita Romenko-Kovenko, who was born in Wielun' on March 12, 1869, received from his father Anton, in about 1892, a portion of *Krasnyy Dvor*, he married Anastasiya Semenovna Yanchuk, born in 1873, who came to Brest after receiving an inheritance in Wielun', a small town about 12 kilometers from Brest. Nikita and Anastasiya set up house in their newly acquired section of *Krasnyy Dvor*. The setting of their property was breathtaking. There were two rivers, Muchawiec and Bug, running through it. The forests, mostly coniferous trees, sheltering hoards of wonderful mushrooms and wild berries, wide stretches of unbroken, lavish groves, and vast meadows of fragrant grasses, would have been heaven for any landscape painter. Unfortunately, none of the Romenkos displayed any talent for painting. In addition to the ample, beautiful fields, the area also encompassed a marshland with coral and cranberries. It is no wonder the area, which was known as *Polesie* (Marsh), was often referred to in Polish poetry and song as *Czar Polesia* (the Enchantment of Polesie).

Anastasiya bore Nikita nine children: Anna, who was born February 13, 1893, Sergey, who was born September 13, 1893, Mariya, born in 1894, Fiokla (died in infancy), Pyotr, born in 1900, Sofiya, born August 18, 1902, Yelena, born in 1904, Yelizaveta, born November 30, 1906, and Olga, born June 24, 1910. Most siblings got along quite well with each other, although Mariya and Anna had their ups and downs, Anna, apparently, being mostly at fault. Sergey, just a few months younger than Anna, was a favorite storyteller for the younger children. He often made toys for them and the youngsters simply adored their older brother. Nevertheless, harmony was not always 100 percent. The siblings liked to pick on and tease each other. Yelizaveta, often telling tales on her sisters, got the nickname *lyska yabida* (tattle-tale). On the other hand, they did not need much to be happy. All in all, the Romenko children had endless opportunities for imagination and entertainment. During the snow season, there was lots of sledding and sleigh riding, as well as skating on the frozen Muchawiec River, and ice fishing. In the spring there were many activities on the estate in which the children liked to participate. Come summer and fall, swimming was the most popular. During harvest time they "helped" eagerly, while playing in the hay. In general, there was lots of fun, even without having many toys. The children were very inventive and never bored.

The Romenko clan was a happy one. Life was prosperous and peaceful, until Anastasiya contracted typhoid fever and died in 1910 in the prime of her life at age 36, leaving Nikita with eight children, the youngest child being only a few months old. Anastasiya was buried in the *Brestskoye Trishinskoye Kladbishche* (Brest cemetery). Sofiya and Yelena contracted typhoid fever as well, but miraculously did not succumb to it. The loss of his wife really changed the life of Nikita. He was heartbroken and almost suicidal. He knew many lady friends, including one in particular who happened to be the widow of a general, who were anxious to marry the handsome and well-to-do widower. Not being able to cope with all the small children while at the same time running the estate, out of necessity rather than love, he chose in about 1911 to marry a widow, whom he met at a friend's house in a nearby town, where she worked as a private nurse in a local hospital. It was an arranged marriage. Within that same year there were three weddings in the Romenko family: Nikita's, and those of his two daughters, Anna and Mariya. Ustin'ya Danilovna was 52, Nikita 42. He chose her thinking primarily of the welfare of his young children. He felt they might get better care from an older stepmother. Ustin'ya had a twenty-five-year-old son, who upon hearing that his mother was planning to remarry, told her he would disown her if she did. After her marriage to Nikita, her son came only once for a visit and nobody ever saw him again. Ustin'ya filled more the role of a housekeeper at the busy household rather than that of stepmother. She wore black clothing, long skirts almost sweeping the floors, and a head covering. Having worked at the hospital, she had learned some home remedies, like using leeches (*pijawki*) for high blood pressure, drinking different herbs for this or that, and cupping people's chests or backs with cupping glass (vacuum cups) (*stawiac banki*) as a cold remedy. Her health was failing and soon severe arthritis set in, crippling her back and leaving her with her body bent over. Although she was devoted to Nikita and was good to the children, the younger children feared her, not because of her behavior but mostly because of her looks, since she resembled a witch. I recall that often, after accomplishing her seemingly endless tasks around the house, she would stretch out her crippled body on a large benchlike surface behind the huge tile stove. She said that the warmth would help her bones to get straight. Very often she would take a catnap there, after which, she felt refreshed and all set to continue her chores. Once, when there was no one in the house to fetch some well water, Ustin'ya decided to get a pail of water herself. The children were playing nearby and heard a frantic voice coming out of the deep well. When they looked, they saw Ustin'ya hanging onto the pail, trying not to fall in any farther. One of the children ran for help to the fields where some estate hands were working. It is not clear to me how they managed to get Ustin'ya out. Despite being scratched all over, bruised, and wet, she was otherwise not harmed, except that she was still trembling, thinking that she could have drowned. In her very crippled, weak body there was a strong and very hard-working woman. Only later on, when grown up, did the children give their stepmother, whom they called "Machekha," lots of overdue credit for her hard work.

Yelizaveta, my mother, called Liza by everyone, being of frail health, had a certain way with her father. Despite being a very fair person, he could not help showing favoritism toward his second youngest daughter. When still quite young, she was quite anemic, and at the suggestion of the family doctor Nikita made sure that his daughter would get milk almost straight from the cow. Yelizaveta would not touch any milk unless it came from a cow that had been milked by her father. Poor Nikita often would get up at night, go to the barn, milk a cow, and bring it still warm to his daughter. When Yelizaveta was bedridden for a longer period of time, he allowed her to keep a tamed fox that the workers had caught for her to play with. The fox was always tied down in the attic for the night, but unfortunately one morning he was found strangled on his chain. Another incident took place involving Yelizaveta's pet pony. The pony one day was horsing around in the vegetable garden. He must have lain down on his back and kept rolling himself back and forth, from side to side, ending up in the furrows of the vegetable patch. This sort of rolling is a horse's favorite way of scratching its back. The furrows being quite deep, he soon became trapped and could not get to his feet. Fortunately, while struggling, he was noticed by the workers. They came to his rescue by tying him with ropes and pulling him out of his entrapment and onto his feet. He galloped away, happy to be out of his predicament.

Next to Krasnyy Dvor, there was an estate, which Nikita was leasing from a *Hrabianka*, a Polish noble woman. Nikita used to spend a goodly amount of time at this estate, very often taking his favorite daughter Yelizaveta with him. He thought that the location of this estate was better than that of Krasnyy Dvor, which was located near the river, and thus too damp for his frail daughter. (This Polish woman was a widow who, according to rumors, had been a lover of the Czar Alexander the First, and bore him an illegitimate son. This son had been an ardent horseback rider. At the entry to their estate there was a huge stone, which bore the inscription that the son, riding his horse, had been thrown off the horse onto this stone, which killed him.)

In 1911, the year Nikita remarried, the first Romenko-Kovenko sibling married. After Anna's marriage to Nikita Nikolayevich Padukow, the newly-weds lived in Biala Podlaska, where Nikolay held a teacher's position. They took Anna's sisters, Lena and Sofia, to live with them, in order for the two girls to attend the local school. The arrangement did not last long, as Nikolay, being a strict disciplinarian, seemed too harsh for the two young girls. They pleaded to be returned to their father. Their wish was granted, and since their older siblings attended school in Brest, the very young ones had a ball growing up on the estate, playing with the children of workers or with children from nearby Zakiy, Pugachovo, and Kamienitsa Zhirovetska. Later they formed friendships with the children of people stationed at the Brest *Poligon*, an army training center, which had family quarters and a clubhouse.

1914–1918

In the years from 1914 to 1918, during World War I, heavy fighting took place on Belorussian soil. One day in June or July of 1915, during the busy harvest time, while Nikita Antonovich Romenko-Kovenko was supervising his workers in the fields and his children were at home, a Tsarist officer on a horse showed up at the house, looking for the owner of the Krasnyy Dvor estate. He came to deliver a notice of imminent evacuation, stipulating that by the next day the Romenko family and all other nearby occupants were to leave the region, as the enemy was advancing into their territory. Nikita, on reading the notice, immediately gave an order to his many workers to submerge all farm equipment in the River Muchawiec, which flowed through the property. They also dug a huge hole in the ground to bury belongings that could not be taken along. For the cattle that Nikita had to leave behind, the authorities paid him 3,000 rubles in gold, which was hidden in the false bottom of a jug, guarded at all times and carried by hand by different members of the family throughout the long journey out of the area. They were, however, permitted to take horses, one cow, some pigs, and some chickens. Finally, when the wagons were loaded with their belongings and the family was ready to leave, the estate was set on fire, so that there would be nothing left for the approaching Germans. Their aim was to march east, so as to arrive in Moscow in order to join the older son Sergey, who, together with his cousin Vasiliy (son of Nikolay Romenko-Kovenko), was studying architecture at the university. Their itinerary was soon altered. At Kobryn they had to abandon practically everything, and with only what they could carry they boarded a cattle train, ending up riding in and on top of the engine car. The escaping Romenko family consisted of Nikita, his second wife (Machekha), Sonya, Yelizaveta, Pyotr, Lena, Olga, and Anyuta with her son Arkadiy. Anyuta's husband, Nikolay Padukow, a teacher by profession, was in the army and serving at the front, stationed in Dvinsk. The oldest sibling Mariya, married to Ivan Boguta, stayed behind in Brest with her husband and their daughter Nina. The older son Sergey, mentioned above, was still in Moscow. As the train continued east it was stop and go for most of the trip. The railroad was jammed, the roads were crowded with fleeing people, and with cattle everywhere, it was a very chaotic situation. During one of the many stops, at the Minsk station, Lena got off the train to fetch some water for tea. The station was crowded with trains, civilians, soldiers, officers and railroad personnel. The queues for water were many and very long. While Lena was still waiting to fill her container, the train, one of many at the station, got the signal to depart and it slowly began leaving the station. Lena ran toward the train, trying to jump back onto it. An officer standing nearby, wanting to save her from a fall, grabbed her and pulled her back down onto the platform. Since there was no way of getting in touch with the train that had just departed, the officer took Lena to an orphanage and left some money with her. She must have been 10 or 11 years old. (She was the shortest of the six sisters and the only brunette.) The family, unaware of the fact that Lena had been left behind, noticed her absence later down the line. Instead of continuing their journey to Moscow as planned, the family got off at the next stop, in Vyazma, in order to search for the missing Lena.

Vyazma

After leaving the train during their evacuation from Krasnyy Dvor, the Romenko family stayed in a little village near Vyazma, in a hut without floors or indoor plumbing, but at least there was a cooking facility and they had a roof over their heads. Nikita promptly bought a cow in order to have milk and butter for the children. A short time later, to try to improve their living conditions, Nikita moved his clan to an industrial area in the Vyazma outskirts, near a hospital, jail, and factories. The owners of one of the factories, the Lutovs, let the Romenkos use their house basement as their new quarters. They settled into this basement, which they felt was an improvement over the cold and damp hut in the village. After all, they were now near a town and civilization, and Nikita could focus on the search for his missing daughter. The new arrangement, however, did not last long. The basement, after prolonged rains, flooded badly, and the family was forced to leave. This time the Shchukins, owners of the *liteynyy zavod* (a steel foundry) who lived two houses down from the Lutovs, allowed the Romenko family to move into their house, giving them two rooms. Anyuta, Arkadiy, and Yelizaveta occupied a small room, in which there already lived a 100-year-old woman. She was a relative of the landlord. The old woman was filthy and infested with lice. Sonya and Anyuta bathed her in a portable tub and applied kerosene to her hair to get rid of the lice. Eventually, the old woman was moved into the kitchen, where she slept on the landing behind a tile stove. The rest of the family occupied the other room.

During this time, while in Vyazma, Nikita used some of his gold coins to buy another cow, and then he rented from the Ivanovs a store nearby and opened a grocery outlet. The store was started primarily to provide the large family with a livelihood, and also to have a supply of fresh vegetables, dairy products and meat. Apparently, all the siblings, except Sergey who was still in Moscow in the army after graduating as an architect, and Mariya back in Brest, had a tough time adjusting to their new lifestyle. Everyone had to pitch in. Soon, Nikolay Padukow was given leave from his army unit at the front and was able to join his wife and Arkady in Vyazma. He, Anyuta and Arkady were given one-room quarters at the Shchukin's factory. Their daughter Taisya was born there, but shortly thereafter died of smallpox. She was buried in the Vyazma cemetery. Shortly after he had arrived, Nikolay left the family once more. This time his mission was to visit various orphanages in search of Lena. Finally, back in Minsk, he was able to locate her. Upon meeting with her, contrary to everyone's worries about this poor, abandoned child, it turned out that Lena was having a good time with the many orphans and had had no time to miss her siblings. Nevertheless, when she saw her Uncle Kolya (who actually was Lena's brother-in-law), she wanted to leave with him immediately. Since it was already late in the evening, he promised to come back for her the next day, with a new dress and coat to bring her back home in. Next day, however, when the time came to say good-bye to all her friends at the orphanage and especially to the woman in charge whom she had become so fond of, Lena began crying bitterly, not wanting to leave her new extended family behind. Eventually, after a very dramatic departure scene, Kolya and Lena left for Vyazma, where, after the long eight or nine months of separation, she was reunited with her father and the other siblings. For a while she seemed to be overjoyed to be home, but once things got back to normal, she begged to return to the orphanage saying, "I want to go home." On many occasions she showed a preference for her friends rather than her siblings. She also missed the orphanage supervisor, who most likely had become a mother figure for her. The Romenkos ended up living at Vyazma for three years. At times it was a difficult arrangement for everyone, but at least they were housed and had an income from the store. The children attended school, helped with house chores, had plenty of milk, butter and other fresh produce, and they had each other's company.

Kolya soon had to go back to his unit in Dvinsk, but eventually returned again to join Anyuta and their son Arkady. Shortly after their return to Dvinsk, their son Georgiy was born. Once again there were four of them.

While in Vyazma, a well-to-do childless couple, friends of Nikita, became very fond of Yelizaveta, whom they called "Lizochka." They showered her with gifts, took her places, and on many occasions she was allowed to spend nights and days at their house. They virtually adopted her. At one point the couple got Nikita's permission to allow Liza to accompany them on a trip. Liza soon found herself on a train bound for Moscow. But shortly into the journey, she got cold feet, became hysterical and demanded to be taken back home. An officer, a friend of the couple, agreed to return with Liza back to Vyazma. For some reason, Liza felt she was being abducted and became frightened.

It was in Vyazma that Liza contracted a mysterious ailment. Her pretty face was covered with ugly dark brown-black warts. She was taken to different specialists and they could not find a remedy for it, presumably not knowing what caused the warts. She was seen by different healers. One told her father to tie strings on as many sticks as the number of warts she had and then at a certain time of a special night to throw these sticks over a fence. The belief was that a spirit would take the warts away. There were over a hundred sticks, one for each wart. Unfortunately, this hocus-pocus failed, as did all other remedies. Then one day Nikita was visited by a *fel'dsher* (doctor's aide), who gave him a simple ointment to apply to the warts. After just a few applications, the warts dried out and, as mysteriously as they had appeared, they one day disappeared, leaving Liza's pretty face with a peachy, flawless complexion for years to come.

Return to Brest

In March 1918, under the Treaty of Brest-Litovsk, the independent state of Belorussia was established under German occupation, so the Romenko family decided to return to Brest. Once again the family, together with its menagerie, boarded a cattle train, heading west. During their return trip they witnessed many atrocities committed by the Bolsheviks. One day, when the family was attending a church service, some Red Army soldiers rounded up the parishioners, stole all the church icons and destroyed the altars and virtually all the interior of the church. They tied the priest to a military wagon and dragged him away. There were massive robberies, rapes, and killings. Then, just before the Romenko family reached the newly formed German/Bolshevik border, the Russians took their cows and other animals before allowing them to continue on to Brest. When they came to the other side of the border, the Germans ordered that all the evacuees get off the train in order to put everyone in quarantine. But, thanks to Nikita's intervention and a hefty bribe, they were permitted to remain on the train and to continue on to Brest. Upon their arrival in their deserted and almost completely destroyed hometown, not sure what to do next, Nikita turned to his sister for assistance. "Lyolya" Lapchinska, who had arrived in Brest shortly before them, graciously offered to share her house with the many newly arrived family members. While Nikita and Petya (a nickname for Pyotr Romenko-Kovenko) would go back and forth to Krasnyy Dvor, at times living there for lengthy periods trying to restore the estate, the children were getting used to living in town at their aunt's house and going to school. All the surrounding villages had sustained terrible devastation. Most of the properties were either destroyed or burned down. At Krasnyy Dvor, the many things that had been buried could not be found. They had apparently been discovered and stolen, either by locals or by the Germans. The submerged farming equipment, however, was still at the bottom of the river. The main mansion, originally built of stone, stood roofless, and tall trees were growing inside it. All the other buildings, structures, and barns had been burned by the Russians when they gave the order to evacuate.

Finally, almost three months later, when the house had been reasonably restored, Nikita, his wife, and Petya returned to Krasnyy Dvor permanently, while the other members of the family moved to Brest once more. This time Nikita had rented from a pharmacist a large house that gave much promise. After a renovation, the basement was transformed into a *kolbasno-masterskaya* (meat products mini-factory). The ground floor facing the street became the retail store and the floor above that was turned into ample family quarters. It was back to communal living, with everyone having a job to perform. The older kids, who attended school, when at home had to look after their younger siblings as well as do house chores. Kolya Padukow supervised the store, the operation of which was organized and financed by Nikita. Sonya provided assistance during the day and attended evening courses at night. Kolya, a strict taskmaster, took everything in his hands and even Nikita, who had provided the means for the store, equipment, and inventory, etc., had very little to say. The store crew was an unhappy bunch.

At this point it had become clear that Sergey, despite his father's pleas, had decided to remain permanently in Moscow and become a professional army officer.

Nikita once again settled into maintaining his estate, rebuilding, replanting orchards, sowing many fields, and harvesting new crops. His dream was to bring his family eventually back to where they belonged. His wife, crippled by severe arthritis, was busy keeping house. But just when things seemed to be getting back to normal, Nikita's family was struck with three tragedies. One day when Liza was babysitting, rocking to sleep Padukow's little son Georgiy, who was sick, the infant died in her arms. Then in January 1919, when the Bolsheviks took Brest and the proclamation of the Belorussian Soviet Socialist Republic was being announced, Petya, who had just finished high school and was eager to continue his education, was ordered by the Bolshevik authorities into forced labor, lifting heavy items and transporting them on horse-drawn wagons. To add to the harsh living conditions, no housing or food was provided. He sometimes ate raw vegetables taken straight from the fields along the way. He contracted dysentery and, unable to work, was allowed to go home. While Liza was at his bedside, he died. Both little Georgiy and Petya were buried next to Anastasiya at the *Bretskoye Trishinskoye Kladbishche* (cemetery). During the same period, Nikita's brother Nikolay Antonovich was stricken with blood poisoning, which started in his leg. Doctors, trying to save his life, amputated his leg, but he could not be saved and soon died. Ironically, some years later, when Nikita himself had an advanced case of blood poisoning in his arm, the doctors likewise wanted to amputate his arm, but Nikita preferred to take the risk and did not agree to the amputation. In his case, he guessed well; the poisoning was stopped and his arm was saved. Some years after, when Yelizaveta (my mother) had a ruptured appendix, she was taken to the army hospital, where she was operated on by Lt. Col. Leonard Szmurlo, M.D. In this case, the surgery went well, and the patient was sent home. But soon after, Liza had a great craving for something salty and spicy. She found a barrel full of salted herrings, one of her favorite snacks, and couldn't resist eating more than one, skin, head, and all. She became violently sick and had to be rushed back to the hospital with a ruptured incision. Because of this the recuperation time was much longer. Dr. Szmurlo was one of several department heads at the Garrison Hospital, which in 1919 had 400 beds, and which in 1921 became Regional Hospital No. IX.

Another relative of Nikita's, his nephew Luka Romenko, with his daughter Nina (who later became the wife of the Reverend Lukashuk), returned by horse-drawn carriage to Brest. Before he started his trek back home, he hid his gold coins in the wheels of the wagon. Luka's wife and a second daughter Katya followed them later. While in Russia, they made their living by making candy. Upon their return to Brest, they continued making handmade candy, which they called *krowki* (little cows).

Life in Brest, 1921

On March 18, 1921, still another change took place in the status of Brest, when the Treaty of Riga gave Poland the western sections of Belorussian territory. New borders were put into effect. Brest became a Polish city. The Romenko family was divided. Sergey Romenko remained in what became the USSR, as did most of the extended Shlykov and Padukow families. However, Anna and Nikolay Padukow (married in 1911), with their sons Arkady and Sergey, were now living in the city of Brest. So were Mariya and Ivan Boguta (married in 1911) with their children Nina, Lydia and Leonid, and Sofiya (Sonya) and Mikhail (Misha) Shlykov (married January 25, 1922) and their infant son Igor. Lena, Yelizaveta (my mother), and Olga were living in Brest at Krasnyy Dvor with their father Nikita and stepmother Ustin'ya. Pyotr died in 1920 and was buried next to his mother.

At this time, Lena, because of her beautiful contralto voice, was urged by a music conservatory professor (in Minsk?) to be permitted by her father to enter the conservatory (free of charge) in order to train her voice, so that she could become an opera singer. Her father, although aware of his daughter's potential, nevertheless wouldn't give the permission. Perhaps the agony he went through when Lena was lost and away for eight months reminded him of what it would be like without her once more.

In Brest, Nikita helped the Padukows (Anna and Nikolay) establish a grocery store and also financed the purchase of a prime location, a city block parcel with a small structure that included three or four stores that were rented. On this parcel the Padukows eventually built a hotel, premises for stores, and their own residence. Padukow had become ill and, following the family doctor's advice, they built a little wooden house behind the hotel in order to be in a healthier environment than they were in the brick building. When that failed to help, Dr. Korol suggested to Kolya that he spend some time in the mountains in Zakopane. When that also didn't help, Dr. Korol insisted that the family should go to Italy for the winter season. Kolya had a serious case of tuberculosis. Anyuta, Kolya, and their young son Sergey left for San Remo, with Kolya being carried onto the train on stretchers. A month or so later Yelizaveta followed them, in order to take care of Sergey, since Anyuta was busy helping Kolya to recuperate. Kolya recovered, but the TB left him with only a very small part of one lung functioning. Yet when he came back to Brest, he was well enough to run his hotel, build a *dacha* and plant a huge orchard around it. The only evidence of his bout with TB was that he walked lopsided, which was quite noticeable. Dr. Pawel Korol, in addition to being the doctor for our whole family, was also a close family friend. A Russian and a resident of Brest, he was chief of the private Polesie Clinic of Medical Specialists (*Poleska Lecznica Lekarzy Specjalistow*), as well as president of the local branch of the Russian Good Deeds Society (*Rosyjskie Towarzystwo Dobroczynnosci*). In the 1920s for a few years he was also a deputy in the parliament. In January of 1937, a cavalry officer, Captain Sadowski, who was madly in love with Dr. Korol's beautiful wife, shot her and then committed suicide on the porch of the Korol's handsome villa. This tragedy was followed by many more that befell the Korol family, which in many ways was typical of what was happening to the families of many whom we knew. When Brest was occupied by the Soviets in September 1939, Dr. Korol, as a major in the Polish Army Reserves, was almost immediately arrested and later presumed killed by the Soviets in Katyn, as were so many other Polish officers. His sister was sent to Kazakhstan, where she died of starvation. His sons, Mikolaj and Igor, escaped from the Bolsheviks to Poland, but in 1946 Mikolaj was arrested by the Soviet authorities and deported to Siberia, where he spent about six years in one of the many gulags. When he returned home, his health was totally ruined and he soon died. Igor, who followed in his father's footsteps and became a doctor, specializing in pulmonary diseases and radiology, was living in Czestochowa, Poland, when in 1949 he was arrested by the U.B. (Communist Poland's Security Service) and deported to the Soviet Union. In Moscow, at the Lublyanka Prison, he was accused of anti–Soviet activities during World War II and after nine months of harsh interrogations, received a death sentence, which later was commuted to 25 years' hard labor in a gulag near Irkutsk, Siberia. While serving his sentence at the isolated and heavily guarded gulag, he attributed his skill as a doctor, which was often needed by the guards, for saving his life. In 1957 Igor was released from the gulag, "rehabilitated," and returned to Poland. His first wife Janina (Sosnowska), after five years of waiting for his return and not knowing his whereabouts, decided to start a new life without him. In 1960 Igor married Nelly, daughter of Prince Leszczynski-Trojekarow, whose estate "Ruda" was about 35 kilometers from Brest. Members of Nelly's family met fates similar to those of Igor's family. Her mother died tragically during the Warsaw Uprising and her brother Mira (Miroslaw) in 1948 was sentenced in the Soviet Union to 25 years in a gulag. He was eventually released, returned to Poland and died in late 1990. In 1996, Igor and Nelly went to visit their hometown of Brest. They found Dr. Pawel Korol's villa on ul. Zygmuntowska in pretty good shape and now serving as a preschool. They couldn't locate any familiar prewar faces. They found the Ruda estate completely in ruins, which made a devastating impression on them, although they were met rather warmly by its neighbors.

In 1998, I was able to locate Dr. Korol's son Igor, who lived together with his second wife Nelly in Warsaw. He informed me about the fate of various mutual friends from Brest times. Unfortunately, most of them perished during World War II, or have died since. He remembered my many relatives as well as Mother. Soon my letters were not answered and through a mutual friend, I recently found out that Dr. Igor Korol had died, leaving Nelly in despair. In her declining years, she was left to spend the rest of her life in solitude.

Sonya and Mikhail Shlykov, being newly married, very young, and with no profession, also needed financial support. Nikita bought them a store and a place to produce meat products. The *wedliniarnia* (meat production establishment) was run by Sonya and Mikhail almost across the street from the Padukow's grocery store. There were six children in the Shlykov family: Ivan (*Iwan* in Polish), Mikhail ("Misha," *Michal* in Polish), Vera (*Wiera*), Lidya (Lydia in English, *Lidja* in Polish), Vladimir (*Wlodzimierz*) and Yevgeniya ("Zhenya"). Vladimir Shlykov, who had stayed with his parents in Moscow, tried to join his two older brothers in Brest. But, being a Russian, he had a hard time getting into a Polish University, so with his brothers' help he had left for Yugoslavia, where he was able to get his higher education. When he

My aunt, Sonya Romenko (later Shlykov), in Brest, 1920.

"Bar at the Barrel," Brest, 1936. Marusya von Brevern (in white), at her left, Serafima Chwiedczuk, and at extreme right, Misha Shlykov.

came back to Brest, Sonya was sick with an acute respiratory problem. Again, the family physician, Dr. Korol, was called to the rescue. He suggested she take a long airplane ride, thinking that a rapid change of altitude might do her some good. She was afraid of flying so did not follow his advice. Not being able to get better, she was forced to quit her job at their business. Vladimir's return was a godsend in helping his brother. Volodya was promptly put to work. Unfortunately, while the brothers were in charge, the business went quickly downhill and Misha was forced to declare bankruptcy. Nikita once more had to bail out his not very industrious son-in-law. Many different enterprises followed, some more successful than others. Some years later, the Shlykovs, together with their friends, the von Breverns, attempted to run a restaurant, which they named *Bar Pod Beczka* (At the Sign of the Barrel). Although at first Nikita had many doubts about Misha's capabilities, as time went by he grew very proud of the Shlykovs' achievements.

In the beginning of 1923, Misha's sisters Vera and Lidya came to Brest from Moscow. Vera also brought her very young son Boris. Vera was married, but free at the same time. Her husband had left her and was living with another woman in Gallipoli. Their visit was about one year in duration. Their parents, Vasiliy Filipovich Shlykov and Aleksandra Georgiyevna Charynskaya Shlykov, stayed behind in Moscow, as did the third daughter Yevgeniya and the youngest son Vladimir. The two sisters, Vera and Lidya, while in Brest, lived in a house

My mother, Yelizaveta (Liza) Romenko (later Kucharska), second from left, with members of a school musical, Brest, 1926.

next door to Ivan Shlykov, who at that time was married to Marta. Marta came from a very wealthy family, which owned a factory in Luck. She had four brothers and a sister. Their mother was German and in addition to Russian, Polish and German also spoke Czech. The Romenko family, primarily the siblings, spent many wonderful and memorable holidays at Marta's parents' estate. One of Marta's brothers, Edward, was Liza's suitor. But his younger brother said to Liza one day, "If you break up and will not marry my brother, I would like to marry you." Liza (my mother) eventually broke up with the older brother, but she also did not settle for the younger one. (I'll have more to say later about Liza's numerous romances!) The others also had romantic adventures. Vera was very fond of a young man, but was too shy to contact him. One day she had a brilliant idea and told Liza to dress up in a servant's dress, apron, and cap and deliver a letter to the young man. Liza eagerly complied, but when she arrived at the fellow's house, he recognized her as one of the sisters from the Romenko estate and burst into laughter, calling her by her name. Liza, very much embarrassed, explained her mission, handed him Vera's letter and left in a hurry.

The Romenko girls, along with Vera and Lidya Shlykov, were taken under Marta Shlykov's wings. She being the oldest, married, and very well off, was their leader and mentor. Ivan, her husband, being a successful engineer, was constantly out of town supervising various construction sites. Marta, perhaps out of boredom, needed diversions and she spent many happy moments with the Romenko sisters, whether at their estate or just being in their company.

Liza Romenko (in a borrowed Polish officer's uniform) with other costume party revelers. Those I can identify are (standing at left) Ivan Shlykow, and, standing at right, his wife Marta. About 1929.

Krasnyy Dvor was next door to a large *poligon*, an army training facility that had a fabulous, for those times, officers' club, also known as *Bialy Palac* (the White Palace). Many informal picnics, as well as quite formal balls took place there, so there was always something going on that the girls could attend and at which they were always welcome. Nikita Romenko introduced Lidya to a *rotmistrz* (captain of Polish cavalry). She fell in love, but the suitor was slow to propose. He may have been hesitant because she was Russian, while he was a Pole. When her time came to return to Moscow, she had already left in the morning and was gone when the officer arrived later that day in order to propose. He rushed to the border to catch up with her, but by the time he arrived she had already crossed it. Later on, she married the border guard that she had encountered that day. They had one daughter, Ludmilla Mentelhof. (Eventually, Ludmilla dropped her father's last name and took her grandfather's name Shlykov, thus, after she married she was known as Ludmilla Shlykova Lobachev.) It was Ludmilla who eventually helped brother Vladimir Shlykov cross the Brest border.

The ladies had many fun times, but one day things went badly. Marta,

Left to right, Ivan Shlykow, his wife Irina, Sonya Shlykov and her husband Mikhail (Ivan's brother), Warsaw, 1943. Ivan preferred the Polish spelling of his surname; Mikhail, the Russian.

Vera, Lidya and Liza were going to the theater, where a new group of out-of-town artists was to perform. As they were approaching the theater they saw Marta's husband Ivan coming out of a hotel, which was next door to the theater. With him was Kilczewska, the leading actress of the visiting theatrical group. Marta, seeing her husband and realizing that he must have been spending

Standing, left to right, Sonya Shlykov and her sister-in-law, Vera Shlykov, the latter visiting from Moscow. In the baby carriage, Igor (Sonya's son) and Boris (Vera's son). Brest, 1923.

Liza Romenko (left) and Lidya Shlykov in Brest, 1923.

time with the actress rather than "being out of town working," immediately returned home. She packed a few personal things and the next morning departed for her parents' house in Luck, leaving Ivan behind. Soon after, they divorced and Ivan married Kilczewska. One day, when he arrived home unexpectedly, he found his new wife reading a letter from home. It was in Yiddish. Soon Ivan's second wife disappeared with an actor and never came back. Their marriage had lasted five years. Ivan obtained a divorce, and soon after was introduced to a married woman, Irina Raubel. Later he even carried on his romance with his new lover while living in our Hoza street apartment in Warsaw. As much as I loved Ivan I could not stomach his new love, and we objected to their rendezvous at our house. One day, Ivan's future father-in-law came and sternly insisted that Ivan marry his daughter, who was still married to another man. The Raubels finally got a divorce and Ivan then married Irina. During their marriage, on and off, Irina's son and daughter would live with them. Eventually, when Irina's ex-husband became seriously ill, he moved in with them as well. Ivan's "extended family" stayed together until Raubel's death, which was soon followed by Irina's passing. Ivan, free again, met Anna ("Hanka"), a granddaughter of a Polish general, who also had once lived in Brest. This marriage was fated to be "until death do us part." Ivan died first. Ivan loved children very much, but as far as we know he never fathered a child.

Ivan Shlykov, one could say, played an important role in Liza's life. Having two brothers in Brest and living there while married to Marta or while building this or that throughout Poland, Ivan kept returning to Brest. And so

Left to right, Mrs. Niemierwrzycki, Liza and Sonya Romenko examining a tree stump in the Bialowieska Primeval Forest, about 1929.

it happened that when he was contracted to build a new *ubezpieczalnia* (a health center similar to a *Krankenversicherungsanstalt* in Germany) in Hajnowka near Brest, he visited Krasnyy Dvor, bringing along some friends, Mr. and Mrs. Niemierwrzycki and their little dog, as well as the director of the project, Feliks Kucharski. And thus, this Polish bachelor, who eventually became my father, was introduced to the Romenko family. After a huge party, the visitors eventually left, but when they arrived back at Puszcza Bialowieska, they realized that they had inadvertently left the dog behind at Krasnyy Dvor. Feliks was more than happy to go back and fetch the pooch. Although Liza was engaged to someone else at the time, she fell in love with Feliks, thirteen years her senior. After many visits by Feliks to Krasnyy Dvor, Liza broke off her engagement to the other fellow, and so, after six weeks of courtship, Liza and Feliks were engaged to be married. Mother, being Russian Orthodox, needed the special permission of the Archbishop in order to be married to my Catholic father in a Catholic church. After it was granted, they were married by Dziekan Ks. Kazimierz Bukraba (who later became the Bishop of Pinsk) at the Holy Cross Church (*Parafialny Kosciol pod wezwaniem Podwyzszenia Sw. Krzyza*) on ul. Unii Lubelskiej in Brest. In agreeing to conduct the ceremony, Monsignor Bukraba made the stipulation that any eventual children would be brought up in the Catholic faith. The church ceremony was followed by a reception at the Shlykovs' house.

Winter in Warsaw, 1934. Left to right, Ivan Shlykov, Kazimierz Niemierwrzycki, Mikhail Shlykov.

Since Hajnowka, where Feliks was working, was on the outskirts of the famous *Bialowieska Puszcza* (National Forest) and close to Brest, it was no problem for Liza to stay in close touch with her family. *Bialowieska Puszcza* is a Polish (and Belorussian) national heritage. It is one of the largest surviving areas of primeval mixed forests in Europe. The age of most of the trees is

160–180 years, with a height of 32–35 meters, but one can find record-breaking 200 to 350-year-old pines. Being able to live in that fabulous environment, the newlyweds were happy as larks. My father was an administrator for the health care system. He was *Dyrektor Ubezpieczalni* (Director of Insurance Clinics) in charge of establishing hospitals in new areas of the country. Eventually, the health center in Hajnowka was established and running well and Feliks was sent to set up another health center in Tomaszow Mazowiecki. Then came Sierpc, Miedzychod nad Warta, Rowno, Szamotuly and Kutno. It was during the short assignment in Miedzychod nad Warta, where my parents occupied the upper floor of the health facility, that that facility became my place of birth.

1931–1936

For sixty plus years, my life has been like a dream. To be precise, a somewhat bad dream that turned into a good dream. Not until recently, when I went back to my country of origin, looking up my birthplace and obtaining for the first time my birth certificate, did I feel a sense of belonging. It confirmed that I indeed had parents with the names I knew them by, and that I was born in that faraway place, that I had only heard of when it was casually mentioned now and then. Although I knew who I was, where I was living and what had been happening, I could not help having certain doubts and thoughts—was every aspect of my life real? Looking back, I cannot imagine now how it was possible for a defenseless human being to put up with and overcome so many of the obstacles that were constantly blocking my path to a normal childhood and adolescence. In 1990 it was an emotional moment for me to step down on Polish soil in Warsaw, forty-six years after having been removed from the city by the Nazis. After all, I had left as a teen and was coming back as a grandmother. It felt strange to walk in the bright, warm sunlight, on streets that had once no doubt been familiar but now seemed so foreign. Every corner, every old, rebuilt building gradually brought back many memories, some haunted with gruesome experiences. Some memories came back very vividly, some appeared as if coming through a thick fog, slowly clearing and becoming vivid. There were so many places I planned to visit, to look up people I might find, to gather as many facts about the past as possible. But, as usual, as on any other trip, there was not enough time. Although I could have spent more time in the country I so often remembered in my daily prayers, once there I felt like a stranger, with mixed feelings and no sense of belonging. I realized that, other than the past, nothing, no tie whatsoever, was binding me to this place. Shortly after the plane touched down in Warsaw, I felt the urge to turn around and go back, to run back to the plane that had brought me there. I felt sad and confused, with a sense of disbelief. Why, after all, with mostly sad memories remaining, had I come back—what was the need for my return, even though it was only to be a brief one and under tolerable circumstances? Maybe the trip was to convince myself that indeed the nightmare that had taken place there was now over, and the rays of sunshine were suggesting a rainbow over the horizon. There was no more fear of being shot, of dying of hunger or disease, while dreaming of freedom. I had to prove to myself that I am who I am, that all is well now and that the "bad dream" had been real but had come to an end.

I remember having a blissful, carefree childhood. I have a vague recollection of my early childhood, just a few incidents here and there. After leaving Miedzychod, in a new place of residence, we had a housekeeper whom we called Gosposia and to whom I was very attached. Gosposia was with us for about five years. She was a mother figure in my carefree environment. Since my father's job very often took him out of town for inspections, meetings, etc., quite often Mother would accompany him. For me it was no hardship to stay behind. I had my Gosposia all to myself and she loved to treat me royally! Once, Father was to leave alone for Warsaw for a few days of meetings. Mother packed him up for the trip and could not help admitting how she hated to stay behind. After all, she felt, there was no reason why she couldn't come along, and with friends in Warsaw she could keep herself busy while Father is attending to business. Father, after making arrangements with Gosposia for my care and without revealing his plan to Mother, asked her to take him to the railroad station. There, sitting in his assigned compartment, Father delayed Mother's getting off the train. As the train started to move, Mother, panic-stricken, rushed to get off. Only then did he show her a double ticket, telling her not to worry—she was on her way to Warsaw—whatever she might need for the stay she can have fun shopping for. I, during their absence, as usual, had a great time with Gosposia, who in my eyes was the best! Even having to take a daily dose of cod liver oil was not so bad, as Gosposia, making a game out of it, would run after me in the garden, managing to distract me long enough to pour some of the terrible-tasting oil into my mouth. The first crisis in my young life was the day my beloved Gosposia announced her departure. Her sister had died and her brother-in-law, who was left with several young children, needed her help. I was inconsolable and so was my Gosposia. After she left, she kept returning, just to peek through the fence of our house to see me play. She once was allowed to take me for a day to play with her nieces and nephews. But since good-byes were always full of tears, my parents did not permit any more such get-togethers.

Not long after Gosposia left us, I disappeared for most of one afternoon. Some older playmates had come by, taking me for a walk without informing Mother. We went here and there. After a few hours of fun, I grew tired and seeing that it was getting dark, I pleaded to go home. I do not know whose idea it was, my friends' or mine, to bring some flowers from the park for Mother, perhaps to soften the guilt of my disappearance. I arrived at the door of our house holding a bouquet of freshly picked flowers behind my back. To my great surprise, I was met by a tearful and at the same time very angry mother, who had been looking for me for many hours, notifying the fire station, the water maintenance people, the police, and so on. In tears, we all decided that nothing like that would have taken place if only Gosposia had been there. Everything was blamed on her departure. There were other housekeepers over the years, but none could be an equal substitute for Gosposia.

The many moves and changes did not make a big impact on my little world—I seemed to make friends easily; grown-ups, especially childless couples, liked and spoiled me. We frequently visited old friends and relatives in various places. Whenever we would arrive in Warsaw, we would take a *dorozka* (horse-driven carriage) to bring us to my godfather's house (Stanislaw and Stefania Chabowski), where we would spend a few days. Taking a *dorozka* was much more fun than taking a taxi, as I would sit up high, next to the driver, and I was permitted at times to hold the reins, getting the horse to walk, trot, or gallop. Also, by taking a *dorozka*, it would make the trip of several kilometers last longer than by taking a taxi. The Chabowskis had an apartment in a huge modern two-story complex in Zoliborz. Across from them lived Stanislaw's sister, Jasia (Janina Chabowska-Piasecka), and their mother (A. Chabowska). Jasia had been married, but her husband died in military action. While my parents socialized, I had plenty of playmates of my age with whom to play in the well-equipped playground. After dinner we all usually took long walks through the many wide avenues shaded by huge trees. Chabowski was a notary at the *hipoteka* (city archives office) in the old town. He took a streetcar to work, which was a very convenient means of transportation. They were a very warm, close-knit family. I always begged to stay with them longer, but other than visiting with my parents, I never got my wish. Only when I was already a teenager was I able to go back and forth by streetcar and spend many hours with the three women (Stefa, Zofia and her mother) while Stanislaw was at work.

Now and then, Mother, Father, and I paid a visit to Father's parents in Lodz, who lived on ulica Sienkiewicza 42 (or 62?). The house was right across from a funeral home, which had a large front window in which coffins were displayed, and was within a stone's throw from the church where I was baptized. My grandmother had a pillow on the windowsill and, while lightly leaning on it, could sit for a long time, watching life on the street below go by. Sometimes my grandfather would join her and then the two would compare notes as to what they were observing. My grandmother, a tiny little lady with gray hair smoothly combed back, was very kind and quiet in manner. As a young person, she once had been grinding meat in a hand-grinder, pushing the meat down the tube with one hand while cranking with the other, and her left index finger was inserted too far. I guess, out of confusion, instead of stopping, she continued to turn the handle. The finger got stuck in the machine and was deformed quite badly. Once, sitting on grandmother's lap, listening to her read a story to me, I kept cutting her finger with a little knife. (I guess the knife just happened to be nearby. I don't think it was a premeditated surgery!) Grandmother was so absorbed with the reading she did not notice what was going on until blood started to ooze and she felt a sharp pain. When asked why I did this, I reportedly told her that I didn't like the looks of her finger and wanted to cut the bad part off.

My paternal grandfather, at the time I knew him, was retired from being a chemist at one of the large textile plants in Lodz. He was a slim, rather short man, with a thick, brown mustache. Both my grandparents adored my mother and were very pleased that Father had married her even though she was Russian. Whenever we came for a visit to these two retired people, who led a quiet, secluded life, it was like a national holiday. For me it was a treat to be left with my two babysitters, while my parents were busy visiting their many friends. In about 1936, Grandmother died unexpectedly of liver cancer. Later, Grandfather, shortly after learning of Father's (his stepson's) death, succumbed to throat cancer. Both grandparents were laid to rest at the Lodz cemetery.

My parents led a very active social life. They attended very formal balls, at which Mother would often take first prize for her unusual, but stunning designer gowns. Although Father was a reluctant dancer, he made an effort to follow protocol and dance with ladies of importance. Mother, on the other hand, loved to dance and rarely got the chance to sit out even one dance in order to catch her breath. In connection with the balls, one incident comes to mind. When Mother was getting dressed to attend a formal function and was ready to slip into her new gown, I, seeing this full-length, multilayered black gown, for some reason became very annoyed. I took a pair of scissors and managed to cut it in many places. Fortunately, not enough damage was made for Mother not to wear it. I cried bitterly, trying to convince Mother not to wear this "black and ugly" gown. My parents, despite my hysterical fit, left for the evening. I remained in the doghouse for several days thereafter with Mother primarily, as Father thought it to be a very funny incident. They also entertained a lot and attended many formal dinners. Their circle of friends was an interesting one, including doctors and administration people connected with Father's line of business, military friends from World War I, and active duty officers. Several friends I vividly remember, such as Major Waclaw Lipinski, who was adjutant to Marshal Jozef Pilsudski, the Polish leader at that time, and a military historian. While in Warsaw, we occasionally stayed as guests at his apartment, which was located in the *Bialy Dom* (the White House). Others included General Edward Pfeiffer ("Radwan"), deputy commander to General Bor-Komorowski during the Warsaw uprising in 1944, Major Zygmunt Chabowski (brother of my godfather), Colonel Edward Nosek, Colonel Platek, M.D., Major Pacholski, Major Zygmunt Rosinski, and Gen. Mieczyslaw Rys-Trojanowski.

Sisters Sonya Shlykov (left) and Liza Romenko (Kucharska), strolling in Brest, 1936.

During this period before the war, when Father was frequently being reassigned to some different city in Poland, wherever he was his typical day at the office started at 8 A.M., then he was at home for lunch and a short nap, and then back to the office until 3 P.M., when his day at the office normally finished. Because the day was still young, he would most times meet Mother at a *kawiarnia* (coffee house) for dessert and coffee. There, almost always, some friends would join them. Should no one come by while they were there, they would stay a while, read the daily papers, and perhaps go for a walk, go shopping, or go to a restaurant for a bite to eat. The evening meal would consist of light food, since the early afternoon meal was the main one. If nothing was planned for the evening, they, including me quite often, would go for a long walk. While I walked with Father, playing games, or humming a song, Mother, wearing high-heeled shoes rather than sensible walking shoes, would trot behind us. Father and I called it *trzymac sztame* (being a team). My parents also played cards as a group (preference or chemin-de-fer rather than bridge), or Father would play chess with one of his friends. On Fridays Father liked to go for *na sledzika* (herring and a drink) at a local pub. We spent Catholic holidays with Father's mother and his stepfather in Lodz, and for Russian Orthodox holidays we would go to Brest to join Mother's family. On national holidays, like *Trzeci Maj* (3rd of May, Constitution Day), we traveled to Warsaw to see and be a part of the many festivities. During one of the many military ceremonies, I was asked to greet and hand a bouquet of flowers to General Boleslaw Wieniawa-Dlugoszewski, who had been an adjutant to Marshal Jozef Pilsudski, and who in 1941, while living in New York, was asked to serve as ambassador to Cuba for the London Polish government-in-exile. A day prior to taking the post, General Wieniawa committed suicide by jumping off the balcony at 12 East 97th Street, New York.

Now and then my parents liked to play the national lottery. One day, on an impulse, Mother called the main office, which was in Warsaw, in order to buy a lottery ticket. She was told that it being so late, only a few tickets were left. They gave her the numbers and Mother wrote them down, separately, as if they were tickets. She asked me to pull one of the "tickets" and dictated the number to the person in Warsaw. After the drawing, a representative showed up at our house, saying that our ticket had won first prize, which was 100,000 *zloty*! He offered to pick up the winnings, but Mother turned the caller down, because if she dealt with him she would have had to give him a commission. Instead, my parents went to Warsaw and collected the whole sum. They promptly invested the money in a commercial property in Brest. There were stores on the street floor and offices on the second floor. The building was next to the Padukows' hotel and house. The income from this investment was very sizeable. Later on, Mother bought a lottery ticket together with our housekeeper. That ticket was a winner as well, but not a first prize.

Despite being active and leading a prestigious way of life, Mother seemed to be homesick for her family and Brest. It was in Kutno that Father had expressed a desire to become the director of the health center in Brest, but for some reason, despite the fact that he was a very successful leader in his field, he was unable to secure this position. He was offered another position, but he declined that and instead took a lump sum of separation money and retired, following which we settled permanently (we thought) in Brest. Having a good income from the commercial property bought with the lottery winnings, plus money from the sale of land in Krasnyy Dvor, enabled Father to become a partner with Misha Shlykow in a meat products business in Brest.

Brest, 1936–1939

That's me seated with my friend Nina Polanska in Regensburg, 1948. Nina is wearing the angora sweater that my mother knitted while tending shop in Brest in 1936. It's the one she was wearing when rounded up in the Uprising and that later kept her warm working in the forced labor camp in 1944–45.

Misha, in order to take over an established meat products plant, needed the capital and connections that Feliks had. Brest, mostly a military town, had many military facilities, and Father, being a veteran of World War I, was very well known among Brest's military commanders and their subordinates. As a result, Feliks and Misha became the sole distributors of meat products to the military, which accounted for the major part of their income. The main meat processing facility, which until Feliks and Misha took over had been known as *Pietkiewicz-Golownicki Wedliniarnia*, if I can recall correctly was located at either ulica Dluga 3 or Trzeciego Maja 62. It had several retail outlets. Mother ran one, in a fashionable part of town, Sonya supervised one in the business section of town, and a hired manager ran the third store, which was near the market area. Mother's clientele consisted mostly of wives of military and professional men. She knew them all; many of them were personal friends, thus she never had a dull moment. Her friends

After a family meal at Krasnyy Dvor, 1935. Standing left to right, Arkady Padukow, Olga and Zhorzh Vakul'chik, Anna and Nikolay Padukow, Liza Kucharska, Sonya Shlykov, Nikita Romenko, and Luka Romenko. Kneeling beside "Rex" is Igor Shlykov, and hidden by the dog, Sergey Padukow.

would do their shopping while also socializing. At the same time, Mother, in order not to sit idle while at the cash register, did a lot of knitting, making sweaters, coats, vests, etc. One attractive jacket made of angora with blue and white stripes became a somewhat "historical" jacket, as it later accompanied Mother to a labor camp in Germany, helping to keep her warm, and later it was lent to my friend Nina during cool days while she was visiting us (it is visible on the picture of me and Nina in our backyard at Weissenburg Str.). The store's windows, in particular at Mother's shop, were tastefully decorated. I still can recall one especially: a huge ocean liner made of lard, complete with promenade decks and cabins, a replica of a real ship. In the evening, lights would go on in the cabin windows and you could see people promenading on the decks. From the large ballroom music could be heard while the passengers were dancing. Crowds of people would marvel at this masterpiece. Another display during the Easter holidays was a large egg, made also of lard, which was full of ornaments. The egg was decorated like *Pisanki* with the usual Slavic motifs. The master artist responsible for the decorations was the chief butcher, who was called *Majster* (Maestro). Misha was in charge of production, Feliks, more or less, of sales. Father's job was also to relieve Mother for lunch, or for whenever she needed time for other activities. He did it reluctantly, as he never really felt comfortable in his new profession. The firm also did lots of business

Nikolay Padukow in San Remo, Italy, recovering from tuberculosis. On his left, wife Anna and her sister Liza Romenko (later Kucharska). Standing in front, Sergey Padukow. 1926.

with other countries, since their hams were widely known as the best one could get.

And so, the years between 1936 and 1939 were pleasant, more or less carefree. All members of the Romenko clan were settled down and looking optimistically toward the future. Grandfather and Machekha were busy at the estate. Grandfather leased out an orchard and a vegetable garden to a Jewish fellow who, during the summer season, lived in a temporary hut on the premises while tending them and protecting them from the nearby villagers across the river, some of whom were eager to steal the ripe produce. The property extended to the river. To protect the orchard and the vegetable gardens from trespassers, a chain was stretched out along the banks of the river on which a large dog ran back and forth, thus keeping strangers at a distance. In addition to profits from each harvest, the leased orchard and gardens left Grandfather with a large income. However, he had his hands full supervising and running the big estate.

The Padukows were the owners of the *Hotel Europejski* (or was it *Hotel Rzymski?*) on Steckiewicza Street and lived next door to it. They had a capable, but very grumpy housekeeper. She loved cats, and in addition to her own cats most neighborhood strays congregated sitting side by side along the back fence facing the kitchen window, waiting for their meals. She was happy to

Raft ferry operated by my uncle Mikhail Shlykov for transporting people, horses and vehicles across the Muchawiec River, Brest, 1934.

see them, knowing she was in charge of the hungry brood; nevertheless, as soon as they lined up, she scolded them: "Why can't you be here when I'm ready for you, not just when you want to eat? You scavengers, loiterers, good-for-nothing freeloaders!" She would repeat this, day after day. It was a daily amusement to watch the ritual with the cats. At the hotel they employed a bellboy, a very friendly, jolly fellow, who constantly was joking and making puns. We all suspected he had one or two screws missing. The guests thought that Kazik (we called him *Glupi Kazio*, Silly Kazio) was a great clown and tipped him generously. Arkady was attending a university, so I did not see him a lot, except when he was back at home for the holidays. Sergey attended Russian high school and kept to himself most of the time, staying in the little house in the garden where he had his studio. At that time he used to do quite a bit of sculpting. I recall posing for him when he did my head. He was dead serious, while I could not sit still and constantly was moving around. It turned out to be a very good resemblance of me after all. Among many busts, he made one of Marshal Jozef Pilsudski. In addition to the house and the hotel near the railroad station, the Padukows also had a summerhouse with a huge, young orchard. My uncle Kolya was becoming an expert in crossbreeding different trees, thus producing unusual fruits.

The Shlykovs, in turn, were busy at the meat products plant, Sonya at the store, Misha supervising production and purchasing the swine and cattle. Igor, their only son, also attended the Russian high school, in the same class with Sergey because there was just two weeks difference in age between them. The Shlykovs had a *dacha* on the Muchawiec River and nearby, parallel to the *Kovelskiy most* (bridge), Misha owned a ferry that plied between the banks of the river. Since the house was built on a ridge overlooking the banks, one could

Mikhail Shlykov holding his son Igor (left) and nephew Sergey Padukow. On grass, left to right, Mrs. Komorowska, Mr. Komorowski and Sonya Shlykov. At the Muchawiec River, about 1930.

see the busy ferry from the *dacha's* windows. At the *dacha* there were many get-togethers with the old and the young of the family and their friends. The river, being clean and not too deep, was safe for swimming. Igor often used to jump off the bridge into the deeper parts of the river. The Russian Orthodox Church used the bank opposite the *dacha* as a place to perform the ritual of christening. After each swim there was always a hearty, home-cooked dinner prepared by Sonya. One such event I remember clearly was when a huge banquet table was set for many in a fairly large room (maybe it seemed larger than it was since I was quite little then). The guests, after sunning and a swim, came casually dressed to eat. All sorts of odd chairs were assembled, but a very old and squeaky one was meant for me. It was next to Misha's, who was to sit at the head of the table. When all were seated, Misha got up to propose a toast, at which point I quickly tried to switch chairs. I moved his away, but unfortunately did not manage to push mine in its place. And so, Misha made a short speech, after which he tried to sit down not realizing that his chair was not there! His 200-plus pounds plummeted to the floor, hitting and cutting his head on the radiator behind him. I was not only embarrassed, but scared as well, seeing that he was hurt. Misha in turn tried to make a joke of the whole incident, which made me feel even more embarrassed. Very often Misha would carry me on his shoulders, while I would sing a song in Polish:

Misha Shlykov on his motorbike with friend Kazimierz Niemierwrzycki on the jump seat. Brest, 1929.

Bije nas Moskal, gryza wszy ... (The Muscovite is beating us and his lice are biting too), which sounded very funny, as I was sitting on a Russian's shoulders singing an anti–Russian song.

The Vakul'chiks lived in town, Georgiy working as a high school teacher at the Russian school, and Olga housekeeping and taking care of their young son "Yura."

The Bogutas also lived in town, but I have no recollection of them or their two daughters, Nina and Lida, or their son Leonid, as the three cousins were much older than I. For some reason the Bogutas rarely participated in the family activities. My aunt Mariya died in 1929 of cancer, and perhaps her absence was the reason that her husband, who was a chief forester, felt more like an outsider than he did while their family was intact. At one point the children of Mariya and Ivan moved in with the Padukows and attended a local school, but soon after, Ivan took the children back. Their housekeeper became Ivan's second wife and they in turn had a son.

Another Romenko daughter also died early in life. Yelena was briefly married to Devyatnikov, but they soon divorced. She fell in love with a married man. Although another, single man had asked for her hand, she, not being able to marry the man she loved, one day drank poison and although found still alive, she could not be saved. This happened in the year 1928,

The children of Nikita and Anastasiya Romenko-Kovenko as adults above and following pages. *Top, left*: Anna. *Right:* Sergey. *Bottom, left*: Mariya. *Right*: Peter.

Yelena

Olga and her husband Zhorzh

Left: **Elizabeth**. *Right*: **Sonya**.

when she was 24 years old. Lena was buried at *Bretskoye Trishinskoye Klad-bishche*.

As for the Kucharskis, the move to Brest was a good thing. Father had his many friends, Mother her siblings, and I got plenty of attention as many young relatives of Mother's family lived nearby. And being the youngest grand-daughter, I became the apple of my grandfather's eye.

In the beginning, we shared housing with Misha, Sonya and Igor next door to the factory. I was enrolled at a private Polish school (*im. Gorskiej*). Mother or Father would walk me to and from school. I had to wear a school uniform, a gray dress with a large red bow at the neck and a red beret with a triangle on the top, with the number of the grade on it. Mrs. Gorska, the prin-cipal, a widow of a Russian general, was a very stately looking woman. She often gathered her pupils at her side, her shoulder covered with a black shawl, while she played the piano accompanying the pupils singing. The principal was very strict about the upbringing of children. One day my parents took me to a coffee house for a soda and a pastry. I was spotted in the room by the principal. She found it inappropriate for a child to be in a room full of smoke, exposed to adult conversations, often full of jokes in questionable taste, so my parents were reprimanded and asked not to take me to such places in the

Sonya Shlykov (left) and sister Liza Romenko (later Kucharska), circa 1926.

future. She thought it reflected badly on the school, since I was wearing the school uniform. After school I would go to the factory, where the chief butcher (*majster*) would give me anything I asked for. Sometimes I would try so many sausages, or cold cuts, that come dinnertime I could not touch a thing. Also, after school I had to float between Mother's and Sonya's stores. Occasionally, when both Mother and Sonya were too busy at the stores, Father and I would have some special activity, which was always lots of fun. One day before Christmas, business was more active than usual. I was visiting Aunt Sonya's store, when she noticed she was getting short of change in the register. She asked me to take a 20-*zloty* note and change it at a nearby store. I liked that kind of assignment; it made me feel responsible and grown-up. No sooner did I leave the store when a very polite girl, a teenager, approached me, calling me by my first name. She asked for the 20 *zloty* and told me to wait, that she would change it, as she knew a place where they always had small change. And so I gave her the money and she left, telling me it will be just a few minutes. It was cold and dark out and I waited and waited. The girl never returned. I went back to my aunt's very embarrassed and minus the 20 *zloty*. No matter how much Sonya tried to console me, nothing would soothe my feelings and pride. After all, I was trusted with a 20-*zloty* bill and was cheated out of it. Many days later, while being escorted to school by Mother, I recognized the girl who took my money. The girl was arrested and prosecuted in court, where I had to testify under oath against her. I felt very proud that justice had prevailed!

Eventually, our communal living came to an end and with it came an end to my fun times. We moved to a house at Sienkiewicza 62(?), owned by a Jewish man named Fuksman, which gave us more room and privacy, but I had no company. I felt lonely and every chance I got, I ran back to the other place. There was always action there, delivery horse carriages, many workers, household help, my beloved uncle and aunt, and Igor. My favorite horse there was Kasztan (a chestnut), who was my friend and who waited for me to feed him with endless sugar lumps. Mother was often horrified, seeing me under the horse, scratching his tummy, or giving him a sponge bath. I had no fear and enjoyed being with Kasztan and having him follow me like a puppy. Whenever I was indoors, he would come to a window and rub his nose on it, smearing the pane with his saliva. I wonder if all the sugar he was fed was really that good for him.

In general, life in Brest was very family-oriented. There were always numerous relatives that often joined us at Grandfather's place. Holidays were most memorable, as the house, although big, sometimes could just barely accommodate us all. For us children Grandpa would bring straw from the barn and make bedding in one of the rooms. There was lots of play and very little sleep while the grown-ups in the adjacent room would celebrate till dawn. My cousins, who were quite boisterous, teased me a lot, and on many occasions I was the scapegoat. In order not to be called a sissy, I did whatever they did or was told to do. They kept daring me to no end, whether it was jumping into the river without knowing how to swim and almost drowning, or jumping over a rose bush full of thorns and not making the jump, ending up covered with scratches and bleeding from head to toe. Acrobatic stunts on the handles of a bike were very scary, but at the same time lots of fun!

Maybe the very first recollection of my grandfather goes back to an incident, when Grandpa put me on a potty. Sitting on it for quite some time, I suddenly called to him: "*Dziadek, Dziadek!* (Grandpa, Grandpa) Come quick, there is a little tail wiggling!" He came rushing to investigate, and sure enough, the tail that wiggled was a long tapeworm! I thought it was very funny at the time, but later I had to be treated to make sure none of the worm was left behind. (I had to drink lots and lots of castor oil, and that was not funny at all!) Excursions with Grandpa to the fields with a blanket and a picnic basket were quiet fun times. Grandpa would feed me, tell me Russian stories, not in Russian, but in Polish. (Whenever we were together with Mother's side of the family, although they all were Russians and spoke Russian among themselves, when father and I were present, they spoke with us in Polish. Although Father could speak Russian, he disliked speaking it, because as a typical Pole he disliked anything Russian—except the Romenko family.) Becoming sleepy after plenty of good food and fresh country air, we would fall asleep, lulled by the wind and the birds singing. Once on such a field outing, I awoke before my grandfather did and noticed a persistent bee flying and buzzing around Grandpa's head. Since

I could not make it fly away, I took an empty bottle and tried to aim at the bee. I missed the bee and instead hit Grandpa in the face, giving him a big shiner.

There were many horses and so there were many horse-driven carriage rides in summer and sleigh rides in winter. During harvest time, the children were allowed to ride home on top of the wagons full of hay. To this day I can smell the freshness and feel the softness of the newly mown hay. Sometimes we were allowed to help gather the mown dry wheat and tie it into sheaves. We looked at it as fun and games. I am sure if we were told to help we would disappear from the harvest scene. This way, the encounter with nature became a lifelong memory. For many years a stork made his home on top of one of the barns. After each departure for a warmer climate he kept coming back to the same spot, needing to do some improvements to his nest after the harsh winter at Krasnyy Dvor, a good place to nest for there were plenty of frogs in the nearby ponds and lakes. Grandfather was able to recognize him as being the same stork because one of his wings had been injured and was not the same as the other. After the young ones hatched and later were ready for a long flight south, the stork parents first checked their flying abilities. If a baby stork showed weakness, or was crippled, the parents killed it. Only the parents and healthy young ones would leave for the south.

Grandfather knew how to keep us happy and playful, but at the same time we obeyed and respected him. Grandfather Nikita, whom we called *Dedushka*, was a tall, handsome, very strong man, physically as well as in character. A great human being! A decent fellow, always fair and peace loving, who created a harmonious atmosphere among family members and among the people who worked for him. He was greatly admired by everyone who came in contact with him. His advice was always down-to-earth and respected. He was a real wise man. The sun and a hard life, rather than age, prematurely etched his face, for it was he who had to shoulder the burden of leading the large family. He was a caring shepherd to his flock. His eyes, always alert and smiling, projected warmth and kindness. He was a very gracious man, not only a father to his eight children, but also to his workers, who often sought his help and guidance. He never made any barriers between his family and the helpers. When one of them decided to get married he arranged a wedding for him or her as if for one of his own children. The estate hands often said, "In addition to being our *khozyain* (estate owner/boss), he is like a father to us." In his simplicity, he was a noble and very brave man. He was a skilled horseman. He performed many supervisory chores in and around the estate and in the vast fields on horseback, often riding without a saddle. He was a born estate owner. When asked what he thought of life in general, he said: "The years flow like the sea's waves, or clouds in the sky. Life amounts to your going in through one door, and going out through another." When celebrating a birthday, he always made a wish for two more years. When he was no longer able to stay at Krasnyy Dvor, his son Sergey took him to his house in Ordzenikidze,

Mikhail Shlykov in his Polish Army uniform, after being called to duty in the Quartermaster Corps, 1939.

now Vladikavkaz, Russia, where he was cared for by Sergey, Sergey's wife Dora, and the rest of the family. He died at age 87 on March 12, 1956.

Brest, 1939, on the Eve of World War II

The years between 1936 and 1939, as I remember them, were peaceful; everybody did their own thing in Brest and no one seemed to complain about life in the then free Poland. The Poles lived in their circles, the Russians had their schools and Orthodox churches, and the Jewish population, which was quite substantial, enjoyed freedoms that were greater in Poland than in any other country. After the end of World War I, Brest Litovsk became a part of Poland again. By 1921 its Jewish population was estimated to be only 15,630 (35 percent of the general population), chiefly because during the war all the Jews had been evacuated by the tsarist government. Later the town was almost totally destroyed by fire. After 1918 a small part of its former Jewish inhabitants returned, and with the aid of the American Jewish Joint Distribution Committee, several Jewish quarters were rebuilt and a large number of new houses were erected to be occupied by Jews. In 1931 the Jewish population of Brest Litovsk had again risen to 21,440, or 44.3 percent of the total. However, the policies adopted by the now Polish government restricted this increase very greatly. A large number of Polish officials, storekeepers, and artisans settled in the town, and many Jews who had formerly been engaged in these occupations were forced out of their trades or positions. Despite a growing acceptance of Jews by most of the Polish population, there was still a strong anti–Semitic sentiment among many ordinary Poles and government officials.

On May 17, 1937, a pogrom occurred that drastically changed the economic situation of the Jews of Brest. This pogrom occurred after a Jewish youth, the son of a local butcher, stabbed a Polish policeman who had entered the shop to see whether the Jewish proprietor had slaughtered an animal in accordance with the Jewish ritual law. Early the next morning there began an attack on the Jews of the town that lasted hours, during which many Jews were robbed by mobs, windows of many Jewish-owned shops were smashed, and merchandise was cast into the streets. Nothing was done by the police to check the rioting or restore order; indeed, in many instances the police prevented Jews from defending themselves. Two Jews died as a result of their injuries, and hundreds were injured. The property damage amounted to more than a million *zlotys* (about $200,000).

The actual purpose in this attack was clearly described in an article published in the anti–Semitic organ *Dzennik Narodowy* of May 17th: "The occurrences at Brest Litovsk will indeed give impetus to the process of Polonizing the city, which is so strongly Judaized. For it is clear that if before these events there were thirty-eight Jewish bakers in Brest Litovsk and only two Christian ones, and if all the Jewish bakeries are now in ruins, the situation will have to change. It is probable that the majority of the Jewish enterprises will not be able to be reestablished, and their places will be taken by Polish businesses." A popular Jewish saying was: *Wasze ulice, nasze kamienice* (your streets, but our buildings). This was generally true. Most stores, with the exception of meat product outlets like ours, most apartment and office buildings, and most factories were Jewish-owned. Two days after the pogrom, a number of Poles from Posen, Silesia, and Pommerania entered Brest and started to buy up Jewish-owned stores and businesses. The Jewish merchants of the town quickly formed an organization that prevented more than a small number of Jewish-owned business-houses from falling into the hands of the Poles. However, a boycott against Jewish merchants started soon afterwards, which was so severe that many Jewish stores and business-houses were forced to close; Polish-owned shops were set up in their place. In addition, a large number of Jewish artisans were greatly affected by the boycott, for circulars were spread among the soldiers demanding that the soldiers and officers refrain from buying from Jews and from giving any work to Jewish artisans.

My mother and I both remember this pogrom, when all hell broke loose. A group of vandals tried to get into my uncle's hotel, but my father rushed out and assured them that there were no Jewish guests present in the hotel. All I could see were mobs of people running, shouting anti–Jewish slogans, and the whole city, it seemed, was covered with the white goose-down feathers that were being ripped out of people's bedding. Needless to say, for me, it was a very scary sight to watch and experience. The pogrom lasted until the evening. The next few days were quiet, as if in full mourning. Many rumors began going around about Jewish acts of spitefulness toward the Christians, and the latter began to mistrust Jewish tradesmen and shopkeepers, and neighbors. One version of many such rumors was that a Jewish merchant was in the habit of adding urine to cans of fuel. Apparently, adding the urine did not seriously diminish the fuel's strength, it simply increased its quantity and so the merchant's profit. Jewish salesmen were also suspected of cheating when weighing goods. Scales were frequently checked by the authorities (a practice that also took place at our meat products stores), but suspicions of cheating continued. In Brest and the surrounding towns there were many synagogues and *yeshivas*, and observance of the Sabbath was a very common sight. Non-Jews were regularly asked to assist, for instance, in the lighting of furnaces or stoves, a practice forbidden to Jews on the Sabbath. With all the Jewish men and boys with their corkscrew curls, hats, white stockings, knickers, and long coats, any Sabbath day in Brest made it look like a little Israel. Most of my school friends were Christian, since most of the Jewish children were sent to a *yeshiva*. After school, however, there was no difference, whether the child came from a Russian, Polish, or Jewish family; we all played together. Mother recalled that one of her close friends at this time was a Jewish woman named Zylberszteyn.

3

Occupied Warsaw

Our journey toward Nazi-occupied Warsaw and away from the Soviets, who from the East were advancing toward Brest, took longer than we had anticipated. Although Warsaw was not very far from Brest, we could only move at a very slow pace. The roads were packed with people like ourselves, who were going west, trying to escape from the Soviets, and people going east, primarily Jews, who were escaping from the Nazi occupation forces. The lively exchange of news and rumors from each side was unbelievable. Some tales were quite true, but some were highly exaggerated, which spread a fear of the unknown among us all. We "marched" it seemed endlessly all day, stopping only to give the horses a chance to eat and rest. Finding a night's shelter was always a problem, but with sheer luck we were always able to get some kind of lodging. After a few days of hardship and all sorts of discomforts, we finally arrived at the outskirts of the city, and then found the Fuksmans' apartment, which was located on the other side of the Vistula River, in the very center of downtown.

Warsaw's population then was about 2.1 million. Although the Polish capital covers quite a large area because of many spread-out districts, because of its relatively small center, it was often referred to as "Little Paris." (All of Poland is roughly the size of Colorado. At the lowest point the elevation is 2 meters, at the highest, the Tatra mountains, 2,499 meters.) When we arrived in Warsaw in late September, 1939, we were shocked to see the damage that the fighting had already left. Many houses were destroyed, the streets were in constant repair. It was far from what we remembered of the Warsaw of just a few months earlier.

Once there, Roman Rajpold, not having a place to go to until he could decide what to do with himself, was invited to stay at our newly acquired apartment. No sooner did we arrive at Hoza 19, Apt. 6 (tel. 8 17 79), than we discovered that the Fuksmans had allowed their housekeeper Nina Makowiecka Drzewiecka and her friend Alla Maksimowicz to stay in the apartment. Alla, a military nurse, after the capitulation of Polish forces, was stranded in Warsaw, and was reluctant to return to her hometown of Brest. Nina, who came from Pruzany (near Brest) still had family there, but had decided, or was asked by her employers, to stay at the apartment in order to guard their domain. And so the two ladies ended up occupying the master bedroom. Roman was given the smallest room, which once was used as a maid's room, and was supposed to be my room. What was to be a short stay became an almost permanent arrangement that lasted until he obtained a divorce and remarried. He was not only housed and fed, but he took part in all our family activities. When he did move, it was not very far, just across the stairway from our service entrance. As I will describe later, our Warsaw apartment became a shelter for many members of the family, friends, and sometimes strangers.

Shortly after we had settled down, Ivan Shlykov managed to cross from (now Soviet-occupied) Brest and joined us for several weeks. No sooner did he leave, than Misha, Sonya and Igor fled Brest and also joined us until they found an apartment at Nowogrodzka #43. The von Brevern family (Dmitriy, Mariya and Wanda) also arrived and the Shlykovs decided to house them in their spacious apartment. Eventually, the Padukows arrived in Warsaw as well, but just Nikolay, Anna and Sergey. Arkady, being at the university, stayed behind and later went into hiding at his fiancée's family home in Lutsk. The Padukows stayed briefly with the Shlykovs but soon after moved into their own apartment on Wilcza. They decided to move, not only because the Shlykov's apartment was getting too crowded, but also it was on the fifth floor, smack in the center of town and the railroad station, and living there made Anna very anxious. During this time there was an order that the city should be kept dark, and all windows had to have black shades on them. There were frequent air raids, during which all tenants had to run for the shelters. Anna, being a scaredy-cat and very nervous, did not run to the basement shelter but would literally slide down on the banister through all six floors, thus being the first one in the shelter area. Most of the family, stranded in a city with just a few friends, somehow managed to make a living. Misha as usual put his inventiveness to work and started not one but several businesses. The Padukows, using their savings, dealt on the black market, primarily exchanging foreign currency, gold dollars, rubles, Swiss francs, etc. They also were selling jewelry, mostly watches and diamonds. Mother got into this business as well, which brought her a good income. I acted for her and the Padukows as a courier between them and their clients.

Since Grandfather, Machekha, and Yuriy with his now pregnant mother Olga (Georgiy, her husband, was missing in action at the front) had stayed behind in Brest, Mother crossed the border twice in order to bring them the means for survival (money and things that they could not buy in Brest.) She chose to cross the river, where it was solidly frozen and at night, with the help of guides, which made it easier to avoid the guards. The first time the escapade went smoothly, but during the second crossing she was caught and all her money was confiscated. While she was bravely crossing the border, Father and

I with great anxiety waited at the apartment for her return. While waiting for such a return, Father and a few of his friends got together for a game of chess and a catered dinner, which we ordered from the Hungarian restaurant downstairs. Of course, what is dinner without vodka? One shot followed another to drown their sorrows, until no pain was felt. Father (I recall as if it was yesterday) started to act silly, trying to cheer me up, calling me "the hostess and lady of the house," as I had grown angry with the *popijanka* (the drinking bout), when at one point Father sat on the very edge of the sofa and slid down to the floor, as if on a slide. Then he repeated it several times. I refused to be amused, and in an angry voice said to him: "If I were your wife, I would divorce you!" He looked surprised and shocked, and only then realized what I meant— while his wife was taking a chance crossing the border, he was having a party and not feeling a bit worried about any possible consequences. The next day he felt ashamed and begged me not to tell on him to Mother. I did not, but he told her himself. This was the first and only time that I ever was cross with my father. Despite the necessity of communal living, I certainly felt no pain. Until Father's arrest, there was never a dull moment.

Relocation to Warsaw for our family was not, it now seemed, as bad an idea as we had feared. Despite many oppressions and tragic events, life went on. We (the Shlykovs, Padukows and the Kucharskis) were housed, each having separate apartments, we did not have to rely strictly on ration cards, and with time many of our friends ended up in Warsaw as well. Nevertheless, the occupation times were not easy for most and were quite difficult for many. Many of my father's friends went into hiding, having to move from place to place, sometimes spending each night, if lucky, in a different house or apartment; if less fortunate they had to hide in villages or forests. The underground's work flourished, leaflets were published and distributed, subversive action against the Germans took place and quite often, and when partisans were caught, they were punished, in most cases quite severely. Arrests were common and constant. Immediate punishment, such as hanging "perpetrators" in a city square or from a balcony, and street executions, were gruesome sights to see. During those years of war, people did not speak careless words and idle talk did not take place. Everyone was afraid of being overheard. Friends conversed in subdued voices. Common were so called *lapanki* (round-ups), or *oblawy* (ambushes) when all of a sudden a Gestapo vehicle would stop and randomly pick up people from the streets; for no rhyme or reason those arrested would be taken to a prison, and then, if they were lucky, they would be released, or sent to Germany to do forced labor. While German men were fighting at the fronts or occupying different parts of Europe, Germany needed a labor force to keep the economy going, thus they "imported" foreigners to do those tasks. Those less fortunate ended up in one of the many concentration camps. Such a fate met my father, who was arrested "from the list," meaning the Gestapo received a lead (in this case, that he was housing a Jew) from one of the many Polish *szpicel* (informers).

The Nazi occupation forces were trying to destroy the Jews of Europe, first by identifying them with an armband with the Star of David, then putting them in closed ghettos, and eventually transporting them to different concentration camps for "final elimination." The tragedy of the Jews is very well documented, but stories of other targeted groups, in particular of the *Roma* or Gypsies, could use more exposure. The Gypsies met a similar fate as the Jews. They had to wear armbands with the letter Z (for *Zigeuner*). Many were taken from the *Umschlag-platz* (reloading center) to a camp in Treblinka, although the earliest organized preparatory center for mass extermination of the Gypsies—which was called *Zigeunerlager-Litzmannstadt*—was at Lodz. The largest extermination center of the Gypsies, however, was the *Oswiecim-Brzezinka* Family Camp (*Auschwitz-Birkenau-Familienlager*). We heard stories of the Gypsies and their fate while we were still in Poland, but we never imagined that we would come into personal contact with one of the Auschwitz survivors. While we were living in Frankfurt in 1953–67, it turned out that one of our housekeepers, Lisa M. who was a Gypsy by origin, was one of the survivors. She told us of the different experiments that the Germans did on Gypsy children. As a result of one such experiment, Lisa became sterile. She still had, tattooed on her forearm, her Auschwitz prisoner number. After the liberation, in Poland, one of the Gypsy's songs was often heard: *Wprowadzili Nas Przez Bramy, Wypuscili Kominami ...* (They brought us in through the gates, they released us through the chimneys ...).

There were lots of underground activities going on, which the Nazi occupation forces were constantly struggling to suppress. Secret schools continued to function during the occupation. So-called *komplety* (make-up classes) were held. A group of children and their teacher would meet each day at a different house, making it harder to be detected by the occupation authorities. Books were difficult to obtain and reading was often hindered by the lack of electricity. Carbide oil lamps or candles were used when the electricity was turned off. At night, starting at dusk, blackouts were ordered. Air raids were frequent and occurred at various hours of the day or night, during which the population had to run to the shelters. If caught by a siren while on the street, one had to run into the nearest house and join the occupants in their shelters, which usually were in the basements. Our basement later on was equipped with benches, as sometimes the raids were long in duration and sitting on the damp floor or standing against the walls was very strenuous. The corridors were quite narrow and the space was too limited to provide any comfort. There were no toilet facilities, but if nature called, and, because of the stress of the situation, that happened more often than one would think, it caused many predicaments, to say the least. There were times we were caught by surprise by a siren's wail and there was no shelter, or time to find one, nearby. In those instances we had to stay put and seek temporary cover, such as under the entry gate to a house, while the bombs were exploding around us, and wait there for the "all clear" (*odwolanie*) sound in order to leave the area.

During World War II, ghettos were established by the Nazis to separate and confine Jews in walled-off areas of Eastern European cities. Adolf Eichmann was the author of the Final Solution, a program for the systematic removal of Jews from all areas of occupied countries into designated controlled areas with the intent to eventually eradicate Jews from Europe. The first large ghetto at Tuliszkow was established in December 1939 followed by the Lodz Ghetto in April 1940 and the Warsaw Ghetto in October 1940. The ghettos were walled off and guarded. Any Jew found leaving them was shot. The Warsaw Ghetto was the largest of the ghettos in Poland confining 380,000–450,000 people. The Lodz Ghetto held approximately 160,000–200,000 persons. The ghetto of Brest-Litvosk, established in December 1941 and evacuated in October 1942, held 20,000 prisoners.

The situation in the ghettos was brutal. In Warsaw, Jews now lived 9 persons per room. In the ghetto of Odrzywol, 700 people lived in an area previously occupied by five families, between 12 and 30 persons to each room. The Jews were not allowed out of the ghetto, so they had to rely on replenishments of food and supplies by the Nazis—in effect, a starvation diet. In Warsaw 253 calories of food were allotted per Jew, compared to 669 calories allotted per non–Jewish Pole and 2,613 calories per German. Because of the densely crowded living conditions, lack of food, and improper sanitation (in the Lodz Ghetto 95 percent of apartments had no water or sewerage facilities), hundreds of thousands of Jews died in the ghettos of disease and starvation.

In 1942, the Nazis began the second phase of the Final Solution: Operation Reinhard. Jews were deported from every occupied country in Europe to extermination camps. The ghettos were emptied out into concentration camps established specifically for the systematic murder of large numbers of people. Almost 300,000 people were deported from the Warsaw Ghetto alone to the Treblinka concentration camp over the course of three months in 1942. At the start of the deportations, the Jews believed that they were being deported to forced labor camps, but by the end of 1942, it was clear that the deportations were to death camps. Many of the remaining Jews decided to die fighting. Against all odds, resistance groups organized uprisings in many of the ghettos. None was successful however, and the Jewish populations of the ghettos were almost entirely killed. In Warsaw, the first instance of armed insurgency occurred on January 18, 1943, when the Germans started the second expulsion of the Jews held there. The roundups stopped after four days when the insurgent organizations took control of the ghetto. The Germans were frustrated for three months. Additional reserves were sent to squash the Jewish resistance. The inhabitants of the ghetto prepared for what they realized would be their final fight, armed as they were with only pistols and revolvers, a few rifles and one machine gun.

Support from outside the ghetto was limited, but Polish resistance units from *Armia Krajowa* (Polish Home Army) attacked German sentry gates near the ghetto walls and attempted to smuggle weapons inside and prisoners out. However, in the end, the resistance efforts proved to be not enough against the full force of the Nazis who fought with a daily force of two thousand men, armored tanks, flamethrowers, aircraft, and artillery.

The final battle started on the eve of Passover, April 19, 1943, when the German troops stormed the ghetto. Jewish insurgents shot and threw Molotov cocktails and hand grenades; the Nazis burned the houses block by block, blowing up basements and sewers and rounding up or killing any surviving Jews. The fighting lasted until the end of April. The uprising ended officially on May 16 after the deaths, most by suicide, of the remaining leaders of the resistance. During the fighting, an estimated 13,000 Jews were killed, either shot or burned alive in bunkers. The remaining 50,000 people were sent to the Treblinka extermination camp. The final daily report of SS Commander Jürgen Stroop stated: "180 Jews, bandits, and subhumans were destroyed. The former Jewish quarter of Warsaw is no longer in existence. The large scale action was terminated at 2015 hours by blowing up the Warsaw Synagogue. Total number of Jews dealt with 56,065, including both Jews caught and Jews whose extermination can be proved."

After the fighting, the ghetto area was leveled and the *KL Warschau* concentration camp was established in the ruins. During the later Warsaw Uprising of 1944, 380 Jews were liberated from this camp by the Armia Krajowa.

During the occupation, food for the general Polish population was rationed. Everything was bought with ration cards. A lot of people were just barely getting by. If one had had to depend only on the rations prescribed by the authorities, the infirmaries would have been filled with people suffering from malnutrition. The less resourceful ones, forced by hunger, would periodically take their household goods and treasures to the *Kercelak* (Warsaw flea market). There they could get some money for their goods, or exchange them for something they needed. Soon, being very inventive in situations like that, the Poles quickly started black markets, including illegal transportation of produce from the country into the cities. The entryways to many apartment houses were transformed into improvised bakery outlets. There, primarily women were selling freshly baked breads of the really best quality out of their baskets. The police would chase them, but as soon as the police presence was no longer visible, they would continue their business. *Szmugiel* (smuggling) flourished. It became for many a lucrative livelihood, even though those who were caught were severely punished. Traveling from the countryside, on any given train that was heading for a city, especially Warsaw, one could see the smuggling in progress right there on the train. The average smuggler, most likely a woman, once she boarded the train, would unpack her goods and hide them wherever she could. Her body might be wrapped with slabs of bacon, eggs might be hidden in overhead lamps, under the seats, and virtually anywhere she would think to be a good hiding place. Train passengers were often left undisturbed, depending on the guard on duty, but those suspected of illegal transport were searched and sometimes stripped naked. All their goods were confiscated, and sometimes they were detained. There was much ugly swearing in Polish and in German. Sometimes, when the guards were aggravated with a smuggler's behavior, they would use their firearms to strike him or her. Despite all the unpleasant circumstances the average smuggler had to endure, she would not be discouraged, but would turn around, go back to the country, get more goods, and head for the city again. On many trips from Terespol to Warsaw, Mother and I, or I alone, would bring by train goods that Mother's friends packed for us to take back home. It was frightening, especially when the German police boarded the train and conducted a search. Somehow, they never searched us, and especially when I traveled alone they did not seem to suspect me of *szmugiel*.

The most popular mode of transportation in those days was primarily the streetcar, then rickshaws, trains, and taxis. Private cars were scarce, because not only was the upkeep high, but also gasoline was hard to obtain. Travelers, who in particular had to depend on streetcars, were subjected to widespread professional thievery, examples of which I have given in another chapter. The overcrowded cars forced many simply to hang onto the outside steps of the moving car. Trolley drivers did not care if the car was plastered with people; they just rang a bell and proceeded to the next stop. Many people purposely waited for a full car, and at the last minute would jump up and stay on the outside steps. Those were people who were going a short distance and wanted to avoid paying or did not want to be blocked off inside the car when their time came to disembark, or (like me) were persons who were carrying a delivery of underground material. In the latter case, it seemed to be safer. One could jump off in case the car was undergoing a search. Overcrowded cars on the inside also were a hazard to one's bones, especially during the holidays when the crowds shoved without any scruples. On several such occasions, Mother sustained broken ribs and bruises and by close calls missed other injuries. It was very common to see lice crawling on your co-passenger's coat or jacket. Also, in a very crowded car one could encounter cases of lewd conduct. I heard a secondhand account from our tenant's secretary, who arrived for work at our apartment outraged at what had happened during her trolley ride. Holding onto a handle, she was standing in the back of the streetcar surrounded by several men. All of a sudden one of the men reached under her skirt. She told us: "I instantly looked at each of them and I chose the one that looked the most suspicious and hit him on the head with my umbrella!" There was no protest from him, so she assumed her choice was the right one. In every case, of course, Germans who were going to board the streetcar had priority for entry and seats.

In Terespol, Mother's friend, Emilia (Mila) Szyszkowska and her sister, Izabella, opened a produce and dry goods store. It became a barter exchange

My friend Izabella Szyszkowska (left) and I are sampling poppy seeds in a field in Terespol, 1943.

type of store, where women from the country would bring eggs, fowl, butter, and cheeses. In exchange they would get sugar, flour, stockings, socks, material, scarves, blouses, combs, and other things such as one might buy in an American 5 &10 cent store. Once a month, or more often if they needed, Mila or Iza would come to Warsaw to purchase these goods. Many things they would get from Mother; thus their connection with us was not only through friendship also business. Very often, during my vacation or holiday times, I would go to Terespol (usually with a suitcase or two filled with stuff ordered by Mila) and instead of just loafing around, I would be put to work at their store. I never objected to this arrangement, as I liked this, so to speak, manager's function at the store. Whenever the business was slow, having fresh eggs and lots of sugar on hand, I would often make myself a *kogel-mogel* (egg yolk and sugar mixture). I wonder what my cholesterol count was like then, after consumption of all those eggs! I remember one of my desires then was to have a large store of my own. I realized that the profits were quite good and the job was pretty easy. Whenever the store was closed on Sunday or a church holiday, Iza and I would take long walks all around Terespol, which was not much more than a little provincial border town. Halfway over the busy bridge that crossed the river Bug was the border between Soviet-occupied Brest and Nazi-occupied Poland. The border was heavily guarded and we could only watch from a distance the people crossing by foot or in a carriage of some sort. There were not too many cars going back and forth. All people, whether going to or from Brest, were subjected to a thorough search. Sometimes, for one reason or another, they were not let through. Then they would beg the guards, cry, or swear at them in their native language. If the guards became angry enough, the travelers were often beaten or arrested. On some occasions, depending on which guard was on duty, and after a hefty bribe, the travelers would be waved through. There were and still are two railroad stations, one in Terespol, on the Poland side, the other in Brest on the Belorussian side. (The official border is still in the middle of the railroad bridge). After leaving Terespol, the train would stop in the middle of the bridge. It would be surrounded by armed guards, while the crew would change from Polish to Russian (or Belorussian today) and the passengers' luggage, currency, passports and visas would be checked. Passengers found to be illegal or of a suspicious nature were taken off the train. Once the inspection was completed, the train would continue to Brest, or Terespol, depending on in which direction it was going at that moment. For Iza and me it was fascinating to watch all the commotion that was involved in crossing the border. We liked to speculate as to who was legitimate, who was a smuggler, and why this or that person needed to cross the border. No matter how many times we were there, there was always something new or different going on. For me, it was painful at times to realize that we were just a stone's throw, so to speak, from my grandfather and the other relatives that had stayed behind in Brest. Knowing that on our side of the border, despite being under German occupation, we were so much better off than they, and no matter how much it hurt, we could do little to help their situation.

Iza's father, Kazimierz Szyszkowski, being still employed by the railroad authority in Terespol, knew practically everyone, and thus Iza was known by many as well. Whether we were on foot or riding a bike (with me sitting on the frame), we had to wave or say hello to almost everyone along the road. Very often Iza would beg me to go by bike with her to the nearby little town of Biala Podlaska, where she had an admirer. I never could understand why she needed my chaperoning, since she was almost six feet tall, while I was only about five feet four. I guess she needed me for moral support, or maybe to hide the real reason for the trip. Behind the Szyszkowski's house there were fields of poppies. While biking through them, we would often stop for a break. We would break a few poppy heads off, open them and pour the ripe seeds straight into our mouths. Little did I know then how potent these wonderful poppy seeds could be. Nevertheless, I do not recall ever being "high," even after consuming quite a few of them. Sundays, both Iza and I dressed up, she very often in a fancy hat, and would go to the local church. The rest of the family would attend earlier or later masses. Because of the difference in our ages and especially in height, we were nicknamed *Pat i Patachon* (the Polish version of

"Pat and Pataszon" (Izabella and I, the little one) strolling on a country road in Terespol, 1943.

Mutt and Jeff). We got along fabulously, and had lots of fun and laughter while in each other's company. Iza, being the youngest of four siblings, apparently needed a younger sister, while I, not having any siblings, had a need filled by Iza. In their little house there lived Iza, Leon, Hipolit and Mila (my mother's bosom friend) and their parents. All four siblings at that time were still single. When everyone was at home and I (sometimes with Mother) was visiting, it seemed rather crowded, but there was always a close family atmosphere. Mrs. Franciszka Szyszkowska looked after the house, cooked, and tended to the few animals that were kept in the barn in the backyard. They were well supplied with fresh eggs, chickens, rabbits, and lamb, and they had all the milk and butter they could use. There was not much in home entertainment, other than playing cards, listening to music, reading, or dancing to a very good record collection of tangos, fox trots, etc. When we danced, Iza and I preferred to dance together although Iza's brothers were available. We would tease the men that an elephant must have stepped on their ears, meaning they had no sense of rhythm. Both Iza and Mila sang quite well, and in addition Mila and I could whistle in duet. So, there was never a dull moment!

All the Szyszkowskis were quite religious, but especially the mother, who would not miss a daily church service. She also was the one who, it seemed, attended all the funerals in Terespol. On one such occasion, there happened to be a severe storm, with thunder and lightening. No sooner had the storm blown over, when word reached us that a young boy of nine or ten, who I think was a shepherd in the field tending some cows, had been struck by lightening and was killed instantly. Next day, Mrs. Szyszkowska, dressed all in black as in mourning, was ready to go to view the boy's body. She kept insisting I come along. "It is our duty to pay our respects," she told me, thus convincing me to accompany her to the house of the deceased boy's parents. In those times, there were no funeral houses in small towns and it was the custom to have the deceased on view, until the day of the funeral service, in an open coffin in his home. Once we reached the house, which was full of relatives, neighbors, and people like ourselves who had come more out of curiosity than out of "respect," there was so much praying, crying and wailing that the two of us just barely could get through the crowd. The atmosphere was so strange for me that I did not want to go in, even less to actually view the body. I would have preferred just to turn around and run, but Mrs. Szyszkowska, holding my hand tightly, insisted I follow her. Once we approached the small coffin, it was for me an unbelievably scary moment. Not only was this my first viewing ever, but in addition it was a sight I could never have imagined. During the bombing, at public executions and the like, I had seen dead bodies, but this was an entirely different experience. The young boy was all charcoal brown and black, as if made of ashes. The mourning parents, siblings and relatives, sobbing and chanting uncontrollably, made the ritual even worse. Mrs. Szyszkowska wanted to stay a bit longer in order to say a prayer, but I took off, shaking, frightened and shocked, and I ran back home. Mila, who did not know about my being taken to the viewing, when she heard of it from her mother, was very angry. I tried to soften the whole incident, trying to protect Mrs. Szyszkowska, and assuring everybody that I didn't mind doing it, although later that night I could not sleep, having the terrifying picture of this poor burnt boy in front of my eyes. For many years after I avoided funerals or even discussions about death. Just hearing of someone passing away and picturing this person lying dead in the coffin would scare me and bring back that memorable viewing day in Terespol. It was a very poor introduction to how to deal with the dead, funerals and mourning.

Leon Szyszkowski was the first of Mila's siblings to get married. He and his wife moved to a nearby town, just north of Terespol. They eventually had a couple of children and they operated an automotive business. Leon died prematurely; his wife only a few years ago. Although Mila had some admirers both in Terespol and in Warsaw, she had a hard time settling on anyone in particular. Mother, being a true friend, kept coaching and introducing her to potential suitors, but with no success. Then one day, when Mila was near a window at her house, a handsome gentleman happened to be walking by. She did not know who he was, but she almost screamed and called her mother to come to the window. She exclaimed: "Mama, this is the man I will marry!"

Her mother looked at Mila as if her daughter were out of her mind. Mila kept repeating: "You will see, this fellow will be your son-in-law!" Some time passed and Mila was formally introduced to this bachelor, who was a doctor of veterinary medicine at Zalesie near Terespol. They courted briefly and were married just before the Warsaw uprising.

After the war, we were reunited with these friends first by mail, then Mother visited them in Poland, and my husband Chester and I got to meet them and their family on our first visit to Poland in 1990, which was exactly 50 years to the day after they got married. We were saddened to learn that Mila's husband, Stanislaw Kulczynski, had become blind a few years prior to our meeting. When he greeted me, he asked if he could "Braille" my face. After a few hugs, he said that I haven't changed—what a gentleman! He added that he remembered me as a very smart and capable kid. While visiting, we stayed at the little house where he lived alone. He claimed he preferred being there, rather than living with Mila at their apartment in Poznan, or in Terespol. He liked his quiet daily routine, listening to his favorite radio programs or recorded classical music. His younger daughter, Elzbieta, with her husband Jacek, and the two grandchildren (Marta and Karol) visited the sightless man daily. Despite having been handicapped for several years, he was very agreeable, never complaining, a very humble and noble man. We were amazed at how beautifully he was able to manage his situation. The family just adored him. A couple of years after our visit, he passed away. Mila, in her nineties at this writing, lives in Terespol, running her hotel, which not long ago burned down and had to be rebuilt. A former handyman from Brest started the fire out of spite. Instead of giving up her business and moving back to Poznan, where she has several apartments, being stubborn by nature, she not only rebuilt the hotel, but also enlarged it. Her older daughter, Anna, lives with her husband and son in Salzburg, Austria, while Elzbieta still lives in Poznan. Both daughters have been to our house in Santa Barbara for brief visits. Mila and I have a mutual name day (Emilia and Lucyna), which is the 30th of June. While in Poland we celebrated this day together. As a teenager, out of respect, I addressed her as *Pani* Mila (Mrs. Mila), but once we met and both of us are now mature, I call her by her first name and use the informal thou form (*ty* in Polish).

Hipolit Szyszkowski, Iza and Mila's brother, was very fond of my mother, but he was not the only one who had high hopes of marrying her. He was the first member of the Szyszkowski family whom Mother met when he helped her during her attempt to cross the border illegally in order to see her father. From then on Mother became part of the Szyszkowski family. Shortly after Poland was occupied, Hitler took a motorcade trip through conquered Poland. On his way to Brest, he had to drive through Terespol. The commandant of local authorities was a neighbor who lived across from the Szyszkowski family, Mr. Poznanski (who before the war was known as a Pole but now

announced himself as a *Volksdeutscher*). The Germans issued an order that all
adult males had to be arrested and kept out of sight until Hitler's motorcade
passed through the town. Thus, Hipolit was kept under arrest by his apolo-
getic neighbor. After this incident, Mr. Poznanski (who wore a German uniform and had the rank of Lieutenant, I believe) actually did more good than
harm. In particular, he often helped people, jailed for crossing the border, get
out of jail. After the liberation of Brest by the Russians, Hipolit was arrested
by them for being an active member of the *Armia Krajowa*, the Polish underground army, and on March 13, 1945 was executed by Soviet authorities in
Terespol. He left a wife and a one-year-old daughter Bogunia, (Boguslawa),
who presently lives in Switzerland. Hipolit's widow remarried, and died a few
years ago. His neighbor, Poznanski, met with a similar fate and died at about
the same time. His widow left Terespol for good and no one has ever heard
of her again.

Iza, my friend, got married after the end of the war, but the union was
short-lived and very unhappy. She never remarried. I lost track of her, and
only through my renewed correspondence with Mila did I get news of her; she
had developed terminal cancer. Fortunately, I wrote her a long letter in time
and through Elzbieta and Mila conveyed my sorrow at her misfortune. I tried
to tell her how much she meant to me as a true friend. I was told she was
pleased on hearing from me. Unfortunately, I was not able to see her again,
as she died in the Poznan hospital on May 30, 1977, one day after her 54th
birthday. I was told that Terespol could not remember and will never have a
more festive funeral than the one that was given Iza. She was deeply loved by
everyone who knew her. She was a stately lady, not only because of her looks,
but character as well. She was the "belle of Terespol!"

Kazimierz, Hipolit, Izabella, Franciszka and Stanislaw (in this order),
died and are buried in Terespol. My connection with Terespol is warm and
joyful. In those difficult times, the Szyszkowski's house in Terespol for me was
a true home away from home.

With her 2002 Christmas greetings, Mila, 90 years old at the time, sent
me a haphazard letter, full of warm, touching recollections of our friendship.
In the letter she writes how she cannot understand why my family and I won't
return to Poland and do not possess more patriotic feeling for our country of
origin. In this letter, she recalls how when a little girl during World War I,
she and her family were evacuated to Moscow. Even though she was quite
young at the time, she missed Poland and yearned to return. She also recalls
an incident when, having returned to her hometown, after eight years in exile,
she was placed in a school in Terespol. Her new Austrian (not Polish) teacher
one day conducted a dictation. Mila, being used to a different alphabet (Cyril-
lic) used at school in Moscow, made three mistakes in the dictation. Her
teacher, as a punishment, spanked her on the hands. To avoid such treatment
by the Austrian teacher, a friend of the family managed to transfer her to

another school in Brest. She closes the letter saying that now in her old age, she is very lonely and cries a lot, thinking with sadness of times long gone. She apologizes for the contents of her letter and her bad penmanship, of which at one time she was very proud. Her daughter Elzunia reads my letters to her and she enjoys them very much. She enclosed two small photos of me and her sister Iza (my best buddy), which were taken in the back of the Szyszkowski house. How good it was that Mila had the desire to connect with us and managed to write this letter, but also, how sad it is to recognize that old age has robbed her of her former sensibility and wit.

4

Coping with Daily Life

Much of our life during the occupation in Warsaw involved various hardships. One of these was the need to get coal or briquettes for our huge, tiled stove. It was not easy to get a decent amount and to have it delivered in time for the cold weather. Most dealers took advantage of people, but if you were willing to pay the going price, you would be warm in winter. The coal was stored in a cubicle in the basement, where usually we stored some potatoes as well. It was my duty to bring the coal up to the apartment in a medium-size bucket. It was no great hardship to carry the not-very-heavy bucket, but the idea of going down to the fairly dark basement was unpleasant and a little scary. During occupation times we only heated one stove in order to economize on the coal. Thus, the dining room, which we heated and which was also Father's, Mother's and my bedroom at night, became a sitting room for all the occupants to congregate in during the day. The other rooms in the winter were as cold as could be, but the rest of the year they were very livable.

The curfew was in effect and stiff punishment was given if it was not obeyed. If somebody decided to have a gathering, it had to be an early one, or one would have to put the guests up for the night. Once, I remember, I had a disagreement with Mila while visiting at her house in Terespol. I quietly packed my suitcase and took the train to Warsaw. One thing I had not figured out was that the train would arrive in Warsaw during curfew hours. Since it was impossible to return back to Terespol, I exited from the Warsaw railroad station onto the nearly empty streets and rushed home, hiding between the gates to the houses, and quickly crossing streets when no cars were moving on the road. Eventually, I reached the Shlykovs' apartment house. The gate was locked. A sleepy concierge came to open it and could not believe his eyes when he saw me standing there with my suitcase, looking very scared. He most likely thought I had run away from home, although in those days young girls stayed put, even if they contemplated an escape. I ran upstairs and found Misha and Sonya quite surprised to see me as well. Once I explained to them what had happened, I called Mother to tell her where I was and why. She was not aware that I had left Terespol and had arrived in Warsaw at this late hour.

Mila for quite some time was annoyed with me, but I think, after this incident, she respected me more, and in the future gave me even more responsibilities at the store.

Thievery during the occupation was very common and widespread. Pickpockets were very common then and in fact there were quite a few of them. One time Misha was standing at a trolley stop, waiting for the next streetcar. A young, very polite girl stopped next to him and asked for the time. Misha opened his coat, gallantly took his pocket watch on a gold chain out of his side pocket, and told the girl what time it was. She thanked him warmly and went away. The streetcar soon arrived and Misha and many others got on it. Shortly thereafter, some people around Misha made a commotion, as if wanting to move to the front. Misha was shoved a little in the process, but did not think much of it, as one expects closeness on a crowded streetcar. At the next stop some people got out, but Misha continued. Just before his destination, he wanted to check the time, but discovered that his watch and the attached chain were missing. Only then was he able to realize what had happened. The girl found out where he keeps his watch, told her accomplices, and they in turn staged the artificial commotion, during which they were able to steal his watch. It was a Swiss Patec Phillipe gold watch! Another time, also during a streetcar ride, thieves cut out the whole back of Sonya's Persian coat, and soon after that, on another trip, someone cut off the tail of her silver fox. This time, when she noticed it, while still in the trolley, she shouted out: "Has anyone seen my tail?" The whole car burst out in a loud roar of laughter. In the case of the lost back of her fur coat, she noticed it was missing when she got off the trolley into the cold of the snow-covered street. Her back felt light and cold, and when she ran her hand over it, she could not believe what she discovered. No doubt quite a few hats, collars, or hand muffs were made out of the stolen back of her fur and later sold at the flea market.

There were not too many apartment break-ins, as each apartment house had its own *dozorca* (a live-in doorman or concierge), and in the better districts the gates were locked at all times, while in less affluent houses the gates were locked after dark, thus making it harder to break in. On the other hand, there were many break-ins into the basements, as their little windows, even though they had grates on them, were in most cases facing the streets and thus easily accessible.

As a civilian, to survive any war, or as in this case a five-year occupation, one has to be inventive, to know how to help oneself, and be able not to lose faith in tomorrow. One has to be brave, and with a little luck on the side one can survive. The things we did during the war times I am not particularly proud of (such as black marketing, illegal activities with the underground, smuggling food, crossing borders illegally, etc.), but in order to survive it was necessary to break the laws that were imposed on us. Except for the unjust laws that were imposed on us, I feel we led an honest life just trying to stay alive and

Friends "struggling" over a jumbo bottle of wine at the Shlykov dacha in Piastow. Holding the neck of the bottle is my uncle Misha. 1943.

in fact, we lived quite well despite the limitations and ever-present dangers. We didn't know then just how bad things could get.

The Shlykovs kept busy and were financially well off. They made many friends, mostly Russians. They were very popular, since they liked to entertain, and when they had friends over, some parties went on and on. If the party broke off the same day, they sometimes repeated it the next day and the day after. Whenever Misha overindulged or misbehaved during one of his parties and made Sonya cross, he would later send her flowers. Sometimes the bouquets were so large they barely fit through the doors when being delivered. One time I remember, in the middle of the worst winter ever, the florist brought in a huge lilac bush. I guess they must have got it from the south of Italy. Sonya was extremely proud and pleased. But Misha insisted on another party, just to show off the beautiful and fragrant lilac tree. Of course, as always, Sonya complied, and the partying went on once more.

All in all, they led a pretty normal life. Their apartment, No. 10 at Nowogrodzka 43 or 41 (during the occupation the street was known also as *Neue Burgstrasse*) corner of Poznanska, was on the 5th floor overlooking the final stop of the suburban electric train. (Sixty or so years later, while talking with a local Santa Barbara Russian woman and recalling that the Shlykovs had lived on Nowogrodzka, it turned out that she apparently lived in the same house. Unfortunately, she did not remember the house number, but described the building as being across from the electric train stop. It's a small world!) From this station we used to take the train that would bring us to the various little towns (Piastow, Podkowa Lesna, Swider, Piaseczno, Pruszkow, Otwock, Michalin, Jozefow, etc.), which during the summer months turned into resort areas for the many Warsaw inhabitants who were eager to escape the summer heat of the busy city. One could live at the height of luxury, renting villas with balconies or verandahs, surrounded by pine trees, with flowerbeds in the sandy soil, and hedges or iron fences. These little suburban towns, being on the electric train line rather than the regular rail line, were easy to get to from busy Warsaw. The trains ran on a frequent schedule and the tickets were inexpensive. One had only to leave or come back before the curfew hours began.

Come the end of May, the Shlykovs were already on the lookout for a nice roomy villa to rent. They needed a big mansion in order to be able to accommodate not only us, the family, but quite a few free-loader friends. I, as a rule, went with them as soon as school vacation time started. Mother, because of her demanding "business," often had to stay put in Warsaw, but occasionally was able to join us for a short visit. Most of Shlykov's Russian friends usually came for a day or two, and some stayed as long as the Shlykovs would have them. One of the villas that the Shlykovs had rented in May/June of 1944 was in Piastow, Krasinskiego 21. Having lots of room in their Warsaw apartment, they were able to share it with the von Breverns (Dmitriy, Mariya and their daughter Wanda.) For a very brief period of time the Padukows lived

The orphan Wanda, seated second from left, in the orphanage in Brest before she was adopted by the von Breverns. About 1938.

there as well. It seemed that the Breverns were at the apartment constantly and because of that, I suspect they did not work, but used their savings to cover their living expenses. Before World War II, "Dima's" (Dmitry's) aunt was a very wealthy woman, who owned a huge estate with many lakes in the eastern part of Poland. Von Brevern was of Russian/German descent, but was recognized by the Nazi authorities as a *Volksdeutscher* (an ethnic German living abroad). Because of his status, von Brevern was able to intercede for his good friend Mikhail Shlykov to get him excused from curfew restrictions and allow him to visit restaurants and other establishments normally accessible only to Germans. His wife "Marusya," who was a nurse, was Polish. As part of her nursing job, she frequently visited orphanages. Once, during such an assignment, she grew to love a little girl, Wanda, whom the Breverns eventually adopted. They loved this little daughter and smothered her with affection. Since the Shlykovs were very generous, I had the impression that the Breverns were not only housed, but fed as well, and were entertained whenever the Shlykovs had a gathering of friends, which was quite often.

    Misha and Sonya had a very young girl worker who came from the country. Sonya trained her so well that she became a very capable housekeeper. Her name was Wacka (pronounced "Vatska"). She was a shy girl, quite simple, short and plump, and always in a good mood, just a sixteen-year-old girl when

My uncle Misha and I in the countryside, Swider, Poland, 1943.

she arrived at the Shlykovs with a little suitcase. After a very brief time, Sonya, on very short notice, could entertain a whole batch of guests simply by telling Wacka what to prepare and for how many. She kept their house in immaculate order, did most of the day-to-day shopping, had a flair for flower arrangements, and fulfilled every wish that Sonya and Misha had. Whenever they went to one of the resort towns, Sonya always took Wacka, as she alone could not cope with the constant entertaining and cooking. Wacka, being devoted to the family, would have been insulted if she had not been asked to come along. During the time when Igor was still living at home, she covered up all his escapades and mischief. If interrogated by Igor's parents about his doings, or whereabouts, not wanting to get him in trouble (Misha happened to be a very strict father), she just turned her eyes up, her rosy cheeks getting bright red, looked dumb, and simply pretended she did not know anything was wrong. Sonya made one small room into a pantry. Having to entertain so frequently, she wanted to be absolutely sure that Igor, Misha, or the Breverns did not eat up whatever she and Wacka prepared for a given party. Therefore, as soon as something was cooked, it was put away into the pantry, which was kept under lock and key. One time, Igor knew that many nice things were being stored, especially his favorite cakes and cookies, so he asked Wacka, to please let him have some, but she would not agree to open the pantry. He did not wait long to find a solution. He went to the room adjacent to the pantry and going through the open window got onto the outside ledge of the building, and, inching his way along the ledge, climbed through the open window into the pantry. He ate what he wanted and returned the same way he came in. The windows overlooked the busy street below, where many people usually waited for the electric train. It must have been a sight to see and a scary one to say the least. Fortunately, no one reported a burglary in progress. "Guga," as we called Igor, was a daredevil and always ready for any tricky challenge. Wacka also looked after Misha's hygiene. After a busy day and a long party, sometimes Misha would think of going to bed without taking a shower. At those times, she would plead with her boss, pointing out that the bedding is so very clean and indeed he should not get into it unwashed. Not getting his agreement, she would make a deal with him, and offer to bring a basin to the bedroom for a quick wash. Usually, a very reluctant and tired Misha would give in and get into bed clean.

There was a very strong sense of togetherness for the Russians that lived or ended up in Warsaw. They were anti–Soviet Russians who were called "White Russians" and bore passports (*Generalgouvernement Kennkarte*) stamped with the letter R. There were different organizations that tried to recruit Russian youth, send them as partisans into the then Soviet Union. One such outfit headed by Sologubov convinced Igor, son of the Shlykovs, and his cousin Sergey to become fighters attempting to abolish the Soviet regime. Both of them and many other of their young friends joined this outfit and left for their assignments. Sonya fought to the last moment, not letting her young son go. Igor one day finally said to her: "If you won't let me go, I'll run away." She felt she had no choice and very reluctantly gave her blessing for his departure.

The White Russians, being anti–Soviet, were treated by the German occupation authorities somewhat less harshly than the Polish population. There was still a distinction between them and the so-called *Volksdeutsch* and *Reichsdeutsch*. The former indicated those who were ethnic Germans (like von Brevern,) and the latter were those recognized as nationals of the now extended Nazi Reich. The only White Russian collaboration with the German authorities, if any, involved their common aim of fighting the Soviets, like the outfit of Sologubov.

Despite the good times and their prosperity, both Sonya and Misha were very unhappy with Igor's decision to leave for the unknown. They were hopeful, but knew that they were not apt to see their beloved and only son ever again, which is exactly what happened.

The Padukows in their turn were faced with the same dilemma. Their son Sergey's departure was a final blow to them, as they already knew that their older son Arkady was missing and might never return. They were also not able to stop Sergey from leaving. Thus, the two cousins, although so different by nature, shared the same cause for freedom. Sergey survived, but Igor was captured near Smolensk and was brutally executed by the Bolsheviks. The fear

Der Polizeipräsident

Abt. **Nachtausweis** Nr. } 33077

Przepustka nocna Nr. }

Нічна виказка Ч. }

Gültig von Ważna od dnia важна від }	26. Mai	bis do dnia до }	25. August 1944. 1944 r. 1944.

Name Nazwisko Прізвище }	Szlykow	Vorname Imię Ім'я }	Michael

Geburtsdatum Data urodzenia Дата народження }	28. IV. 1900	Geburtsort Miejsce urodzenia Місце народження }	Brest-Litowsk

Beruf
Zawód
Звання } *Kaufmann*

Wohnung (Stadt, Gemeinde)
Mieszkanie (Miasto, gmina)
Мешкання (Місто, громада) } Warschau

Straße und Hausnummer
Ulica i Nr domu
вулиця і число дому } Neue Bürgstr. 41

beschäftigt bei (Arbeitgeber, Firma)
Zatrudniony w (Pracodawca, firma)
зайнятий в (Працедавець, фірма) } —

in
w
в } —

ist berechtigt, in der Sperrzeit
jest uprawniony w czasie zakazu przebywania poza domostwem
має право в забороненому часі перебування поза хомом

von
od
від } 21 Uhr bis
godziny do
год. до } 5 Uhr
godziny
год.

die Straßen in (Stadt, Gemeinde, Gebiet)
przebywać na ulicach w (Miasto, gmina, obszar)
иступати на вулиці в (Місто, громада, округа) } Warschau

den Wald in
w lesie w
до ліса в } — die Felder in
na polu w
на поля в } —

Nachtausweis. An identity document, issued to Mikhail Shlykov by the police president of Warsaw, 26 May 44, allowing him to disregard curfew restrictions and be on the streets of Warsaw between the hours 21 and 5 (9 P.M. and 5 A.M.) The card was obtained through the intercession of Dmitry von Brevern, who was given special privileges by the Nazi authorities because of his status as a *Volksdeutscher* (ethnic German living abroad).

for Arkady's fate was many years later confirmed by news that he, like his younger cousin Igor, had also been executed.

Thus, considering the fate of my father, of Arkady and Igor, and our separation from my grandfather, it appears that, after all, life in Warsaw, which at the time seemed to be a fairly good thing, was also a time of great loss.

5

Father Dies in Auschwitz

The Warsaw apartment house was a massive building in the center of the city at the corner of Hoza and Krucza streets consisting of approximately 25 apartments. Facing Krucza Street, on the corner, there was a fairly large coffee house, *Cukiernia Paciorkowskiego*, at which one could buy delicious pastries as well as sit at tables, have coffee or tea, and read a magazine or a selection of newspapers, which were mounted onto sticks. Next to the coffee house there was a restaurant from which we used to order catered dinners for our unexpected guests. Our apartment house was a three-story building overlooking Hoza street, with balconies supported on the shoulders of mythological figures. The entrance (a gate for cars) and a separate door for people on foot were closed after dark and one had to ring the bell to get in. The janitor (*dozorca* Kaniewski) who lived at the end of the *wjazd* (gated entry) was the one who would open the gate. Apartment owners had their own keys. Each apartment that faced the street had two entrances: front and delivery. The front staircases were of marble; the back ones were of wood, as were the balustrades of highly polished mahogany. (They were well maintained, since children sliding down on them polished them daily.) On each stairway landing there was a spittoon. One of the duties of the *dozorca* was to keep the spittoons clean, other duties included washing the staircases and windows and generally looking after the overall upkeep of the building. Balconies on the courtyard side were recessed and simple and mostly served for storage of this or that, and in the winter these balconies were a good place to keep things cold. It was also a place from which it was convenient to shake out a small rug or air featherbeds and pillows, but it was not customary to use them for drying one's laundry. You could look out from them onto the courtyard, which had a raised square planter on which trees and flowers were growing. The planter had a sturdy railing that served as a place to beat large oriental rugs. From these balconies many parents called to their children, announcing that it is time to come to eat, or to quit playing for the day. Whenever neighboring parents appeared on the balconies at the same time, it was customary to say hello and chat. At such times the children took advantage of their parents' socializing,

having another chance to continue a game, or make another tour of the courtyard on their bikes. In the courtyard there was an enclosed garbage bin, next
to which were cages with rabbits owned by various tenants. The fairly large
paved area around the planter was used by children of all ages as a playground.
There was never a shortage of playmates—as soon as one child came down to
the courtyard, others joined him/her, to play volleyball or soccer, to ride endlessly round and round the square on bikes, to play hide-and-seek or hop-
scotch. Those children who primarily spent their outdoors playing in their
own courtyards were called *dzieci podworza* (courtyard children). Rarely would
children of one house engage in playtime with the children of an adjacent
house. But schoolmates would sometimes come for a visit and join in the play.

    One of my schoolmates, Cecylia ("Lusia") Wojewodzka, was one of my
closest friends and a frequent visitor to our house. She played the piano beautifully and sometimes tried to show off and put me to shame by playing Chopin
pieces and the like. Although I had the use of the piano, which was in Lissner's (our German tenant's) room, because of the coldness (if a glass with water
was left there, it would freeze solid!) I was reluctant to practice there as I had
to wear gloves with their tips cut off and a coat to keep (barely) warm. My
first teacher turned out to be very lenient, letting me play any which way just
to please me. It was obvious he was only interested in the pay and not in my
progress. Soon, Mother hired a new teacher, a very strict professor of music.
After a few lessons he told Mother point-blank: "This is a waste of my time
and your money." At that, the lessons stopped, but I continued to be envious
of Lusia's ability to play well without any seeming effort. Often when I visited Lusia we would go for a walk and now and then inadvertently or sometimes on purpose go through the "red light" district, a street parallel to Lusia's
street where there always seemed to be lots of "action." We were fascinated by
what we saw, speculated on it, and wondered what it was about. Of course,
nothing was ever said to our parents and we never asked about it.

    Frequently, almost daily in the summer time, amateur street performers
would come by to give a show in the courtyard. They might be a solo musician, gypsy singers and dancers who would also offer to tell your fortune, or
even a three- or four-piece orchestra, which would play the latest popular
tunes, especially tangos. After each number tenants would throw down coins,
wrapped in paper so that they wouldn't scatter all over the pavement.

    When I was growing up, there were no plastic toys. Dolls were often
made at home from old stockings, or socks stuffed with rags. Faces were painted
on and hair was made of yarn. I had such a little rag doll that went with me
everywhere and gave me a great sense of comfort. She was mended, washed
frequently, and dressed to look nice. Since she was my constant companion,
no matter what effort was made to keep her presentable, she showed a lot of
wear and tear. In fact, she looked ugly. My parents tried numerous schemes
to get rid of the doll, "forgetting" her in different places, hiding her from me,

and so on, but they all were unsuccessful. Finally, one day, when father could no longer stand the sight of "Kasia," he pretended to do a little magic. He took my Kasia and making hocus-pocus gestures made Kasia "disappear." Father thought it would be an easy way out, but he did not realize what an impact it would have and how it would affect me by losing my beloved companion. He tried to make up for the disappearance of the doll, but for many, many days I cried for Kasia's return. I was inconsolable.

A vivid recollection I have from childhood is when I received a bright red rubber ball, shiny as if covered with lacquer, and spotted with white polka dots. Just recently I watched a commercial on TV in which I saw the ball of my childhood. I could not believe that there could be another ball exactly like the one I had had so many, many years ago.

During the war years presents weren't as lavish as we give nowadays. One present that I remember made an impression on me when I was a girl was a small oval, red leather shoulder bag. It had many compartments, with zippers, a mirror, and a change purse that contained one zloty! I was so thrilled with it that I slept with it to make sure no one would take it away from me. A small, nicely engraved sterling silver compact with a mirror and a powder compartment was a gift from my cousin, Sergey. When he gave it to me, he warned me to the effect that although I was grown enough to powder my nose, I was not old enough to date his friends! Often on holidays during a meal I would find an envelope under the tablecloth with German marks from the Shlykovs. Also on one occasion I got a bright, shiny five-ruble gold coin from them. It was a piece from their collection.

Our first-floor apartment (second-floor American style) faced the front and back, occupying the whole side to the right of the gate. There were identical apartments above and below us. Under the ground-floor apartment there was a baking facility for the *Cukiernia Paciorkowskiego*. Baked pastries were carried on huge trays through the courtyard to the coffee shop. The bakers were very friendly with the children and often treated them with reject pastries, and if a competitive game was taking place, they served as a cheering section. The owner of the coffeehouse, Mr. Paciorkowski, was an elegant, plump, almost roly-poly man in his fifties, always dressed similarly to a floorwalker in a fashion house in the States or England. He was married, with a son of college age, and he often teased me with the greeting: "How is my future daughter-in-law?" which embarrassed me if said in front of other children. His wife died prematurely. One winter day, returning from a beauty salon, she stopped to talk to a friend on the street, caught cold and died a few days later of brain inflammation. Next to the gate, a shoemaker (Mr. Mazur) had his workplace, where three men sat behind the window, primarily making shoes to order but also doing repairs as well. One could see them through the window, laughing and chatting while plying their trade. Mr. Mazur's wife would bring their meals to their workbench, meals that she prepared in the back of the shop, which in fact was the Mazurs' tight apartment. Their son, Jasio, who was a grade or two younger than I, in exchange for my help with his homework, often let me wear his fancy pumps (*polbuciki*). I would leave the apartment in my ugly high-laced shoes, that Mother insisted I wear in order to have nice ankles, but would quickly change into Jasio's shoes, which he would leave in front of our door. Mother never caught me making this exchange. Not only did wearing up-to-date shoes make me happy, but also the ribbed cotton stockings I also had to wear looked 100 percent better. Of course, these children's stockings didn't compare to my girlfriends' sheer ones, which at that time were silk stockings with a seam in the back, which extended to the upper thigh and were held up in front and back by a garter. As much as I hated to wear the ribbed stockings and the high-laced shoes, in the wintertime, I loved to use a fancy muff to keep my hands warm and a home-knit angora hat that was tied under my chin.

In many entry gates women would sell freshly baked loaves of breads (including my favorite, *pytlowy chleb*, made of sifted flour) and rolls. Other women would sell vegetables and fruit, most likely grown in their gardens in the outskirts of the city, which they wrapped in cone-shaped bags of stiff brown paper or newspapers.

Under the length of the whole house there was a massive basement, with a high ceiling but with an unfinished dirt floor and small windows with iron grates looking out onto the street or the courtyard. Running along the long corridor were several cubicles with see-through doors; each tenant was assigned one of these cubicles for personal storage and to hold potatoes and coal in the winter. During bombings and air raids the basement served as a bomb shelter and during the uprising as a temporary hospital for the wounded. Also, just before the end of the uprising, Mother designated our basement cubicle as the hiding place where her valuables were to be buried, a task she entrusted to the same friend (Roman Rajpold) she saved at the time of Father's arrest and to another friend (Jurek Neuman), who was to know about the site as well, in case one or the other did not survive, so that some day we could retrieve the substantial possessions that would keep us going for many years to come. After all, we expected the war would come to an end and we would return to the ruins of destroyed Warsaw, and eventually find our hidden treasures. According to their accounts, these two friends did bury Mother's valuables as asked, shortly thereafter the house was bombed and destroyed, and the remaining occupants were forced to leave the city. Roman and Jurek, our friends, ended up in London. Roman notified his wife (Ziuta, who survived the uprising by staying in their summer house with their child) of Mother's buried fortune, giving her a diagram of the Hoza 19 basement area. She went to the ruins of the house, to the designated area, but allegedly found nothing. Our friends maintained that someone beat them to it. While in London, Mother tried to meet with Jurek, but he declined. Roman and his wife met with us and claimed to know nothing. Although they were quite poor while living in Warsaw, we were surprised to find them in London as the owners of a three-story house in a good part of the city. He had become an alcoholic and she was suffering with breast cancer. Reluctantly, I accepted their story as the truth and we parted as "friends." (As of October 2000, as reported by a friend in Poland, it appears that Ziuta and Roman Rajpold both passed away and were buried in Wloclawek, Poland.)

Forty-seven years after the August 1944 Warsaw uprising, during my first return visit to Poland, I came back to Hoza and Krucza streets. Hoza now is a one-way street, which seems much narrower but much greener. On both sides of the street, branches of newly planted trees join at the top, forming a dark tunnel. At our former address there is a five-story house of modern architecture, with large windows and with narrow balconies that serve more as decoration than function. There are stores and offices on the street level, with not a single reminder of the *Cukiernia Paciorkowskiego*. The apartment buildings across from Hoza 19 made the picture even stranger—the once familiar place is there no more. I couldn't help but wonder: perhaps, deep under the basement of the new facade, maybe, by sheer chance, Mother's treasures are still lying buried there?

Standing there, memories from the past came back to me, the good, somewhat carefree moments of my early youth and some very sad and tragic times.

The apartment in Warsaw, which we exchanged for our place in Brest, was a very spacious one. The front staircase led to two apartments on each floor. The Paciorkowskis' apartment was on the right, ours across from it, on the left. The ornate, high double door with a peephole opened to a medium-sized central foyer, which, in turn, had three doors. To the right was a double door to a huge living room (*salon*), which was connected to a smaller room, meant to be a library or study, through which one could enter the bedroom. All these three rooms overlooked Hoza Street. The left door from the foyer was to a very small room, originally meant for a child, guest, or maid. Straight ahead from the entry was the dining room. This room had a double door to the study and also had a door to a central corridor, from which there were doors leading to the bedroom, a separate toilet, the bathroom, and the kitchen, for a total of five doors! From the kitchen there was a service door to the staircase, which came out to the courtyard. The layout of the apartment, if it were to be used by one family, was rather sensible, whereas in our case it was quite problematic. When we arrived at Hoza, we discovered that the apartment was far from being ready for our occupancy. The Fuksmans' housekeeper, Nina Mazowiecka, and her friend, Alla Maksimowicz, already occupied the bedroom. The study was temporarily housing a Jewish couple, friends of the Fuksmans, who had fled from Lodz. Shortly after, they ended up in the newly formed ghetto. Roman Rajpold, Father's friend, who came with us from Brest, moved into the very small room. After the Jewish couple had left for the newly formed ghetto, the three of us, Father, Mother and I, had the three remaining rooms to ourselves. But this luxury didn't last long. No sooner had we settled in when we were forced to give over the living room and the study to two German firms, to be used as their offices, thus leaving only the very transient dining room at our disposal. Fortunately, the director of one firm lived in Lodz and commuted on weekends, the other lived in the outskirts of Warsaw; therefore, we could occasionally use these two rooms to house stranded visitors.

The apartment was elegantly furnished with massive Germanic-style furniture, which was imported from Gdynia, a city very much influenced by German culture. The bedroom furniture was more modern, of grayish, highly lacquered walnut. The dining room was of a heavily carved wood that had a jet-black finish. There was a huge grandfather clock with chimes that rang once every quarter of an hour, twice for each half hour, and the appropriate number of times on the hour. This busy black monstrosity, like a coffin standing on its end, scared me on many occasions. It was an expensive antique, which I hated but had to live with every day. A wall-length buffet stood on one side, a double-size sofa bed on the other. A very large round table, supported by a massive cylindrical leg with six or eight chairs stood in the middle of the room. A floor-to-ceiling, imported tile stove in the corner served not only to heat the room but also to warm our backs. In this stove, under the ashes, Roman hid his dollar banknotes during the warm season when the stove was resting. But there came a cold spell and one of us (it may have been me, as one of my duties was to bring coal or briquettes from the basement and start the fire), not knowing of the money hidden there, started the fire. Fortunately, Roman was in the room and remembered in time to retrieve the banknotes, with only the corners being burnt off. Being very laid-back as he was, this was not the first or last near miss in Roman's life. In fact, Roman's laid-back nature made him the butt of several practical jokes, which my friend Hanka Nosek and I played on him. One day Hanka convinced me to lure Roman on a pretext to check something in our basement cubicle. Not suspecting anything, he gladly agreed to give us a hand and went down to the dimly lit basement. While he was engaged in checking out the cubicle, as we had asked, Hanka quickly pushed me out the door and immediately locked the cubicle, with Roman inside it. We both ran upstairs, planning to return soon and free him, but we then became preoccupied with something and completely forgot about Roman's predicament. Finally, a fellow tenant in the building came to alert Mother about Roman's imprisonment. Mother quickly ran down to the basement to release the absolutely furious Roman, who vowed to "kill that devil Hanka" once he got hold of her.

On another occasion, when the very relaxed Roman appeared ready to take one of his frequent catnaps, Hanka offered to give him a facial while he rested and he readily agreed. We began properly, first applying steaming hot towels to his face and then massaging it with cream. Noticing that the treatment had put him to sleep, Hanka proceeded to apply heavy makeup to his face, and then we left him in that condition to continue his rest. When he awoke, not being aware of what he looked like, he came to join us and the others in the dining room. At the sight of him everyone burst into spontaneous laughter. He looked quizzically at the hysterics and was told to go look in a mirror. When he did so, he screamed out of rage and proceeded to search for Hanka, but by that time we both had left the apartment! After he cooled off, I returned, but, fortunately, he felt that Hanka was the instigator of the prank. Hanka, in her turn, waited several days before coming by our apartment again.

Father and Roman played chess quite often. When it was his turn to make a move, it was usually an action in slow motion. It took him forever even to make a simple move. Often, I would come up from behind him and make the move for him, at which he would exclaim, "Splendid! Just what I was thinking of doing."

Since the dining room was the warmest place in the winter and the coolest in the summer, it was the preferred place of all activities. We ate there, played cards or chess, I did my homework there or laid out a solitaire. The solitaires (*pasjansy*, as we called them in Polish) were constantly suggested by Mother. She presumably would think of a secret wish and if the solitaire came out, it meant her wish would come true. I usually agreed to her request and always hoped that the outcome of the solitaire was such so that her secret wish indeed would come true. All sorts of discussions and debates took place in this room — if only walls had ears! When it was our turn to hold classes, we met here as well. Also, in this dark, scary room, by candlelight, we held séances (*wywoly-wanie duchow*, calling forth the dead).

Because the electricity was turned off very often, for a source of light we used carbide lamps. These leaked unpleasant and dangerous fumes if not put together properly. The lamp consisted of two parts. In the lower container carbide chips were placed. Then the separate, upper container was filled with water and screwed on tightly to the bottom part. Through a small opening the water would drop slowly onto the carbide below, creating fumes and then, turning the lamp to the "on" position, the lamp was ready to be lit. Regulating the water would intensify the bright, bluish light. The tiny opening on the top had to be kept clean with a pin in order to have an even stream of light. The lamp would hiss if too much water was dripping, or if there was a gap between the two containers because it was not screwed on tightly or was cracked. Sometimes carbide lamps (as happened in Mother's childhood) would explode and injure the person tending to it. Since I was also in charge of the carbide lamps, after many lectures on how to handle this task, I learned all the tricks and never had any problems. In addition to occasional carbide fumes, the sometimes smoky stove, and cigarette smoke (practically all adults smoked, up to two or more packs a day!) our dining room was literally a smoke chamber! It was fortunate we had the large window and the balcony door, which was ajar almost always.

Until the takeover of our two front rooms, heating the living room with its two large windows and a balcony door and the study, which also had a large window, made too large a space to heat in the winter. Once these two rooms became offices, heating them was no problem for the tenants. They got extra coal and did not have to use it sparingly like the rest of us. One of the tenants was a financial advisor, Alfred Josef Lissner. He paid us 400 zloty a month. He was a *Volksdeutscher*, originally from Lodz, where he had a wife and a son. His secretary was a Polish woman, who became his mistress. The other tenant was Waclaw Kszeminski, a Pole, who had a firm that dealt in chains. Waclaw was married and lived with his family outside Warsaw. In general, all the rooms were often shared with friends who needed shelter while in transit. All in all, it was a large place, but quite small when invaded by a large number of people at the same time.

The kitchen was well equipped, with a huge stove, quite modern for those times, with many burners, which often were all in use at the same time. There was a sliding door to the back balcony and a high window in the bathroom. The floor was of light, unfinished wood, which was kept spotless! There were no washing machines or dryers. A middle-aged woman, who was our housekeeper, came to do the cleaning, laundry and ironing.

When she arrived for work, she would find lunch, often more like dinner, prepared by Mother, and a glass of vodka, which she drank with gusto. This simple woman was rather witty. When Mother would ask her, "Would you like another glass of vodka?" she would say, "*Co do tego to i owszew i owszem!*" ("As for that, indeed, indeed!"). When discussing the laundry, her favorite saying was "*Biale nie biale, byle wode widzialo!*" ("White or not white, as long as it's seen water!"). We called her *gosposia* (housewife), which sounded warmer and friendlier than *sprzataczka* (cleaning woman). She was devoted to our highly polished parquet floors. After applying wax to them, she would have me sit on the polisher, and then she in turn would pull or push the polisher until the floor's shine was to her satisfaction. My weight, she claimed, gave a better and higher gloss and I never disputed the case! Because of the shiny, slippery floors, Mother slipped on them several times, breaking her elbow three times! Gosposia insisted it was Mother's haste and her high heels and not the fault of the beautifully maintained floors.

After being squeezed into the dining room, which became our only room, Father and Mother slept on the double sofa that had drawers under the mattress for hiding the bedding during the day. My bed consisted of two heavy armchairs that were placed face-to-face at night and apart during the day, for extra sitting room. Occasionally, while fast asleep, I would stretch, thus making my bed separate and I'd end up with the bedding and all on the floor. If that happened, often I would stay put on the floor until morning. After Father's arrest, I shared the sofa with Mother. Eventually, Roman remarried and moved to his own apartment across from our service entrance, so I was sure I could have his room for my own. But as it turned out, Mother needed it as a warehouse to keep merchandise she was selling and trading. And so, my dream of having my own room, or just my own bed, had to stay a dream for many more years to come. We missed Roman, even though his laid-back nature occasionally got on everyone's nerves. After he moved out, while mother was cleaning up his room, she discovered many opaque beer bottles with hermetic corks. Knowing that Roman was a nondrinker, we were puzzled until we opened one of the bottles and discovered their true use. It turned out that, in addition to being laid-back, he was too lazy to make the trip to the bathroom during the night and found a different solution. This time it was Mother who said, "I could kill him!"

The whole apartment was wallpapered, not once, or twice, but many times over, with layer upon layer covering the thick walls. Once, the owners of the apartment above us decided to fumigate their place for bedbugs, which had had their home for many years between the layers of their wallpaper. Not knowing of our neighbors' action, all of a sudden we had bedbugs everywhere! They were dropping on us from the ceiling, crawling in through the windows, doors, and the smallest crevasses! Before the neighbors' fumigation, our apartment had been bug-free; now it was the mother of all nightmares! We were plagued with bites and felt disgust just entering the apartment, not to mention sleeping in it. Mother chose to sleep temporarily on the table. Somebody suggested putting containers with water around us, so the bugs would drown. But nothing helped. We had to remove all the layers of wallpaper and fumigate our place as quickly as possible!

The apartment was a happy one—despite the fact that all its occupants had their problems and worries of what the future might bring—until the night when Father was arrested, imprisoned, and sent to Auschwitz. Life for Mother and me from then on was not the same. Mother became the sole breadwinner. While Father was still in Auschwitz, Mother would try to move heaven and earth to rescue him. She would often leave for Krakow to go to the Gestapo headquarters to see if she somehow could get Father freed. On those occasions, although I was glad to have the sofa to myself, I dreaded her being away. I thought that she, too, would disappear and no one would know where to, and that she, like Father, would never come back.

In 1940, a few months after we settled down in the new apartment in Warsaw, Oleg Fuksman (*Oles Fuchsman*), the son of the apartment owners and a young man in his early twenties, came to the city and stayed with us for a few days. He came primarily to pick up his parents' hidden jewelry. While living there we were not aware that the massive leg of the huge round dining room table was literally a vault. Taking all the valuable belongings, Oleg returned to Brest. Someone, a neighbor who recognized him perhaps, informed the Gestapo that Father had been "hiding a Jew and had released to him Jewish valuables" (they called this *Judenbegünstigung*, doing favors for Jews.) Shortly after Oleg's visit, in the middle of the night on July 3, 1940, the Gestapo came and arrested Father. While he was given a few minutes to get dressed, Mother managed to warn Father's friend, Roman, to hide under his blanket and pretend to be a woman, not an easy task to do as he was over six feet tall. When asked if there were any men other than Father in the apartment, Mother firmly denied it, thus saving our friend's life. Father chose not to wake me up to say what would have been his last good-bye. Together with a full truck of other arrestees, Father was taken to the infamous *Pawiak* prison in Warsaw.

During the early years of the German occupation people were taken from the streets at random during so called *lapanki* (roundups), or arrested from a list, as was Father and so many others on the 3rd of July 1940. One could be on a list as a suspect for working in an underground organization, for being denounced as a Jew-lover, or for being part of the *intelligentsia* (clergy, teachers, doctors, lawyers, and other professionals). One could also become detained for resembling a Jew. For example, in an ambush on the street a detainee's genitals would be quickly checked behind the gate of a nearby house. If found to have been circumcised, that person would be arrested for being a Jew, inasmuch as only Jews and not Poles were normally circumcised.

While at *Pawiak* Father managed to send us little messages via people who were being let out, or we would go to the walls of the prison and catch a *gryps*, a tiny note that was shot out of the prison window with the help of a rubber band. In one of these notes, Father addressed me separately, ending with the words "be obedient and kind to your mother." Mother and co-residents of our apartment were constantly called to *Aleje Szucha*, the Gestapo offices, for interrogations. The German interrogators were rough, demanding more information about the Fuksmans, any knowledge of underground activities, names of people who could be of interest, etc. In a few weeks after Father's arrest, on August 14, 1940, we were advised that he had been transferred from *Pawiak* and taken to Oswiecim to *Koncentration Lager Auschwitz* and on August 15, 1940 given the number 1515. In 1990, when together with my husband Chester I visited Poland for the first time since the end of the war, I immediately went to the Pawiak prison to see if they had any more information on my father's stay at that prison and on his transfer to Auschwitz. The curator of what is now a museum could only confirm what I have stated above, but he suggested I might find more information in the *Gestapo Prison Chronicles 1939–1944*, compiled by Regina Domanska, and published in 1978 by the Ksiega I Wiedza Publishing House, Warsaw. An excerpt (page 80) from that publication gives a few more details, as follows: "1940—14 August: the first transport departed for the Oswiecim (Auschwitz) concentration camp. Five hundred and thirteen prisoners were taken from the Pawiak prison. Seven trucks making several trips were used to transport prisoners to the railroad platform on Zelazowa Street. In the transport operation among others were included the members of RKS "Skra" arrested on 3 July 1940, a number of lawyers, physicians, officers of the Polish Army, political and public officials, and priests. Along with the Pawiak prisoners there were transported 1153 men caught in street round-ups. The prisoners arrived at Oswiecim on 15 August and received numbers from 1513 to 1899 and from 1901 to 3179. Those taken from the Pawiak prison included ... Kucharski, Feliks."

Although I had been aware that people were "disappearing"—were being arrested, executed or sent to ghettos or concentration camps, no matter their origin, faith, or walk of life, until July 3, 1940, I would never have imagined that my father's safety was endangered or that some day he too could be one of those unfortunate people. From that day on, in my young world, life was never the same. Although now, when I look back and recall my teenage years, I can say that I was generally a happy, easily pleased, lively child. Father's departure had put a tremendous damper on my disposition. I became moody and melancholy, and yet, despite it all, I could often still laugh through my tears. While sitting in our makeshift classroom listening to the voice of the teacher, I often didn't absorb a thing that she was saying. I kept looking out the window (if there was one) just staring, daydreaming, or thinking. Now and then during recess, one teacher in particular, a very compassionate woman, noticing my sadness and distraction, would ask me if she could comfort or help me in some way. She would say while hugging me, "Lusienko, everything will be all right. The war will soon be over and we all will be reunited with our loved ones." There were happy voices full of laughter around me and I envied them in a way, and wished I could be like them—carefree and happy. Among these friends, there was only one friend who was in a situation similar to mine. Hanka's father, Col. Edward Nosek, was considered lost in action after the Polish surrender in September 1939, but actually he had gone into hiding where he became an officer in the underground army. Periodically, he would show up at their house and then disappear again for weeks or months, just sending his family a signal now and then that he was still alive. The last time he left, his wife was pregnant with their second child. Hanka, in contrast to me, acted as if she did not care that she might never see her father again. She was full of mischief and happy-go-lucky, and because of her misbehaving, sometimes I also got in trouble. Her mother counted on my being a good influence on her daughter, hoping that it would help curb Hanka's behavior, but that was next to impossible. Hanka was a devil in disguise! Sometimes she not only acted like one, she even resembled one! And because of her attitude, so different from mine, despite our mutual problem of missing fathers, she was of little consolation to me. We just could not share the same grief. Coming home after classes to an often empty apartment was painful. Many friends and those that lived at our place tried to support me and cheer me up, and they showed concern by asking if there was any news about Father. They kept assuring me that he was well and would return. Many nights I woke up crying and shivering from fear that soon bad news might arrive. On the one hand, fearing the ultimate bad news became like a paranoia; on the other hand, I would imagine that Father was just on a business trip and that one day soon, unexpectedly, the doorbell would ring and I would see him, with his usual warm grin, waiting to be let in. No matter what went through my mind, either way there was no comfort, especially at night, when I simply had to wait for the morning to come, hoping that the new day would bring good news—news from Father via someone from somewhere. Day or at night, it seemed, Father's presence kept moving across my field of vision. After a sleepless night, I couldn't care less when crossing the street against the red light or jumping in front of a moving streetcar. Just the thought of life without Father seemed senseless.

Mother's utmost appeals for Father's release remained to no avail; she was left with promises that never materialized. Finally, at one point, in the Krakow Gestapo headquarters, she was promised Father's immediate release from the camp. A sum of money, via a middleman, was to be deposited after his release. Despite all the hope, promises and faith—the dreadful day came. A brief telegram from the German authorities was delivered to our apartment stating, "Feliks Kucharski died on February 6, 1941. Ashes and belongings of the deceased will arrive separately." Soon after, a bundle of Father's clothing arrived. We bought a plot at the Warsaw cemetery to bury his ashes, which never came. Symbolically, on *Zaduszki* (All Souls' Day) and his birthday, June 2nd, we would go to the empty plot and light a candle in his memory.

At first, both Mother and I could not and would not accept the terrible news. We could only imagine that the telegram was a mistake, involving a wrong identity. After all, just prior to this, Mother had been assured in Krakow at the highest office, that Father's release was imminent. Many speculations kept going through our minds. It was known that some lucky few did survive—who knows, maybe one of them was Father? Then many days passed and our hope of seeing him at the door dwindled. We developed another theory: He must have run away, on his own, or have been released illegally with the help of the person that promised Mother that day back in Krakow, and now Father must be in hiding. We believed in this possibility and lived with it. The hope was stronger than ever—until the day when Mother met a man, a friend of Father's, who was released recently from Auschwitz and now was again in hiding, "just in case they (the Germans) will be looking for me again." This is why he decided to approach Mother on a street corner, rather than come to our apartment. He was very reluctant to speak to her and told her to give up any hope she had. He told her about seeing Father before his own release, about the poor condition he was in, swollen beyond recognition, and this friend assured Mother he could not see any chance of Father's survival. Mother was crushed by the grim news. Hopeless and defeated, she passed the news to me as gently as she could. Hearing the terrible account, I suddenly felt the rush of the weeks of grief and the ocean of pain pouring forth. I wept uncontrollably. After all, I felt very close to my father and I was crushed by the news that he was dead.

Bringing up the above recollections of my childhood and writing about what is perhaps the hardest segment of all my life experiences, including all the other war and postwar escapades, are very difficult. Nothing can compare to the subject of my father's death, which is so close to my heart.

Mother, at 35 years old, like many other widows, lived many years with false hopes, somehow willing to believe it was possible to have the promise of her husband's release while at the same time holding his death announcement. She lived with the image of him showing up at the apartment. They had been happily married, but for a mere thirteen years.

6

My Father, Feliks Stanislaw Kucharski

Feliks was born on June 2, 1897 in Pabianice (near Lodz), Poland. He was an only son, and was brought up solely by his mother. He never met his father. Mother recalls the following mysterious event. Once in about 1935, while visiting Mother's relatives in Brest, we stayed at the Padukows' hotel. While she was sitting in the living room with relatives, the bellboy came in and told my uncle that so and so (she doesn't remember the name) had just arrived and was checking in. Father, on hearing the name, jumped to his feet and quickly followed the bellboy. When he came back he appeared to be extremely shaken up and upset. Apparently, this new hotel guest was Father's half-brother, who was passing through Brest while traveling to Warsaw from his estate, which was northwest of Brest. That was the last we ever heard of a possible half-brother. As a very young man, Feliks, together with fellow students, joined the *Legiony* (the Polish Legions), which were formed by Jozef Pilsudski during World War I and fought side by side with the Austrian forces against the Russians. On Russian territory he was wounded in the thigh with a "dum-dum" bullet (a soft-nosed bullet that expands when it hits). The bullet tore out part of his thigh, leaving a substantial hole and exposing the thighbone. He was hospitalized for many weeks, but as soon as he felt that some healing had taken place, he left the hospital without permission and started walking west, eventually arriving at his mother's house. Up until that time, she had assumed that he was dead. His mother eventually married Wawrzyniec Maciolek, who became a very devoted and loving stepfather. Feliks' mother died of liver cancer in 1936. His stepfather was simply devastated when my mother brought him the news of the death of his stepson Feliks. Maciolek passed away in early 1944 of throat cancer. Both parents were buried in Lodz, Poland.

Father's military career started quite early and finished quickly. Nevertheless, he remained a very loyal *legionista* (legionnaire) throughout his entire life and kept very strong ties with his military friends of his short-lived World

War I experience. His first official job after recovering from his war wound was as chief of police in a city I cannot recall, possibly Kalisz. Then he accepted an offer to become part of the *kasa chorych* (state health insurance) system and many managerial posts followed.

Father was a very intelligent and skillful man, and because of his strong diplomatic and managerial abilities, the Polish government entrusted him with the task of organizing new facilities all over Poland for the *kasa chorych*, later known as *ubezpieczalnia spoleczna* (social insurance system, similar to Medicare). As soon as a new facility had been built and was functioning well, Father would move on to a similar project in some other city. He was highly respected both by his subordinates as well as his superiors. He was a man of

My paternal grandmother, Anna (Kucharska) Maciolek, 1935.

strong principles, who possessed extremely acute instincts and a natural intellect. He was well read and was a very witty conversationalist who was always sought after by his many friends for a game of chess or an interesting dispute. A very generous man with a warm personality, he was always ready to help. He was a tall man with a military posture and his full head of thick hair, almost black, but prematurely graying at the sides, which he kept quite short, added a few inches to his height. Because of the thickness and darkness of his facial hair, he often took to shaving twice a day. His mustache was thick and neatly trimmed. He did not have the looks of a movie star, but he was quite handsome in his own way. In particular, his bright smile, his very expressive eyes and his very warm handshake were enough to make any stranger comfortable from the first encounter. One could say he was a careful dresser, almost fastidiously so, just as he liked perfect order both in his office and at home.

Soon after my parents' marriage, Mother quickly learned that not being orderly and scattering things all around the house was the very thing Father could not stand. In order to make his point, whenever he was displeased with some disorder she had created, he would simply stop talking to her. She would plead to find out what she had done wrong. Finally, he would give in and say, "I could not find the clothes brush. You failed to put it back in its place." After several such offenses, Mother learned she had better shape up fast, or there wouldn't be any harmony in the house. Even Mother's mispronunciation of Polish words did not annoy him as much, but disorder in the house seemed to bother him the most. Other than this fussy strain in his strong-minded character, he was soft-spoken and demonstrated his feelings without reservation. He was very affectionate and enjoyed it when anyone showed affection toward him. He enjoyed good food and liked to have it served in good style. He liked to entertain and to be entertained. He was polite and considerate to our household help. Only one incident comes to mind that was an exception. Mother had hired a young person to be our housekeeper. After she had been with us a few days, Father refused to eat at home. It turned out that this girl, despite being very clean, had an offensive body odor. (In those days there were no deodorants.) Thus, whenever she approached Father with food, he simply could not tolerate her presence. Eventually, Mother had to find someone else and let the poor girl go. Before the war, he was always wearing, or at least carrying, a black bowler hat. He also wore spats over his shoes, galoshes in rainy weather, and a full suit with a matching vest. He was very punctual and hated it if someone was not. If Mother would delay their departure for a party, he would simply say, "If you need more time, I'll go ahead and meet you at the party." If it came to the point that Mother was indeed going to be late, I am certain he would not leave her behind, but that nudge was a trick and she learned to start getting ready earlier so as not to be left behind. At a party he was always a gallant, very well-mannered gentleman, beaming with pride to show off his beautiful wife, who was always elegantly dressed. Although he disliked dancing and was not much of a dancer, he did not mind when Mother was in demand for every tune that was played. He in his turn made an effort to ask each lady at the party

My father's step-father, Wawrzyniec Maciolek, 1935.

for a spin around the dance floor—
as he said, "So that they could say,
'I have danced with the director.'"
I really can say that he almost
always had a sunny disposition, he
was always happy-go-lucky and
never complained about or criticized anybody. He made friends
very easily and knew how to be a
true friend. He made them for
life! Despite being a chauvinistic
Pole, he knew how to get along
with his many White Russian in-
laws, by whom he was adored and
respected.

My father was a very generous, noble man, one of Poland's
true *intelligentsia* who fell to a
senseless massacre by the Nazi
regime.

Konzentrationslager Auschwitz
was established in a former Polish
military compound in Oswiecim
(50 kilometers south of Krakow) by
Reichsführer-SS Heinrich Himmler in April 1940. In the beginning
it served as a concentration camp

My father Feliks Kucharski, circa 1939.

for Polish intellectuals and resistance movement members, victims of the Nazi
plan called *Terrorisierung und Vernichtung von Polen* (terrorizing and destruction of the Poles). The first prisoners, 728 Poles, arrived in Auschwitz on June
14, 1940. (My father was transferred there from the prison in Warsaw the following month.) Early prisoners also included Soviet prisoners of war, common German criminals, "anti-social elements," and German homosexuals.
These initial prisoners were ordered to construct what would be the first of
many enormous extermination camps. The entrance to the camp was—and still
is—marked by a sign that reads *Arbeit macht frei* ("Work will set you free").
With strange Nazi theatrics, prisoners who left the camp during the day for
construction work were made to march through the gate accompanied by a
prisoner orchestra. After the "Final Solution to the Jewish Question" was
ratified at the Wansee Conference in January 1942, Jews, Gypsies and "unde-
sirables" from all over occupied Europe were brought there to be systemati-
cally murdered. Exterminations began in February 1942 and continued until
November 1944.

The booking photograph of my father (Feliks Kucharski), inmate No. 1515, at K.L. Auschwitz (Concentration Camp Auschwitz), 15 August 1940.

Prisoners, like my father, were initially housed in one-story brick barracks formerly used by the Polish Army for stabling horses. When the number of inmates increased, a second story was added to each barrack. At first the prisoners slept on the floor; later, two- and three-tier bunkbeds were installed. Hard labor, crowding, and poor nutrition and hygiene led to exhaustion and high death rates among the prisoners. Prisoners were also subjected to cruel and inhumane tortures and punishments.

Expanding Auschwitz's capacity was of paramount importance once the method to decimate the population of European Jews was decided upon by the Nazi authorities. By 1942 the original camp was as full as it could get (up to 20,000 people were incarcerated) and work commenced on building a second site, Auschwitz-Birkenau (Auschwitz II), which could accommodate up to 200,000 people at one time. Birkenau (*Brzezinka*) is 2 miles from Auschwitz I. An additional satellite camp (Auschwitz III), the first of a series of forced labor camps, was created to service an oil and rubber factory, *Buna-Werke*, owned by the I.G. Farben company. Thus, the three main Auschwitz camps became one huge complex consisting of the extermination camps plus 45 subcamps, factories, and mines.

People were transported to Auschwitz-Birkenau by trains from all over Nazi-occupied Europe. They were generally sent in freight or cattle cars, usually without food, water, or toilet facilities. Auschwitz II was principally an extermination camp. Prisoners, if they were held, were housed in wooden stablelike buildings. Eight hundred persons were crowded in a space designed for 52 horses. At the height of its operation, most prisoners went directly from the trains to the gas bunkers.

The first gassing in Auschwitz took place at the end of August 1941 when Zyklon B gas was tested on Soviet prisoners of war. Developed by I.G. Farben,

Zyklon B was a cyanide gas originally used as a pesticide to kill lice. When the Birkenau camp was operational, prisoners were sorted as soon as they stepped from the trains into those who would be killed immediately and those who would be used as forced labor or in medical experiments. People were gassed in four gas chambers designed to resemble showers and cremated in four very large crematoriums. More than 20,000 persons could be gassed and cremated in one day. The pace of the murders reached an apogee in the summer of 1944 when more than 400,000 Jews from Hungary were transported and killed in a period of two months.

The number of people who perished is staggering. Auschwitz I was the site of the deaths of roughly 70,000 people, mostly Poles and Soviet prisoners of war. Auschwitz II (Birkenau) is where as many as 1.6 *million* Jews, 75,000 Polish people, and approximately 19,000 *Roma* (Gypsies) were killed. When the Soviet army liberated the camp on January 27, 1945, they found about 7,600 survivors abandoned there. More than 58,000 prisoners had been sent by the Nazis on a final death march to Germany.

After the end of World War II, Mother and I attempted to receive some kind of compensation (*Wiedergutmachung*) from the German government. With ironic logic, because we were not Jewish and since "the imprisonment took place on Polish soil" (Auschwitz being in Nazi-occupied Poland), we were advised by the German authorities to seek restitution from the Polish government!

The thought of my father's sufferings while at *Pawiak* prison and then at Auschwitz is sickening, beyond comprehension, but even worse is the thought of his final moments. He did not die in the comfort of his home with his loving family by his side. He died alone, at best perhaps surrounded by fellow prisoners, giving up all he had held onto—his pride, the strength of impeccable character, loyalty to his country, hope, and foremost, his beloved *Kota* (Kitten, his wife) and his *Myszka* (Little Mousie, me).

7

Handel
(Black Marketing)

After Father's death, Mother had to make a living, and not having any profession, she took up a new occupation so many women and men turned to during the war—*handel* (black marketeering). It was my godfather, Stanislaw Chabowski, who came to Mother's rescue. Mother being in need of help, but at the same time too proud to accept help, finally succumbed to Stanislaw's persuasions. He insisted on lending her some of his savings, so that she would have some liquid cash for purchase of different things that she could resell with profit. From then on, she developed many sources both for buying and then selling out of our little room. At one time, she was offered a huge amount of silk stockings directly by the factory owner, who did it as a favor to her, and she then sold them illegally. In our "warehouse" we had stockings up to the ceiling! Customers were coming and going and now it is hard to believe that this activity went unnoticed. Most of the time, I was in charge of the money, and later did the accounting. My accounting was always correct and every zloty was always accounted for, until once when for several days in a row a substantial amount of money was missing. It turned out that the days when one of my girlfriends would volunteer to help out were the days that we were short. When caught and confronted, she confessed to taking the money, but her parents couldn't forgive Mother for making the accusation. Mother also dealt in diamonds, gold, gold coins, foreign money and the like. At such times, I would be the one to do the pickup and delivery of many pieces of jewelry. As a courier, I was also used to distribute various underground materials for the *Armia Krajowa*, the partisan organization. I usually walked to the different nearby places; to distant ones I took streetcars. If I saw there might be an *oblawa* (roundup), I would jump off the car before it reached the next destination so as to avoid being caught with my loot. While running the business, Mother would often have to leave the apartment for several days at a time. She not only had to get new merchandise, but go to the country to get produce, especially butter, chickens, meat, etc., as almost everything was rationed and hard to get in the stores. On several occasions she had to cross the border. During one of those illegal crossings to Brest, which was under Soviet occupation, she was arrested by the border guards and jailed for about a week. On those crossings, she would bring her family food and clothing, which were impossible to get there. A couple of times she traveled to the border jail where her oldest sister, Anna, and brother-in-law were being held for crossing into Nazi-occupied Poland from Brest illegally. While in jail, Anna contracted typhoid fever, which left her with a serious heart ailment. Although many friends tried to look after me during Mother's absence, I always felt like an orphan. For some reason I preferred to stay in the apartment, rather than visit with one or the other aunt. I felt rather responsible and obligated to stay behind and keep the business going. Whenever Mother was on a trip, there was always someone coming by, wanting this or that. By being there, I felt I was doing my share of work, and the extra income never hurt. After schoolwork and other duties were done, many friends of my age would come for a visit and we would play endless card games. I very rarely would visit the other children's houses. They always came to our apartment—they just loved being where the action was, and Mother's business fascinated them. While Mother was away, I was in charge of my own cooking and had just a few favorite meals: Russian cutlets, pork chops, blintzes, tomato soup with *kladzione kluski* (*spaetzle*), omelets, or the famous Polish *parowki* (hot dogs!).

Often Mother had to leave even while I was sick. I had the bad luck of getting a recurring tonsillitis. No sooner would I get better than I would get another case. And then there was acute appendicitis, which ended up with my having an appendectomy at a hospital overlooking the Jewish ghetto. It wasn't a picnic, to say the least. Still under the influence of the narcotic, I managed to get up and headed for an open window. Fortunately, my godmother was entering the room and pulled me away. My homecoming was very joyful, with all the kids of Hoza 19 welcoming me back! There were many questions from them in regards to my operation—I felt like a real hero! Once while I was lying sick with scarlet fever (during which our family doctor let me stay home illegally instead of admitting me into the hospital, even though it was a highly contagious disease), and with the heavy curtains shut so light would not damage my eyes, I could almost hear whispers, or see the bustle of creatures or people of the past. I would hallucinate that the souls of former tenants were present and I would think that they were hiding inside the massive black furniture that I was surrounded with. I simply hated evenings and nights and the black furniture—it reminded me of a morgue full of coffins.

During one of Mother's absences from Warsaw and four months after Father's death, the date of my first communion arrived, the 7th of February 1941. With no one available to help me get ready for the event, I decided to make the arrangements myself. I already had a beautiful gold medallion with holy images on each side, given to me by my godmother Kazia Osuchowska-

Pegza, which I wore nonstop and still have as a remembrance. My search for a suitable dress was unsuccessful until my friend Hanka's mother, Mrs. Nosek, offered to lend me her daughter's dress. Hanka was more developed than I and the dress was too big for me, but with the help of several safety pins, we made it fit. Hanka's shoes were about two sizes larger than my feet, so I filled them with tissue paper, although the width remained obviously larger than my feet. Next I ordered some flowers for a headdress and for a bouquet. Once my hair was nicely curled, I was ready to join the other communicants at St. Alexander's Church, on Three Crosses Square, which was a few blocks from our apartment. The ceremony was very festive, after which the square was filled with girls dressed all in white and boys in their Sunday best. Afterwards, I rushed to a photographer's studio to have my picture taken and

My First Communion portrait after the ceremony at St. Alexander Church on Three Crosses Square, Warsaw, 7 June 1941.

then paraded in my white outfit the rest of the day. I was very proud of myself for having organized almost everything all by myself.

My most favorite and dearest companion during my lonely days at the apartment was my cousin Igor, "Guga," as he was known, who knew best how to cheer me up and make me happy when I felt blue. But his sunny presence in my life was also short-lived—he left one day to fight the Soviets and never returned.

When we had guests, I was often sent to the store for food, drinks, and, most often, cigarettes. Usually I would be given a large amount of zloty and when I returned with the purchase and there was change, I was told to keep it. My favorite guest was Ivan Shlykov, who, in my eyes then, was a big spender, like a millionaire! And best of all, a very generous one. I rarely spent my "tips"; I liked to see my money grow. The only time I could part with it was when Guga needed to pay his debts and he would persuade me to give him a loan,

My beloved cousin "Guga" (Igor) Shlykov, photographed in Smolensk, Soviet Russia, 1943.

for which I was to earn a nifty interest. Diligently, I kept track of the account, adding the interest and seeing the sum grow from year to year. Since Guga was constantly short of money, I got to see the numbers of zlotys on his account grow fairly rapidly. However, Guga never returned from the front. I would have forgiven his debt if only he could have lived.

Being the youngest of the many occupants of the apartment, I had the privilege of growing up among adults. Although they treated me as a child, often their expectations of me were more suitable for an adult, which made me grow up so much faster. I was proud of having this privilege and saw to it that I lived up to their expectations. They, in turn, knew that they could trust me and rely on me, so no secrets were kept from me. But this didn't stop any of my cohabitants from giving me plenty of lectures, instructions, and advice. Also, they would take advantage of the fact that I was the youngest. I was constantly being dispatched to do something, from very simple to very dangerous errands. The least important and most annoying errand was constantly going to fetch cigarettes from the corner kiosk! Because of that, I decided that I would never smoke or marry a smoker! Growing up surrounded mostly by grown-ups, I felt like wallpaper with ears. Ignored and listening, one can learn a lot. Paying attention, I discovered, is often wiser than being the subject of attention. I was a very busy young girl, to say the least. Somehow I managed to have time to do my homework, help other kids do theirs, attend theater plays, all the current musicals, and many masses (in the summer sometimes two a day—after all, most of the boys of Hoza Street were altar boys!) at St. Alexander's Catholic Church on *Plac Trzech Krzyzy* (Three Crosses Square). And so, despite the fact that the apartment often was full of a great many sorrows, nonetheless it was, and is in my memory now, a special place.

After the end of World War II, we learned the following about the fate of our cohabitants of Apartment #6:

Nina Makowiecka, who had married Jerzy Drzewiecki shortly before the uprising, moved to live with her husband and his mother. They eventually immigrated to Australia. After an on-and-off correspondence, I learned that the three of them had died.

Alla Maksimowicz returned to her hometown Brest, where she became a dentist, married, then divorced. At this writing she still resides there with her sister Nina. We visited her during our very brief visit to Brest in 1991.

Lissner, director of the German firm with offices in our apartment, ended up being a very decent German, who helped us a lot during our stay at the camp. After the war's end, he opened a toy factory in the outskirts of Warsaw.

Kszeminski, the Polish director of the other firm, settled also in the outskirts of Warsaw. During our visit to Poland in 1993 we tried to locate him, but to no avail.

Rajpold, with his second wife and the younger son, ended up living in London. We visited them during one of our visits there. Since then, both are deceased.

We never heard of the Jewish couple's fate.

Just recently I had a short but vivid dream in which Chester and I came to Apartment #6. It looked the same as when we lived in it. While Chester went to the bathroom, I inspected the kitchen. I was startled by the fact that it was ghostly empty and that the door to the back staircase was opened. I tried to close the door, but I couldn't. Then I tried to close the balcony door, which was ajar, and this, too, wouldn't close as well. I woke up with a strange, insecure feeling.

My mother (who is 100 at the time I write this) and I also don't know what became of the Fuksman family, or whether they were aware that Father paid with his life for housing Oleg Fuksman and helping him to retrieve their valuables. An Abram Fuksman of Brest *(Brzesc)*, married with two children, is listed in the online Central Database of Shoah Victims *(Yadvashem)*. It may or not be the same person. Only after the war did we learn of the Bronnaya Gora massacre that occurred in 1942 in which the Fuksmans may have perished.

Early in the morning on October 15, 1942, Nazi soldiers surrounded the Brest Ghetto. The entire population of the ghetto was rounded up at gunpoint, loaded into cattle cars and transported to Bereza Kartuska (a town northeast of Brest). Groups of Jewish men, women and children were unloaded and marched to an area (Bronnaya Gora) where a huge, long trench had been prepared. At the edge of the trench the people were ordered to disrobe. Naked, they were then pushed into the trench and machine gunned by the Nazi soldiers who surrounded them. The killings went on all day, trainload by trainload, and it is estimated that 50,000 Jews were shot and buried that day. In 1944, when the Soviets recaptured Brest, there were only nine Jews (two men and seven women) left alive in the city. They had been hidden by non–Jewish friends.

On hearing the rumors of an uprising in Warsaw and of the strong possibility of the Soviets' imminent liberation of the city, many members of our extended family decided to leave Warsaw as soon as possible. They did not waste any time, as they wanted to be ahead of the situation, to avoid being caught in the midst of Polish-German fighting and especially to be sure of escaping from the Russians. As soon as their decision to depart was made, the Shlykovs, together with the Breverns (and perhaps with their help), packed up their whole household and moved to Czestochowa. Wacka, their housekeeper, chose to return to her village. Sonya and Misha begged Mother to join the exodus, but she would not agree. Thus the two of us stayed behind, for better or for worse. Almost at the same time, the Padukows, together with their friend, the Rev. Znosko, also left Warsaw, heading for Czestochowa as well. As soon as they arrived in Czestochowa, they were able to reconnect with Misha's older brother, Ivan, who had taken up a brief residence there. Igor and Sergey, having joined the anti–Bolshevik movement, were in Minsk fighting the Soviet regime. Arkady, meanwhile, was in hiding near his fiancée's house, while still trying to continue his subversive anti–Soviet activity. All

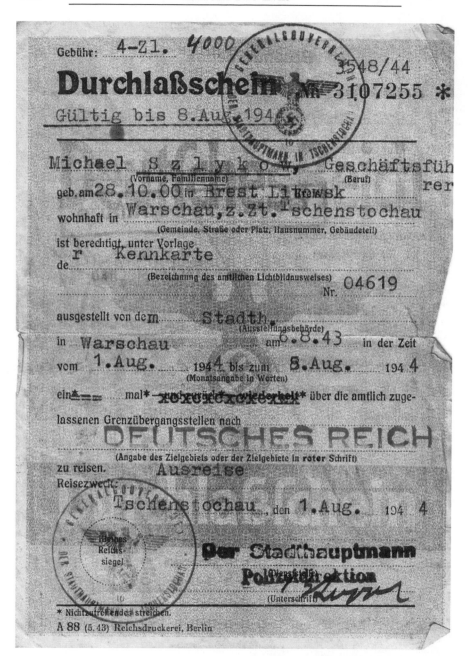

Durchlassschein. The permit allowing Michael Shlykov, a *Geschäftsführer* (shop-keeper) to cross borders within the Reich, issued when Shlykov was leaving Czesto-chowa, Poland, to begin working for a lumber company in Austria, a subsidiary of the German government.

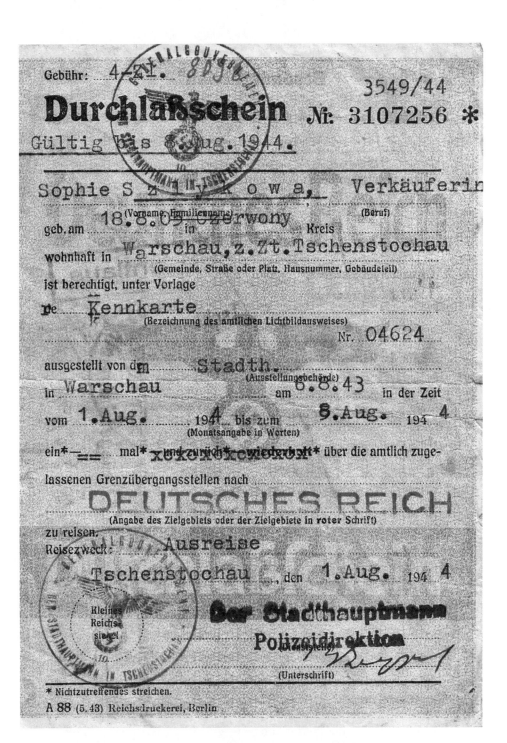

Durchlassschein. The permit allowing Sophie (Sonya) Shlykov, a *Verkäuferin* (saleswoman) to cross borders within the Reich in order to accompany her husband.

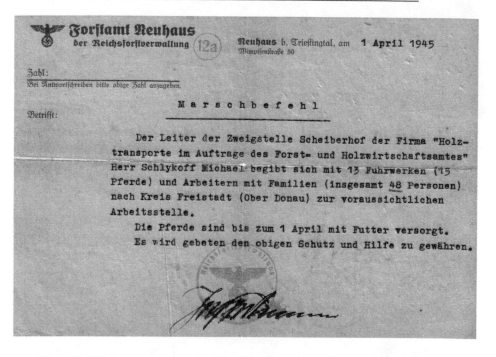

Marschbefehl, a movement order of the Neuhaus Forest Service, a subsidiary lumber company of the German government, allowing Mikhail Shlykov to travel across the border with 13 wagons, 15 horses and up to 48 workers and their families to a prospective new workplace in Ober Donau, Bavaria. The order in fact was issued by a supervisor friend to assist Shlykov and others fleeing the approaching Soviet forces and intent on finding shelter in Germany. April 1, 1945.

three were able to send short letters home, but in time news from or about them came to an abrupt end.

During his stay in Czestochowa, von Brevern obtained a contract from the Nazi authorities to assemble a labor force for timber-hauling work in Kleine Maria Zell, near Vienna, Austria. He offered work to the Shlykovs and Padukows who agreed to join him. Since the Shlykovs were not able to take their furniture along, and Ivan had decided not to become part of the labor force, all their household goods, except for a few important things, such as rugs, china, silver and six sectional mattresses, were left with Ivan. After the end of the war, Ivan settled with his third wife in a house on the outskirts of Warsaw and their villa was full of Misha and Sonya's belongings.

And so, the von Breverns, Shlykovs, and Padukows, together with several other couples that had volunteered for the labor force, with no real clue as to what was awaiting them and now really looking like refugees in transit, departed for Austria. Upon arriving in Vienna, the Padukows decided to stay there, rather than continue on to Kleine Maria Zell. The Shlykovs and another family of four, the Chwiedczuks, settled down in Kleine Maria Zell in a farm-house near the site where the work was to be done. Misha's work amounted to supervising a team cutting trees on the mountainside and bringing the logs down to the valley for transport to a lumberyard. To assist them, they were given very lean, but tough horses and oxen, which were very fit for this task. (We have a painting in our living room that depicts quite well this type of operation.) And so, the labor force, with little prior knowledge of the trade, was hard at work, successfully doing what was expected of them. Sonya and Serafima Chwedczuk were in charge of keeping the ever-hungry force fed. The living quarters were tight, but each family had its own bedroom and ade-quate privacy. They even started their own vegetable garden, and an abundance of gathered mushrooms made every meal even tastier. The foreigners man-aged to make their stay in this remote village a happy one. They were able to find time for an occasional party or two, with Misha, as usual, being the organ-izer.

While the Padukows were in Vienna and the Shlykovs in Kleine Maria Zell, none of them knew what fate had befallen Mother and me. I guess they must have heard of the ill-fated Warsaw Uprising and began to believe that we had perished in it.

8

Warsaw Uprising, August 1, 1944

In the summer of 1944, strong rumors were circulating in Warsaw of an impending uprising. Mother and I were kept informed day to day of the coming action and of the danger of staying in our apartment. Col. Edward Pfeifer (later known as General Radwan, deputy to the commander Bor-Komorowski) urged us to leave the city as soon as possible. We had many offers as to where to go and whom to stay with outside Warsaw, while waiting for the big victory. Nevertheless, Mother could not make the decision to go. She just could not accept the idea of leaving most of our things behind. When the big day for the uprising, August 1, 1944, came closer, our friend, Dr. Bruno Gutkiewicz, who at the time was hoping to marry Mother, convinced her that I should leave the city, while she could stay behind long enough to return different things that she had on consignment, after which she would leave Warsaw and join Bruno and me at Gora Kalwaria, the location of Bruno's work and residence. Although Mother was not quite sure she wanted to marry Bruno, when applying for a new identity card she gave as her address Bruno's residence in Gora Kalwaria. However, when the time came for my departure, Mother wouldn't let me go. She decided that the two of us would stay put until she was done dismantling the business. Only then would she be willing for us to join Bruno at his place. Her plan never materialized.

During those summer days, our day-to-day living had not changed. The gray life went on. I hopped from one house to another for daily schooling sessions, Mother continued her business, and our apartment served for various meetings of the *Armia Krajowa*. There were many whispered, unconfirmed rumors about when, how, and where the real thing would start. The tension was rapidly increasing and spreading like wildfire.

Virtually a few hours before the actual uprising's start, a meeting took place of several AK generals, including General Bor-Komorowski, at which it was decided that the uprising would start on the 1st of August 1944 at precisely 1700 hours. They considered 1700 to be the best time of the day to start

104

Identity card issued to Zofia/Sophie (Sonya) Shlykov by the Warsaw City Commandant of the General Government (Nazi occupation forces), 6 August 1943.

the action, as the streets at this hour would be busy with people returning home from work, going shopping, etc., thus making the AK activity less noticeable to the Germans. It was estimated that the AK would have arms and food lasting for four or five days, at most for seven days. It was expected that help from the allies in the West would be available to assist the AK combatants during the action and that the Red Army, which had already reached the eastern banks of the Vistula River, within a week would enter Warsaw from the east to liberate the city. Part of the overall plan was to divide the city into 8 regions, one of which, the #1 region *Srodmiescie* (City Center), was to be under the command of our friend, Colonel Edward Radwan Pfeiffer.

The *Armia Krajowa* (Home Army) force numbered about 50,000 combatants (women and men), but in actuality only 23,000 took an active part in the uprising. There were also supportive groups from the *Armia Ludowa* (People's Army), a rival partisan organization established by the Soviet Union, bringing the total number of active participants to 28,000 men and women. The combatants, in addition to pistols and rifles, also had some artillery, mostly light, at their disposal. Military equipment, uniforms, and other supplies were sparse, due to the fact that just prior to the uprising some warehouses hiding such supplies were detected and taken over by the Germans. In the end, all in all, only 10 percent of needed equipment was available to the combatants. Since 1942, the Germans had been expecting that sooner or later an uprising of the Poles would occur. Because of that assumption, they kept stationed in and around Warsaw about 15,000 to 16,000 German troops, fully equipped with the best of arms. One German army unit was made up of convicts recently released from prison. These men were extremely cruel not only to captured combatants, but also to the civilian population. They were promised reprieve

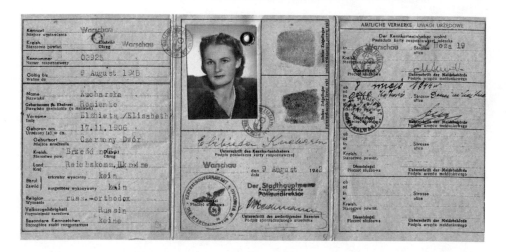

My mother's ID card issued by the Warsaw City Commandant of the General Government, occupation forces, 9 August 1943.

from the death sentence in return for help in overthrowing the uprising. In addition to the convicts, the unit also included German army deserters who had refused to fight at the different fronts. This particular group was responsible for the massive killing of some 40,000 residents of just one district of Warsaw. The Germans used Polish civilians as human shields, making them run in front of their tanks as they approached the Polish barricades. This is how many civilians died.

At 1700 hours on August 1, 1944, Mother was somewhere in town on an errand. I was at my gymnastics class, just a few streets up from our house. The rapid actions of combatants and the population were amazing. As soon as signals were given to start fighting the Germans, barricades appeared like mushrooms everywhere! In just a short time, by the time I left the school, on the way home I could see streets blocked literally with everything from concrete, dug up while making sewer tunnels, to piles of furniture and household goods of every kind. The barricades were rapidly getting higher and higher. Running and alternately hiding behind the gates of houses, I was able to reach our apartment. Only then did I become frantic when, "safe" at home, I discovered that Mother was not there. Nightmarish thoughts began going through my mind—I was sure I would not see her alive again. The phones were not working, so she was not able to let me know that she was safe somewhere, alive, and trying to come home. After a few hours, late at night, Mother came home, exhausted primarily because of the anxiety that she, too, might not find me safe at home. Her run, trying to avoid bullets and the combat in the streets, was more dangerous than mine, since she was quite a distance from home when the uprising started.

A photograph received from Col. Pfeifer during a visit to London in 1958 showing officers of the Polish Legion at the front in Kosciuchnowka, Poland, fighting the Russians in World War I. Left to right, Waclaw Lipinski, who later became a well-known writer/historian, A. Goldenberg-Burski, and Edward Pfeiffer, who, as Colonel Pfeiffer (pseudonym "Radwan") was commander of Region 1 (City Center) in the Warsaw Uprising of 1944.

It took us a couple of days to get used to the overall situation. The sounds of various kinds of explosions, the shouts of *golebiarze!* (snipers on the roofs), the cries of the wounded, and the daily hardships emphasized the seriousness of the situation, which was to continue for many days. Encouraging news included reports of the takeover of various territories, the heroism of combatants, and the spontaneous help of the civilians. Nevertheless, we never exactly knew what really was going on in the different parts of the city. The hope was that soon all would be over, the uprising would end in victory, the liberators would arrive in time, and the allies wouldn't forget us. Little did we know!

A few days into the uprising, all utilities were shut off or destroyed. We had no water, no electricity, and no gas. Supplies of candles and carbide lamps were dwindling, so that at night, except for the light from occasional artillery explosions, there was total darkness. Water for cooking and warm meals was nonexistent. I remember having to go to fetch some drinking water. We knew that a few blocks from us a Russian acquaintance happened to have a supply of water, which he kept just in case. He kept replenishing his supply from day to day, making sure the water stayed fresh. In general I disliked this man, as he always teased me when I passed his house on my way to church. Sometimes

I would take another street just to avoid him. This time, out of our great need for water, I forgot how I felt about him. I went to him and because he was too disturbed with the ongoing situation he failed to tease me and gave me some of his water in a pail to carry home. Since I had to navigate my way carefully, stepping over various pipes in the open sewer lines, ducking into the trenches to avoid possible snipers, I spilled a considerable amount, bringing home about half the water. It was heartbreaking to see the precious liquid spilling, but I could not help it. We continued staying in the apartment for several days, but once the fighting was in full swing, we were forced to take up living in the cellar. Now and then we would go up in order to get something to eat. Mother always kept *zapasy* (stocks) of various foods, so that even when the storekeepers, knowing that food was running out, would sell their inventory at astronomical prices, we could still rely on our own supplies. Although some people used the opportunity to take advantage of the grim situation we all were in, it was hard to believe they could actually become such scalpers.

Within a few days, the number of casualties began to mount. In the hottest August that anyone could remember, the dead bodies deteriorated quickly; sometimes there was no time or place to bury them right after they were killed. The smell of dead flesh was sickening. Our friend Rajpold's teenage son was killed by a sniper as he walked unprotected on the dug-up street. He was killed instantly. Someone helped to make a coffin. We followed the dead boy's box, which was carried by his father and a couple of friends, to the nearby *Plac Trzech Krzyzy* (Three Crosses Square). There, in an improvised grave, we laid the young Rajpold to rest. He was not the first one and not the last one to be buried there.

Because of the unsanitary conditions, I contracted dysentery, with painful intestinal cramps and very severe

My beautiful mother, Elizabeth Kucharska, photographed in Warsaw in summer 1944.

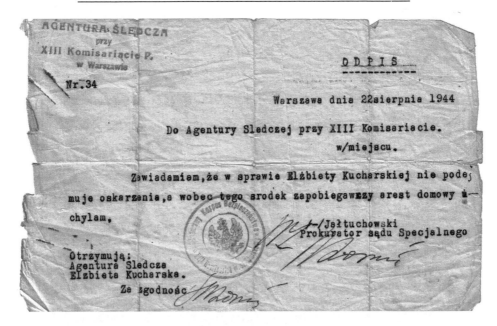

Statement issued on 22 August 1944 by the special prosecutor of the Polish Republic's investigations Branch that Elzbieta (Elizabeth) Kucharska is no longer charged and hence her house arrest is lifted. She was placed under house arrest by the Home Army after having been accused by someone of being a "suspect" Russian, but was cleared through the intercession of Col. Pfeiffer of the Home Army. (Note that during the Warsaw Uprising, Polish government offices in the combat zone resumed operating as they had before the war.)

bloody diarrhea. I was constantly dehydrated and getting weaker every day. On top of my illness another complication occurred. Just as some *szpicel* (informant) had denounced Father for housing a Jew, someone during the first days of the uprising denounced Mother as being a Russian, making her out to be an enemy of the new Polish government. And so, one day, out of the blue, she was placed under house arrest by the AK. She was not to leave the apartment, even to go to the basement to join the others in hiding from German attacks. Fortunately, we were able to send a message to Col. Radwan Pfeiffer. Radwan in turn sent a harsh reprimand and an order to free Mother immediately. I guess the denouncer wanted to see Mother suffer and to punish her for being Russian-born, not realizing or overlooking the fact that she, too, participated in the uprising and in the *Armia Krajowa* underground. Not all the Poles knew that there was a difference between White Russian and Soviet Russian. The house arrest lasted until August 22, 1944. Once again we were free to hide in the cellar, to seek shelter, or go somewhere to get water or medical help.

As the days passed, the German offensive grew stronger. They began using not only tanks and heavy artillery but also aircraft. They began bombing the city. The Polish combatants asked for help from outside Warsaw. A number of AK groups were sent from other areas of Poland, but unfortunately, many units never arrived as they were quickly intercepted by the Germans and destroyed. The Polish partisans who did reach the city's Polish-occupied parts had come from hiding in the forests and were not used to fighting under the difficult circumstances in the city. While in hiding, they were relatively well fed and out of immediate danger. Now, fighting in the city, they often complained of their extreme hunger. Wherever combatants retreated, the Germans took revenge by mass murdering the Polish civilian population.

One day over the loudspeakers and by word of mouth we learned that there would be a period of time set for the wounded, the sick, and women and children to leave the city. Inasmuch as I was very sick and Mother was physically and mentally exhausted, and since we had many places where we could make a temporary home, we decided to take advantage of the two-hour ceasefire. And so, reluctantly, we joined the exodus, which, to avoid snipers, took us mostly through sewer passages rather than over the streets. In haste and confusion, Mother took along a huge jar with butter (in water to preserve its freshness), one of her fur coats (despite the fact that the temperature must have been in the 90s), and a gold mantel clock under a glass dome (a gift to Father from his co-workers upon his retirement in 1936). Of course, both the glass dome and the jar fell and broke almost immediately. We vainly tried cleaning the butter of glass shards, hoping to save some butter for emergency use. Mother was also carrying all her jewelry, until we heard rumors that at the exit from the combat zone everyone was being searched and stripped of valuables. Thus, Mother decided to hand over her jewelry to one of our male friends, who were helping us negotiate the difficult passage, telling him to bury it in our basement. She never saw the jewelry again. During those two hours about 5,000 people were "evacuated."

On the 63rd day of the ill-fated uprising at 2000 hours a capitulation was signed in Ozarow. The number of dead and injured varies, but there were about 17,000 dead and 9,000 wounded on the German side, while on the Polish side the casualties were much higher: about 20,000 combatants killed, about 7,000 wounded, and about 180,000 civilians killed in massive executions or who perished in fallen and burnt houses. The statistics for the mass destruction of national and private wealth are enormous. The city was left in ruins. Between the day of capitulation and the Russian Army's "liberation" on January 17, 1945, the Germans took advantage of the stalled Soviet advance in the suburbs of the city, and decided to level Warsaw to the ground. They demolished the surviving buildings one by one, street after street, detonating them or setting them on fire. Whatever had survived the uprising was destroyed.

9

Forced Labor Camp

As we were leaving our beloved city that was almost totally destroyed and burning, we continued to have the hope that one day soon we would be able to return, primarily to find our buried treasures, and to get our strength back and start our lives anew. Perhaps Mother's silent wish was eventually to marry Dr. Bruno Gutkiewicz and settle down. He lived in a lovely villa at that time in Gora Kalwaria on the outskirts of Warsaw. He had a steady, well-paying job as a chief doctor of veterinary medicine. (Little did Mother know that instead she was fated later on in her life to marry another vet instead, Dr. N. Proskuriakov.)

The freedom we seemed to have after leaving the combat zone of the city was short-lived. At the city limits, when we came to the surface, we were surrounded by German guards and marched several miles on foot to Pruszkow outside Warsaw to a streetcar depot. There we spent several days until we were transferred to a small facility, where we were housed in one of several barracks, all of which were filled to the brim. There was no food, water, or toilets. My acute intestinal problems continued, at times becoming worse. There was no way of getting any medication or to be seen by a doctor.

Now in captivity, after a short stay in a heavily guarded transit camp, we went through a selection process in an open area. During this selection, a German soldier with a rifle told me to go to the left, Mother to the right, but Mother wouldn't let go of me. The infuriated soldier hit her on the head with his rifle butt, inflicting a fracture in her skull that she still had throughout her life. An officer, who was standing nearby supervising the selection process, intervened and let us both join the group on the right. Mother, bleeding from her head, and I, with the worst case of dysentery, together with many hundreds of fellow Warsaw insurgents, boarded a standing cattle-car train, 50 or so people to a car. This destitute flock filled the wagon like herrings in a barrel. It had one tiny window on the top and a bucket in the corner to serve as a toilet. No food, no water! And so, in the stuffy and smelly, closed and locked car, we were taken on a long journey to another transit camp in Erfurt (or Eisenach?) where German representatives, mostly *Lagerführers* (camp supervisors)

111

came to select their future workers. Our future camp supervisor, Volkman (whose first name or his rank, if he had one, I do not recall), happened to be a quite short man, dressed in a uniform and the typical knee-high leather boots. He carried a leather crop. His legs were quite bow-legged and as he walked he wobbled from side to side. One of his eyes was a glass one, replacing one he perhaps may have lost at the front.

Mother and I, together with five Jewish women and other Polish women, who had primarily come from the Prushkow camp, about 45 of us in all, were designated for a camp in Breitungen/Werra, Thuringen. It turned out to be *Lager Kirchberg*, the prisoners of which were forced to work at the *Metalwaren-fabrik Scharfenberg & Teubert GmbH*, producing munitions for use on the various German fronts. Barbed wire enclosed the campgrounds that housed women, who were mostly Russians, Ukrainians, Poles and the five Jewish women I mentioned. A separate section, divided off by a fence, held men, who had come from France, Italy and Poland. The camp was guarded and was a short distance from the factory, in which local German citizens worked as supervisors or foremen. Armed guards accompanied each shift to and from the facilities of the plant. Apparently, because of the high percentage of foreigners working at the factory, the area escaped allied bombing, but supplies that were thrown down from allied planes and meant for the prisoners never reached us, most likely being retrieved by the local Germans. Upon arrival at the camp, we were photographed and we, physically, as well as our clothing, were disinfected. When the German guards, exclusively male, told us to strip, and Mother and I and the rest of us stood naked—I thought I would die of shame! While in a bath en masse we were watched by the guards. We were later issued identity documents (I asserted I was two years older to assure I would not be separated from Mother) and a ration card for food (reissued weekly and stamped each time we were fed), and assigned to one of the many long barracks. In ours, we met two Russian women. One was Vera, who came from Pinsk, and when we eventually became friends, it turned out that she knew Lyolya Ugrinowicz, who was Mother's cousin. In this designated barrack, we were assigned to a cot in a huge room. Since I was only a teenager and too young to be classified as "legally incarcerated," I wasn't assigned a cot of my own and therefore had to share one with Mother. The cots were two-decker type, as narrow as a stretcher. There were about 30 cots to a room. Each cot had a straw mattress, a straw-filled pillow, and a cover. Ours was the top bunk. The barracks were built very poorly, with walls made of thin boards, through which the wind and frost would blow in—there was always a draft of some kind! The roofs were full of holes through which, during the winter months, drops of melting snow fell. The monotonous noise of the drops brought us close to a nervous breakdown. One drop after another, endlessly. In the morning it wasn't unusual to see an icicle hanging over our heads and to find the cover and mattress damp. The walls would be covered with frost, and frost trees formed on the small, broken window panes, dripping and forming puddles on the bare floors. There was a small passage between the rows of cots, and in the middle of the room stood a potbelly stove, often cold due to the lack of wood for burning. The wind would blow the smoke back into the barracks through the long aluminum pipe that extended from the stove to the outside. The smoke was dense and inhaling it created headaches and breathing difficulties. After a while, Mother and I, together with the five Jewish women (the only Jewish women in the camp), were transferred to a small barracks, where there were three sets of cots—again, no cot for me!

Most of the inmates had only one change of clothing, since most of us were incarcerated during the heat of summer. It must have been the hottest August one could remember. All of us were not prepared for the cold days to come. Ironically, when fleeing Warsaw, Mother in the midst of the heat took her fur coat, for which many thought her mad, but in the camp during the bitter cold days and nights the coat was a lifesaver!

A special track ran to the camp from the main railroad tracks, since the huge amounts of vegetables, mostly rutabagas and potatoes, were delivered by train. Dumped on the ground, they were hosed down to wash off clinging dirt, then chopped and cooked in a huge kettle. This watery *Kolrabi Suppe* was portioned out into metal bowls, together with bits of still clinging dirt and worms. A small piece of dark, stale bread accompanied the soup, and that constituted our daily meal. The severe rigors of wartime existence had left me weakened and emaciated, and coupled with prolonged severe bowel problems, I was constantly hungry. To help me recover my strength, Mother somehow was able to share with me her meager portion of daily ration. The German workers were allowed to bring box lunches or dinner pails and eat at designated tables, while those that were especially patriotic and didn't wish to waste time, ate at their machines. For us, regardless of which shift we worked on, there was no pause for lunch or dinner. How often we watched with envy the Germans eating their delicacies! Because of malnutrition, lack of sleep, and the harsh working conditions, it was an enormous effort to keep working until one's shift ended. The plant worked nonstop around the clock! We were allowed to go to an outhouse at a special hour only, not whenever nature's call came. The trip to the outhouse was guarded. During one of the trips to the latrine, we overheard two guards speculating as to whether the five women with us were not by chance Jewish? Once, later on, Mother and I were confronted by the *Lagerführer* with the same question. We both denied it, and from then on while we were in the camp the subject was not brought up again. One picture comes to mind about one of the trips to the outhouse. On this occasion, as usual, I stopped at Mother's station (her machine punched out bullets) when I found her standing but asleep, holding onto her coat, which was hanging on a hook. Her foreman, seeing her in this strange position, which perhaps may have lasted only a few seconds, dropped a heavy iron near her feet, scaring her almost out of her wits! In general, the noise of the several hundred heavy machines of various types was so loud that the foremen, in order to give commands to workers, had to shout at the top of their lungs. They liked to be mean and to make fun of us. Knowing that all of us were intimidated and scared for our lives, they took advantage of any given situation to spite us. The plant was a huge concrete building, poorly ventilated. Machines lined up one after another, leaving very little room for the operators or other equipment necessary for a given operation. Many critical machinery operations were manned by German foremen, sometimes German women. These were the trusted ones! We, the *Ost Arbeiter* (eastern workers) were not to be trusted and had to be watched. After all, what we were producing was ammunition that was used to defend their *Heimat* (homeland) and destroy ours!

I worked on the day shift. After thousands and thousands of highly polished bullets were stamped out by a huge machine, they were brought to my table, poured out, forming a high pile. Once they were on my table, I had to take as many as my open palm would hold, roll them from side to side, check them for defects and scratches. In the beginning I was probably doing a good job, selecting as many rejects as I could find. I did it more out of fright than loyalty. Soon after, knowing and feeling the oppression, I would throw quite a few with blemishes into the pails meant for perfect ones. That was my spite for all the sufferings we had to endure. I was sick and remained sick from day one of the uprising. In addition to the dysentery, later in the camp, the lymph glands all over my body became badly swollen and I was covered with boils. Periodically, I had to be sent to the infirmary, which was run by a Ukrainian woman, a so-called nurse. There were no medical supplies, and she often lanced the boils and applied a disinfectant to them, which burned like hell. At times I couldn't sleep or sit, but nevertheless I was compelled to work. Often in the cot with my mother I was feverish and couldn't find a comfortable position to avoid the hardness and bumpiness of the straw in the mattress that pressed on the boils. Thus, despite being dead tired, I had trouble falling asleep. Those sleepless nights, disrupted by the sound of water drops and the heavy breathing or snoring of nearby neighbors, brought frightening thoughts of realization that we indeed had ended up here in the camp, surrounded by a low, angry element of people, filth, cold, and hunger—those thoughts created a deep despair that, in fact, there is no hope in sight. Life in the barracks began to take on a dreamlike state, full of dreams rather than thoughts that shifted from my carefree years to the tremendous yearnings of my present condition. I thought of Poland, where there was nothing that was left for us and about all that had taken place. The nights became longer and longer in duration, during which I had all sorts of visions, based on the past. While recalling them, they brought more sadness to our now miserable life. After each sleepless night, morning would bring exhaustion. The wake-up call by the commando was always premature. It was sheer torture to lift my head that ached so terribly and get up to stand ready to face another day of hard work. Something must have been added to our food in order for our menstruation to cease—or it might have been from hunger. Mother had developed an edema due to a heart ailment. Occasionally, she was sent to a German doctor in the town of Bad Salzungen, who, despite her condition, wouldn't excuse her from work. Whenever we were outside the camp, for which one needed written permission, we would now and then be spit at by German children and called Polish pigs. Near the camp, in the village of Breitungen, there was a shoemaker who employed a Pole who was sent out to work in Germany. This brave countryman often scrounged bread and whatever else he could and shared it secretly with us. We can probably attribute our survival to his help.

Through the help of the International Red Cross, occasionally people would get a food package or some items of clothing, which were shared with those that were less fortunate. I started to write to friends who we knew were in various parts of Poland, as writing to Warsaw was hopeless—everything and everyone there by then was long gone. One of the people who answered one of my many SOS pleas was our Warsaw apartment tenant, Alfred Josef Lissner, whom I located in Lodz. He responded not only to my fright-laden letters, but also was able to send us a couple of packages, mostly warm clothing that I had begged for. In his letters he described in detail what the outside situation was like. He indirectly indicated that the end of the war was imminent and that our suffering would end as well. Soon after the capitulation of the failed uprising on December 4, 1944, Lissner was able to go to Warsaw, still burning. He went to our apartment building, to the basement, in search of Mother's buried treasures. Unfortunately, even following a second attempt with a diagram of the basement layout showing the right spot in the cellar, he was still unable to locate Mother's things. He said that perhaps it was not the right place, or that someone had found the treasures before him. (In about 1946, Lissner relocated to Otwock, where he owned a toy factory.)

A lucky day finally came our way when we were able to locate Mother's family, which at that time was working in the outskirts of Vienna, Austria. Until we contacted them via the Red Cross, advising them that we were in captivity and in urgent need of help, they were under the impression that we had perished during the uprising. As soon as Misha heard of our whereabouts, he did not lose one minute, but started turning all the wheels available to him. Very soon he managed to obtain a legal certificate and an urgent request for our immediate release from the labor camp because Mother and I were needed for work in Austria and that we would be provided quarters. From that day on, more certificates, letters and postcards were exchanged and our permission to leave the camp was granted. The final approval was given to us by the camp *Führer* who agreed to release us.

Often, those who have heard my story ask how it was possible to obtain permission to leave the camp. My uncle's employer's request for the release of

Russische Vertrauensstelle in Deutschland
Berlin W 15, Bleibtreustr. 27

Bestätigung

Name: *Kucharska geb. Romienko*

Vorname: *Elisabeth*

Geboren am: *17.11.1906*

Geburtsort: *Czerwony Dwor, Bez. Brest-Litowsk,*

Adresse: *Breitungen-Werra*
(Wohnort, Strasse und Hausnummer)

Lager Kirchberg

Eigenhändige Unterschrift:

Der Inhaber dieser Bestätigung hat am *15.12.44*

Nr. *345/44* ein Gutachten betr. seiner

russischen Volkszugehörigkeit erhalten.

Bestätigung. ID card issued by the Russian representative of Germany (a consular office in Berlin) confirming the Russian nationality of my mother (Elizabeth Kucharska) working and residing in the forced labor camp, *Lager Kirchberg*, in Breitungen-Werra. This confirmation enabled her to apply for assistance from the Red Cross. 1944.

two people, a woman and a teenager, was certainly unusual. What could the two of us, worn-out and sick as we were, possibly do in a lumber company, the tasks of which were executed by men only? Our *Lagerführer* could simply have ignored it, or denied it. But, instead, he made it clear to us that he was doing us a favor by acknowledging the affidavits sent by Misha's firm and issuing the work release passes. Mother had a typically emotional explanation, saying that perhaps the *Lagerführer* had a daughter of my age and felt sorry for keeping me captive and doing work unfit for a teenager. I, however, suspected that there were more realistic reasons: perhaps feeling that the end of the war was imminent, he wanted to reduce the number of prisoners in the camp, and he probably hoped to cover up the fact that I was "illegally" incarcerated and forced to work as an adult, reducing any retribution he might face once the camp was liberated. Of course, it's also possible that he was motivated to let us go by not wanting to have Mother on his conscience, should she become gravely ill. Hearing about atrocities committed by other *Lagerführers*, ours, as it turned out, was one of the "better" ones.

We bought our rail tickets, for which we paid with our hard-earned money. I remember that it cost us 58 *Reichmarks*. And so, on March 12, 1945, very sick and weak, with a new work affidavit in hand, the two of us, with our tiny baggage of a few possessions, said tearful good-byes to our few camp friends, and boarded what turned out to be a strictly military train headed for Bavaria. Throughout the long journey, we didn't utter a word and fortunately were never questioned by any of the officers or soldiers. Undoubtedly they wondered about our presence, while we were too scared to open our mouths! Mother slept, or pretended to sleep, throughout the journey with her head buried in the folds of her coat that was hanging from a hook above it. She was deathly afraid that one of the Germans would speak to her and discover that she was not German. Except for bombings—once when all the passengers had to run into a tunnel to seek shelter and another allied bombing in Regensburg, and still another one in Vienna—our train trip to Vienna was uneventful. Although the bombing in Regensburg was quite scary, at the same time, when looking back, it was somewhat amusing. Our train had just pulled into the Regensburg railway station when the sirens started to cry, almost drowning out all other sounds around us. Since railroad stations were among the most popular targets for allied bombing, most likely the siren device was placed right above the station, thus this frightening noise was louder than usual, compared to one that one might hear faintly in the distance. We were to change trains at this point and then continue on to Vienna. Because ours was a military train, there was a sudden air alert, followed almost immediately by bombing. Once off the train, Mother and I did not lose a minute and started to run out of the station in search of shelter. People were running in all directions, therefore it was hard for us to know whom to follow or to guess where the nearest shelter was. We were not able to spot a suitable hiding place, but then we noticed a large

Railroad ticket for two persons, bought for 58 Reichsmarks in Mainingen, Germany, after Mother and I were released from the *Lager Kirchberg* labor camp. Our destination was Kleine Maria Zell near Vienna, Austria, where my uncle Mikhail Shlykov worked for a lumber company.

wooded area, which seemed to be a park of some sort, and we decided to go for it. With great difficulty we climbed over the remains of what was once a very elaborate wrought-iron fence surrounding the badly overgrown grounds. (Most wrought-iron structures in Germany were dismantled during the war and the iron was used for military purposes.) I climbed over the beaten-up, deformed fence first, and kept running with my little suitcase, not noticing that Mother was not following me. When I heard her cry for help, I turned around and saw her literally hanging over the fence, with her suitcase in hand, her clothing caught on some of the sharp spikes of the fence. She remained there, waiting for my help, rather than take a chance of tearing her clothing. It looked mighty funny seeing her in this awkward position. When I helped her down, she was shaking, and almost in tears. Fortunately, her clothing did not tear, but she sustained some scratches on her arm and legs. It turned out we were on the grounds of a beautiful, but obviously terribly neglected chateau, which later, when we came back to Regensburg for the second time, we learned belonged to the Turn-und-Taxis family. There, in shoulder-high weeds, we stayed long enough for the bombing to stop and to hear the allied bombers (once their mission was accomplished) turn around and leave. Once the sirens sounded again to let us know the air alert was over, Mother and I quickly, but this time with caution, climbed back over the fence and returned to the slightly damaged station, which was just across from the chateau park. Fortunately, the tracks leading south were intact, in contrast to the tracks going north. We were also lucky to catch a departing train for Munich that eventually brought us to Vienna. Picked up by a truck full of refugees who happened to be traveling toward our destination, we finally, in the middle of the night and in a snow storm, ended up at a very small railroad station in the little remote village of Kleine Maria Zell. Just the two of us. We decided to rest on the wooden bench, the only ones in the one-room waiting hall, and wait out the storm. By this time we felt free, but lost, still not at home and among our own.

Ironically, the town of Breitungen/Werra, once a center for hundreds and hundreds of forced foreign laborers at *Lager Kirchberg* engaged in the production of munitions and causing misery and suffering for so many, today, together with nearby Meiningen, is now listed as a *Christus Gemeinde* (a Christian community), and is said to be rich in arts and cultural traditions, with a very competent medical center. After the end of World War II we tried to find the Jewish women we shared the barracks with and whom we vouched for as Poles. We wrote to the contact addresses they gave us, but to no avail. Until this day we wonder if they were among the survivors when the camp was liberated in May of 1945. To this day, so many years later, whenever I say that my father died in Auschwitz and that Mother and I were captive in a labor camp, people are astonished and say with surprise: "I didn't know you were Jewish!"

The Jews have rightly done an excellent job of making the world conscious of their sufferings and of the persecution and enormous amount of atrocities inflicted upon them. The Nazis were intent on decimating the Jews of Europe. They were also planning the subjugation and destruction of the Slavs. Poland was devastated by the Nazi occupation. The subsequent Soviet domination resulted in delayed recognition of the enormous Polish losses. To me, as a victim and a survivor, it is very painful to see the Poles forgotten and not recognized for their horrendous sufferings.

10

Kleine Maria Zell, Austria

We must have dozed off at the lonely railway station. After the long-awaited release from the camp, then the departure from Breitungen Werra by military train, the bombing along the rail tracks that we were on, the bombing of the Regensburg railroad station, and bombings on the way to Vienna and in Vienna itself, then being stranded at the Vienna station before getting a lift on a truck that was going our way, finally, arriving at the Kleine Maria Zell station, a final blow was that we had to fight still another obstacle, an unexpected snowstorm. After a rest, a very brief one, just long enough for the storm to cover the countryside with a lush, soft blanket of snow, we were ready for the final segment of our journey. And so, at dusk, after a long walk in knee-deep snow, with a huge and bright full moon above guiding us down the unknown country road, Mother and I at last arrived at the farmhouse that the Shlykovs for the last few months had called their home. Cold, hungry and very exhausted, especially Mother, we simply collapsed! The joy of being free at last was beyond comprehension. The departure from the camp was finally a dream come true. We were going to be warm, not hungry, and among our own. The Shlykovs, who shared this hut with the Chwedczuks (Petr Pavlovich, Serafima Mikhaylovna, and their twin sons Gleb and Boris), made some quick changes so as to accommodate us. Although, once again, I had to share a bed, this one was bigger than the cot at the camp, had a mattress rather than a straw-filled sack, and the clean sheets and blankets felt very cozy. I recognized the bedding from Warsaw times and could not believe that so many familiar things were around us. It was sheer, indescribable ecstasy! To top it all, everyone treated Mother and me with so much love and compassion. They all tried to do their utmost to help us get stronger, both physically and mentally. I am not sure which part of our beings needed more attention and fixing. We spent many hours retelling our tale. They could not believe what the two of us had experienced and endured from the time we all parted back in Warsaw. They had urged us to come along with them on the long journey to Austria, so as to avoid the Uprising. They knew that we should not stay behind, but Mother, even though she realized how dangerous it might be if we stayed, could not think of "leaving everything behind." If we had gone along, "everything" could have been saved. For the rest of her life, the recollection of her indecision to leave Warsaw still haunted her.

The days in Kleine Maria Zell passed quickly, although Mother's recovery to health was slower than anticipated. Most of the warm days she spent in the winter sun in the garden, or in her warm room, lying down, thinking, and being pampered, especially by Serafima, who soon became her best friend for life. They knew each other from prewar times in Brest, but only now became close. Serafima's husband, Piotr, was the one who, after the Bolshevik revolution, had helped Misha and Misha's brother, Ivan, relocate from Gallipoli to Poland. My time, other than eating (because I ate too much too soon I developed a lot of stomach/intestinal problems), was spent gathering mushrooms, which allowed me to wander in the woods, which I enjoyed doing so much. Although there were not many mushrooms to be found because of the cold weather, I was still able to bring some for Sonya to use in meals or to make marinated mushrooms, which Misha would usually have with a shot of vodka. Misha insisted that we have a vegetable garden, since produce and other stores were some distance away and day-to-day shopping was out of the question. By establishing a garden, Sonya and Serafima had most of the stuff they needed for cooking hearty meals, while chickens, eggs and dairy products were available locally. The first "fun" chore I had to do after we were settled was to dig out horseradish root and grate it by hand on a half-broken grater. I almost cried my heart out in frustration and suffered many bloody fingers while working on those hard and sturdy horseradish roots! I often thought to myself, "I'm becoming another Cinderella." I could not understand why it was so important to have horseradish on his plate; could not Misha see how painful it was to make? Anyhow, no sooner did I finish preparing one portion, when I had to make more. They just devoured the hot stuff, eating it almost daily! Misha would swallow, by the spoonful it seemed, the freshly grated radish to which some grated beets had been added, and then he would start sneezing. He could sneeze a dozen times nonstop! I guess for him it was a kind of antihistamine that cleared his sinuses, although he actually had no trouble with them.

My other duty was to walk to the store to fetch needed supplies. It was hard in the cold weather, but in the early spring I did not mind it so much, as it was something to do, and more fun than grating horseradish! Oh yes, another fun-time chore (ha!) that I had was to roll partially dried leaves of tobacco into a thin, tight roll, similar to a cigar. Then I would cut these rolls with a very sharp knife, as if they were dough for fine angel-hair spaghetti. Once it all was cut, I would spread it out on a cloth and let it dry in the sun during the day or near a stove at night. The dried, very fresh tobacco was used by Misha and Mother for cigarettes. They used special thin squares of paper to roll the cigarettes, but if they ran out of those, small pieces of newspaper would do. Sonya and I looked at this process of homemade cigarettes with disgust, but complaining of the smoke got us nowhere. When it was warm out, they would smoke outdoors; if not, they would envelop us with smoke indoors. Little did I think then that really I was their partner in crime! Another annoying thing was Misha's practice, as it was Mother's and anybody else's that came for a visit or a meal, of drowning their sorrows in drink. No matter how hard it was to buy both liquor and tobacco, they always found a way to do so. Often a little bribe made the purchase possible. Again, because I knew some German, I was the compliant one who had to conduct the actual bribing.

As it had been in Brest or Warsaw, there, in a sleepy village in Austria, the Shlykovs were quickly discovered by other Russians. Soon they had more friends than they could feed. But Sonya, as always, knew how to make and stretch any meal, and no one ever left her house hungry!

11

Flight from the Soviets

No sooner, it seems, than we were settled and little by little able to put our nightmare behind us, when the rumors started to circulate of Soviet troops advancing on Vienna. Shlykov, knowing what that could mean to the Russian work crew that he was in charge of, quickly organized a group that was interested and eager to flee from the Soviets. They were sure that staying behind would mean a death sentence for any Russian who might fall into the hands of the Soviet authorities. A fellow Russian and good friend of the Shlykovs was the work supervisor at the Kleine Maria branch of the Lumber Transport Service where Mikhail Shlykov was employed, and he issued a movement order *(Marschbefehl)* allowing Shlykov to take 13 wagons and 15 horses and move them with workers and families to an alleged new work site in Ober Donau. A similar attestation states that Shlykov, on the move to Bavaria, will travel with two oxen, which are his personal property. Having horses, oxen, and wagons at his disposal, Shlykov resolved to pack up, leave the area promptly and join the endless columns of retreating German military forces, which also did not want to fall prey to the Soviets. It did not take long for the actual packing. Everything that was useful was loaded. Inasmuch as the Shlykovs had been able to bring to Kleine Maria Zell everything but their furniture, a selection of things had to be made: what could fit on the wagon and what should be left behind. For instance, they decided to leave their porcelain dinnerware behind, as well as various newly acquired household things they used for day-to-day living in the farmhouse. They made an arrangement with the owners of the farm from whom their quarters were rented, that at the end of the war one of us would come back for the things left behind. In the 1960s, about 20 years later, while Chester and I were stationed in Germany, we drove down to Kleine Maria Zell. We found the owners of the little house that had housed the Shlykovs, Mother and me back in 1945. We asked if we could pick up the things that we had left behind. The farmer and his wife were rather surprised and flustered upon seeing us. They stated that most of the things that had been left with them by us for safekeeping were taken by the Soviets. She did produce a couple of dishes from the set of our china. The visit was otherwise uneventful, but it was somehow strange and almost unbelievable to be again at the place where Mother and I had found shelter and comfort.

From day one of our departure, I was the one designated to make all arrangements that required use of the German language. All of a sudden the family was helpless and the small amount of their German vocabulary was not sufficient to get by. I became their sole interpreter. There were several wagons that left Kleine Maria Zell at the same time. Our group consisted of an oxen-driven wagon and another pulled by two horses. Our stuff, that is to say the Shlykovs' things, as Mother and I had come to Kleine Maria Zell each with only a little suitcase, were placed on the oxen-pulled wagon. Misha, heeding the plea of a young Rumanian Gypsy, who had appeared out of nowhere and wanted to come along, put him in charge of leading the oxen, with orders to keep them in line. Stepan, we soon learned, was a typical Gypsy, very outgoing, fearless, and always in a happy mood, but it was never made clear to us where he came from, or who and where his parents were. He spoke some Russian and we all considered him a cheerful, good-natured fellow who, when not busy with the oxen, would play a harmonica or a homemade flute. He simply adored Sonya, perhaps because she fed him well and was very kind to him. She sometimes said: "I like to be as good to him as a mother would, because maybe, I hope, somewhere there is some good woman looking after my son."

On the horse-driven cart were the belongings of the family Zhgun, consisting of Timofey Ivanovich, his wife Mariya Gavrilovna, their daughter Tamara, and their future son-in-law. Mariya Gavrilovna, with her short and quite plump figure, a wrinkle-free, round face, rosy cheeks, and a tiny, very talkative (nonstop) mouth, usually sat like an adornment on their stuffed-to-the-brim wagon. Being overweight, she was not able to walk alongside the wagons, as the rest of us did. It was, I must say, quite a sight to see this person sitting like a Matreshka wooden doll on the wagon, guarding all her belongings. There was very little conversation among the four of them. Tamara's parents disliked the young man and very often just ignored him. Tamara was very unhappy, but could do little to improve the situation. Timofey often spent time talking to Misha, while the rest of us tried to tolerate his wife. In addition to constantly whining and worrying about the future, she often displayed her very distrustful nature. One day she misplaced the little bundle of jewelry she always carried pinned to her clothing. In a highly hysterical state she accused us of stealing her precious sack. Of course, when she calmed down, she found it right under her on the wagon. Their wagon and ours were almost always together on the long march toward Bavaria. We invariably stopped together for a rest or to feed the animals, and always stopped at the same place for a night's lodging. From time to time, one could hear Mariya Gavrilovna demanding this or that in her high-pitched, squeaky voice. On many occasions her husband would lose his patience with his demanding wife. Once, having heard her complain one time too many, he lost his temper and swung his whip a bit too high, giving her a sharp blow. She, in her amazement, exclaimed a few words like "Oh, Ow, Oy!" and submissively became quiet. Those of us who had witnessed the scene had a hard time keeping from laughing. The Chwiedczuk family was marching with us as well, but they kept company with other people. I suspected that Misha and Piotr Chwiedczuk had had a disagreement prior to the departure, and so our relationship with them was kind of strained.

Since the Soviet forces were rapidly advancing from the south, the main artery leading north was getting jammed, time was running short as we marched day after day only as fast as the oxen could go, and we were constantly being joined by more people trying to move north, away from the Russian front. The roads were already packed with retreating German forces and often we, the civilians, had to give way to their endless columns. It was now April and the weather was getting better, but then came April showers. The roads became muddy and full of potholes, as the heavy military equipment damaged them in no time. There also were areas that had suffered bombings a short time prior to our march. Railroad tracks especially were sorely in need of repair, so that train travel for most was out of the question and those wanting to flee had to turn to the crowded, mostly country roads. There were many civilian horse-driven carriages, wagons, and carts, but ours was the only one drawn by two beige-colored oxen. Wagons were piled to the brim with possessions that people were trying to save, but in time during the flight many of these possessions were exchanged for food or used as payment for a night's lodging in a room, in a barn, or sometimes in a warm pigsty. The long line of masses of fleeing people clogged the roads day after day. When we stopped near Lienz, waiting for the roads to be free in order to continue our march north, we were told of the announcement by Cossack General Shkuro that the Soviets were now closing in on Vienna, Austria.

Lienz was the setting for an infamous, yet little-known, event of the war. Here Russian Cossacks were forcibly given over to the Soviet Union by British soldiers in an action known as the *vydacha kazakov* (handing over of the Cossacks). The Cossacks are a traditional people of the southern steppe region of Eastern Europe and Asian Russia. During the Russian Revolution of 1917, thousands of Cossacks fought for the White Army and the Tsar against the Bolsheviks who later established the Soviet Socialist government. These White Army Cossacks fled to western European countries. When the USSR was attacked by Nazi Germany in 1941, Cossacks were conflicted whether to fight with the Russians against the Nazis or fight with the Nazis against the Soviets. Some chose to continue their self-imposed exile, and some chose to continue their fight against communism by supporting the Germans. At the close of the war, the Cossacks were caught in the middle. At the Yalta and Teheran treaty conferences, Stalin demanded that at war's end all Russian and Soviet citizens known to the Allies be handed over to the Soviet Union. Churchill and Roosevelt agreed to this stipulation and Russians and Cossacks were forcibly surrendered by the Allies to the Red Army wherever they were found. The most notorious scene of this repatriation happened in Lienz a month after we passed through the area.

Toward the end of the war, Cossack leaders persuaded Hitler to allow all civilian Cossacks to settle in the foothills of the Italian Alps. Thousands of Cossacks moved there and established a refugee settlement. When the Allies crossed into the Alps, however, the Cossacks were ordered to retreat northward. On the banks of the Drava River, near Lienz, the British army caught up with them and interned them in a makeshift camp, which at first the Cossacks believed was a refugee camp. But at the end of May 1945, more than two thousand Cossack officers and generals were disarmed and transported in British cars and trucks to a neighboring town held by the Red Army. A week later, the remainder of this group of Cossacks, 32,000 men, women and children were summarily herded by the British into cattle cars and trucks and delivered to the Soviets. Many fought their capture and were beaten into submission. Later, in the USSR, Cossack leaders were tried and executed for treason; the majority of the civilians were sent to labor camps in Siberia where most died. A total of two million people were forcibly repatriated to the Soviet Union by British and American forces; 45,000–50,000 of them were Cossacks.

For our group it was sheer terror, as we helplessly agonized over these tragic events, unable to intervene or help. These were Russians, including some who had left Russia during the October Revolution in 1917, who were being returned to their former homeland, which was now their communist enemy! The cries, screams, and struggles they put up in order not to go as ordered proved to be useless. The more they fought the more force was used on them.

S. G. Korolkoff, the artist of the famous painting *Betrayal of the Cossacks*, was a friend of my family, who on many occasions visited the Shlykovs at their farm when they resided in Lakewood, New Jersey. Another friend and frequent visitor (and one of Mother's admirers) was a Cossack *ataman* (chieftain), Professor Nikolay Fiodoroff, who at the age of 100 was living at the Tolstoy Foundation Nursing Home in Novo-Deveyevo, New York, and still writing books about the Cossacks. He died at the age of 102 on 28 September 2003.

Every night we stopped to rest our tired animals, our savior oxen and horses, and our very tired and sore feet. Now and then, not being well yet, Mother would climb up on the wagon and try to rest. The rest of us just walked along the wagons without stopping, in order not to fall behind. As soon as dusk approached, we would stop, preferably in the nearest village. Once the wagons had come to a halt, Misha and I, the interpreter, would go from one farmhouse to the next, pleading with the farmers to let us use their premises to spend the night. Sometimes we were lucky to find a place right away; sometimes, almost ready to give up, we still were able to convince or bribe the owner to let us in. Nevertheless, on many occasions we either did not get to a village in time before night set in, or we could not find a farmer who was willing to permit us to stay overnight. On such occasions we preferred to pull off the road and stop near the forest's edge, if there was a forest nearby. Being near lush woods meant having better shelter from the wind and frequent rains. We felt lucky if the underbrush was full of needles, rather than leaves, because then it would be much warmer during the night. Sonya and Misha had their mattresses with them from Warsaw. There were six sections of them, so each of us had a small mattress and a Persian rug under our tired bodies. (Forty-five years later, when Mother agreed to move from New Jersey to California and was ready to start packing, she wanted to sell one of the Persian rugs. For nostalgic reasons I did not let her do so. At this writing we still have this rug!) We used our coats and some blankets as covers. When I saw the mattresses being loaded onto the wagon back in Kleine Maria Zell, I could not imagine what a comfort they would be during our very long trip. Now it was obvious what a wise decision it was to take them along. Before we settled down, whether in the woods or at a farmhouse, we would start a small fire outdoors and cook our dinner. Our Gypsy boy knew well how to start a fire and to cook on it. He must have had plenty of practice from his early childhood. Often we counted our blessings and were grateful to Misha for his decision to take Stepan along. You could say Stepan gave us more in return for our favor of taking him along. Thanks to him, on a couple of occasions, we had an illegitimate chicken or stolen eggs for our meal. One time, Stepan was holding the reins in just one hand, rather than in both hands. Sonya noticed that the oxen were going too close to the edge of the road, almost getting off the road, and she shouted to him to straighten them out. She asked him to use both his hands, so as to have better control of the oxen, or the wagon would leave the road. Stepan shouted back that he cannot use the other hand, and as Sonya ran toward him, she noticed that under the green wool cape that he wore a hand was holding an almost dead chicken by its head. Apparently, he had caught it on the road and had kept it under his cape for quite some time, its beak shut so it would not make noise. Sonya scolded him, but with his devilish grin, he answered her, "The chicken will make a nice dinner for us all." He was an expert on drinking the insides of eggs without breaking the shell, except for a tiny hole. Much later, when we were staying at the last farmhouse on our journey, the farmer's wife was complaining to me that she keeps finding eggs under her chickens, but often are empty. She could not understand how it was possible for a chicken to lay an egg that was empty. We could not understand it either, but soon enough our Stepan, after interrogation, admitted that he would make a tiny hole in the egg, suck out the insides and, somehow camouflaging the hole, place the egg back in the chicken's nest. The mystery was no longer a mystery.

Whenever we were allowed to stay at a farmhouse, it did not mean we would be given bed and breakfast. We were simply allowed into a barn to sleep in the warmth of the hay, away from the wind and dampness or rain. At the time it felt like sheer heaven! Usually we were allowed to use the well water for washing our clothes and ourselves and to have drinking water for our cooking, which still was done in the outdoors. Our daily camping continued for over one month! Ever since that time I am allergic to the idea of camping, and if I can help it I will never go camping again! One day, it was extremely cold and I was having a hard time keeping warm, despite the fact that I had walked all day. Sonya suggested I use her Persian coat. I wore it and when it came time to scout with Misha for a lodging, we stopped at a nearby farmhouse and as usual asked for permission to stay overnight. The farmer looked at Misha and me very suspiciously and questioned us more than other farmers had before. Then he asked, "Are you and your husband the only prospective lodgers, or are there others with you?" I laughingly told him that I am the niece, not the wife, and that, yes, there are several of us, but not saying how many, just in case he did not want to let too many in. Only then did we realize that by wearing the Persian coat, though I still looked quite young, it made the farmer somewhat suspicious. Some farmers were hard to bargain with, and often, if it was late or we were too tired to keep looking and begging, we would offer extra money, material for a dress, or a coat, or some other thing that Sonya would not mind parting with. Once the owners saw that they would receive something extra, the deal would be made immediately. And for a little more, we would get milk, eggs and sometimes bacon. Unfortunately, bribing was necessary quite often. On the other hand, if on some occasions we had not done it, our long journey would have been so much tougher and harder to live through.

And so, day after day, no matter how cold or wet the days were, our march continued. The pace was little faster than a turtle's; on the other hand, it was fast enough to be farther and farther away from the threat of the Soviets. We were delighted that our oxen and horses proved to be strong and sturdy. Thanks to Stepan, they were very well fed, groomed, and happy. By the time we reached Bavaria, the roads were crowded with the almost defeated German forces. In many barns there were soldiers and officers waiting for orders they anticipated from their higher-ups to surrender. Once we reached Landshut, it was obvious that the war was approaching its end. We decided to interrupt our journey and try to find a place for a longer period of time, which would give us a chance to decide what to do and where to go next. At the village of Phillsbiburg, the Chwiedczuks and the Zhguns were able to settle down and take a breather, while we continued to the next village of Pfistersham/Binabiburg. There we found a reluctant and yet friendly farmer, whose wife, more than he, made the decision to let us stay at their large farm. Maybe it was smart of us to offer her this and that from the very beginning as pay for a roof over our heads, making our stay possible. Later we found out that the lady of the house was very greedy for presents. No sooner did we receive their permission to settle down in their barn than we discovered that the barn was already housing close to a hundred German military. These men, primarily soldiers, most of the time were lying around, burrowed into the straw, so that only their heads were visible. Their faces were quite lean and unshaven, but their uniforms, despite being sloppy and wrinkled, were still in fair condition. The five of us took over a corner of the huge barn and were happy as larks to be warm, to be able to rest, and to eat more normal meals, cooked by Sonya on a small burner outside. We kept exchanging this and that for milk, chickens, and eggs and for hay for our oxen. Josef ("Seppie") Haegelsparger and his wife had many animals, of the usual farm type, but our beautiful, light cream-colored oxen, compared to their herd, were champions!

During our stay at the Haegelspargers' farm, our life took on a pretty normal course. After we got acquainted with each other and the family felt comfortable with us, they let us use their oven, so that Sonya could cook larger meals. She was also able to do some baking as well. Frau Haegelsparger was eager to watch Sonya in the kitchen and to try our "strange Russian dishes," but once our hosts tried them, they were overwhelmed with how good they were. Now and then, Frau Haegelsparger also shared some of her dishes with us. She was a good German cook, but she was not too generous with portions. Each day there were quite a few people at their kitchen table: Herr and Frau Haegelsparger, their charming little daughter Ottilie, who with her blond curly hair looked like a twin sister of Shirley Temple, Herr Haegelsparger's brother, an active-duty officer, and several farm hands. Frau Haegelsparger, when not preparing lunch or dinner, washing everybody's clothing, or cleaning and milking the cows, also went with her husband and the other workers into the field to gather hay, to help with plowing, etc. She was a very hard worker, and in addition she was the boss of the farm. Her husband was very quiet and reserved, always minding his own business. Ottilie, who was not of school age yet, went everywhere her parents would go, until she discovered that it was more fun for her to be with us. As usual, I did the shopping at the village stores and every day had to make a stop at the local brewery for fresh yeast and to fill our empty beer bottles with delicious Malz Bier. Ottilie usually came along. On the way home we would nibble on the yeast, so instead of buying extra at once, we often had to go back to get more for Sonya's baking. We both needed the yeast, she for growth, and I for supplementing my dietary needs.

We did not stay long in the already overcrowded barn. Once Frau Haegelsparger got to like us and felt comfortable with our presence, she suggested we make our lodging in the granary, which was near the barn. It was there that they kept sacks upon sacks full of various grains. We were able to place, first, our mattresses on top of the sacks, then the rugs, and so our bedding was fit for kings! It was quiet and airy compared to the overcrowded atmosphere in the barn. Stepan continued to sleep with the soldiers. This new room we used only for sleeping, as there was no electricity and no windows, except for small vents for ventilation. Our delight did not last long, when, during the night, we were visited by huge fat rats! Back and forth, they would run over our bodies. Although they never bit us, we hated and feared them.

One night, during a full moon, Misha was snoring more loudly than ever. Sonya and Mother were sleeping, undisturbed by Misha's "music" making, but I happened to wake up to a loud mooing, which was more like an alarm signal, warning of a disaster. I ran out and saw one of our oxen immersed up to its neck in the manure pit. If you picture the farm as somewhat like a U-shaped cluster of buildings, in the center there was a fairly deep manure pit, which was surrounded by the house, the barn, a tool shed, and the granary. The poor animal was crying for help and no one heard him but me. I did not wait a minute, but ran into the barn and shouted for help. Many soldiers ran out, and some immediately took long sticks and various implements they could find to attach to the ox's collar. They pulled and pulled and, finally, they got him out before he drowned. There was a loud "Hurrah" and applause! Many other soldiers, as well as the farmer, his family, and my group slept throughout this terrible ordeal. What must have happened was that Stepan had failed to secure or tie down the ox firmly enough and he was able to get loose and stumbled into the pit. It is hard to say how long he was in it, but if I had not heard his cries, he would surely have drowned. He was black and brown from the manure and stank to high heaven! By morning the manure had hardened and the ox looked as if he were wearing armor. Hosing him off did no good. Stepan had to spend many hours scraping and brushing off the dry, smelly, filthy crust. Eventually, little by little the animal began to look like he had looked before his adventure. Once our ox was clean and handsome again, we felt relieved to still have him alive and happy, rather than being angry over this negligent accident. After all, we would soon need him and his partner to take us to our final destination.

I do not know what prompted our landlady to suggest one day that perhaps we might be more comfortable to stay in their house. She thought that their living room was used very little and therefore it might as well be our new quarters. Of course, she offered us her living room, not so much for our comfort, I am sure, but because she expected that we would pay her one way or another, which we did, and at times Sonya's gifts to Frau Haegelsparger seemed endless. The latter knew exactly how to get them under one pretext or another. She would innocently remark, "We are invited to the wedding of a friend and I would like to have a dress made, but I can't find a piece of material." Sonya's reaction would be: "I'll look, maybe I will find something that might be enough to make a dress." Then Frau Haegelsparger would protest and try to explain that she did not mean to be so blunt or to sound as if she were hinting for a gift. When leaving Poland for Austria, Misha made sure he had enough barter-worthy gold coins, diamonds, and watches to keep them comfortable, no matter what the situation might be. Sonya, on the other hand, stocked up on material for coats, dresses, men's suits, scarves, and the like, thinking that things no longer available in Austrian or German stores would come in handy, and in both cases they proved to be right. In any case, when the offer was made for us to move into the real house, we were overwhelmed and could jump from joy. There would be no more rats or grain, which smelled in its own particular way, instead a warm, large room with real windows (even though the view was of a manure pit that in damp weather was quite smelly.) Misha especially felt that we had achieved something that no one else from our group had.

From day one our life at the house was as normal as it could be. Sonya was able to cook almost any time she wanted, although out of courtesy she stayed out of the kitchen whenever Frau Haegelsparger was cooking, or when the family and the workers sat down for their meals. The barn continued to be occupied by the military, who continued with their meager military-issue meals. Stepan ate with us. The oxen had plenty of fresh water and food as well. Misha, Sonya, and Mother slept in the big room, I slept on a bench in the kitchen. Often, early in the morning, while everyone else was still asleep, even the farmers, Sonya and I would go into the nearby woods to look for mushrooms and wild berries. Since mushroom hunting was a popular diversion among the locals, we had to be out very early, or we would come back empty-handed. The practice was not to pull out the mushrooms, but rather to cut them off at the stem, so that in its place another mushroom would grow for the next seeker. There was a special place in the woods that we discovered, a rather damp meadow full of *rydze* (*Lactarus delicius*) and *kurki* (*Catharellus cibarius*, saffron milk caps). Those were best fried or marinated. But the best, the champion of mushrooms were the *prawdziwe* ("true" mushrooms, known in German as *Steinpilze*), which until this day are considered the best! (Polish *prawdziwe* mushrooms are usually cut, strung and dried, and then sold in markets within Poland and as an export item.) By the time Sonya and I would come back to the house with our baskets full of mushrooms and berries, it was time for breakfast. Out of the berries we made *pierogi* (dumplings), *Dampfknödel* (dumplings steamed in milk), which our landlady taught us how to make, or *blintzes*. And so it went, day after day we passed much of the time just eating. Misha ordered the best beers to go with Sonya's delicacies. I did the shopping and the washing of clothes but also found time to walk in the beautiful woods. One day I got lost and, while looking for my way home, a terribly frightening storm approached. There was much lightning and thunder, followed by a torrential rain! Alone in the dark woods, it was a frightening experience. Hoping to be safe, I hid under the biggest tree. Later I found out that that was the biggest mistake I could have made. Another time, during a similar electrical storm, Mother was pouring tea while her head was right under the ceiling light. All of a sudden lightning struck and the bulb above Mother's head exploded! Mother was shaken, but not hurt. Ever since, however, she was deathly afraid of thunder and especially electrical storms, during which she would run to the darkest room accessible, preferably one without windows, and often accompanied by our dog, which also was afraid of such storms. One day, on a Sunday, Frau Haegelsparger had just hung up her wash. Sonya, in her broken German, tried to shame her by saying that instead of going to *Kirche* (church), she chose to do the wash and also that she had hung it out on the fences for all the churchgoers to see. Sonya jokingly added, "Watch out, God will punish you for not observing Sunday as a day of rest!" By the time the wash was dry and ready to be gathered, Frau Haegelsparger noticed that her laundry was full of holes. It so happened that our oxen had strolled over to the fence and had done the nibbling. Although the landlady was upset, to our surprise, she was not angry. She soon calmed down, admitting that indeed Sonya was right, and that God had indeed punished her for doing the laundry on Sunday. She took Sonya's casual warning with the utmost seriousness and vowed never to do her laundry on a holy day.

While living at the Haegelspargers' farm, there was not much happening around us. The barn was still full of German military, the roads were quiet, and rumors once more started to circulate that the Germans are very near capitulation. And so on May 9, 1945, they did surrender! Soviet forces had already taken Vienna on April 13, 1945. American forces quickly occupied the area we were now living in. Once again the roads became crowded, but this time by American tanks, trucks and cars. The German soldiers and the officers that were staying with us at the farm promptly surrendered and were disarmed and then escorted, presumably, to a prisoner of war camp. The transition was calm and there was absolutely no resistance from the German military or the civilian population. On the contrary, the farmers and other civilians greeted the American forces with warmth. The Americans showered them, especially the children, with candy and chewing gum. We continued our stay at the Haegelspargers' farm for another few weeks. On June 20, 1945, we were officially registered by the Allied Expeditionary Force Government Office as legal residents of Pfisterham/Binabiburg.

12

Via Oxcart to Regensburg

Once we decided what to do next, we packed our wagon and said a very warm good-bye to our hosts. There were even a few tears shed on each side, as we realized that we had all survived living under the same roof in harmony, despite the fact that we came from two countries that had been fighting each other so bitterly. And once more, we found ourselves marching step by step on the road leading north. Once again we had to stop here and there, to bargain for lodging and food. After our long rest in Binabiburg, and because the weather was giving us no serious problems, it seemed that the last segment of our journey was easier than before. We found ourselves spending most nights under the open sky, and often did not need to unload mattresses or rugs in order to be warm at night. Pillows and blankets were often all we needed to spend the night comfortably. Cooking on an open fire was no problem as well. What bothered me the most were the frequent storms, with thunder and lightning. After that memorable and scary storm that caught me alone in the thick forest back in Binabiburg, I have never felt safe and comfortable during electrical storms. We passed many villages and little towns, and finally with great relief we arrived in the outskirts of Regensburg, the town that, for some reason, we had picked as our final destination. But during the approach to the center of town we had to go through an ancient fortress gate. Somehow, Stepan misjudged the width of the gate, probably because the lower part of the wall of the gate had thick concrete footings on each side, making the passage narrower than it appeared to be. In addition, the oxen were reluctant to go through because of the darkness, and so Stepan urged them with the whip. The oxen pulled harder and one of the wagon wheels did not clear the wall. The wheel broke and fell off, leaving the lopsided wagon in the middle of the ancient gate. The chaos it caused was unbelievable. Area residents with long poles came to our aid to set the wagon straight, fix the wheel, and put it back on, and only then could we continue our journey, leaving the spectacle we had created behind us.

Now that several weeks had passed since the war had ended, as refugees we were able to get help through various newly established organizations. On our very first day in Regensburg we met a Polish Jew and his daughter, Rozia, survivors of the Auschwitz concentration camp. Rozia's father (Flaumenbaum, or Pflaumenbaum), while in the concentration camp, in order to save his only treasure of gold coins, swallowed them almost every day in order to hide them, with the hope that one day, after liberation, they would enable him to start a new life somewhere. If I recall correctly, the coins were mostly Tsarist rubles, which were smaller in size compared to American gold dollars, or other coins, which were often double or triple in size. Once he and Rozia were free and in Regensburg, he immediately was able to put his saved treasures to work and start a little business. As compatriots they steered us to a Polish organization, formed under American auspices, which gave immediate help to survivors of the various camps. Mother and I, having lost Father in Auschwitz, were eligible for housing, food and clothing rations, and a small monetary payment. Out of green military blankets we had overcoats made by a local German seamstress, who also altered some badly fitting dresses issued to us. The clothing given in general but ladies' clothing in particular, was out of fashion and rather drab-looking. A so-called *Koncentrazionstelle* (concentration camp post) was run by former concentration survivors, part of an organization called *Zrzeszenie b. Weinzniow Polit. Niem. Obozow Koncentracyjnyc*h (Polish Association of Former Political Prisoners of German Concentration Camps). The person who looked after our affairs was a former theology student by the name of Bruno Gierszewski. He had spent several years at the Mathausen concentration camp. When the American army liberated him and his fellow prisoners, he had to be transported immediately to a military hospital. There he was operated on for a broken spine. The doctors had little hope for his survival, as they had to support his spine with gold plates. His friends teased him, saying that he is a walking gold depository. While on the operating table for most of the day and into the night, one of his friends was busy painting a large image of the well-known Polish icon, the Black Madonna of Czestochowa (*Matka Boska Czestochowska*). He dedicated this painting to his friend's survival. The surgery was a great success, and the image of the Black Madonna was offered for a side chapel of the Regensburg *Dom* (cathedral) where it is housed to this day. During one of Mother's many visits to Munich, she received a copy of this painting with the artist's dedication (Klemens Kwiatkowski, student of medicine). It was dated July 7, 1948. By coincidence, three years later on that same day Chester and I were married.

    Bruno, Klemens, and their friend Jan Kujawa, another concentration camp survivor, were inseparable. They went through hell together and now that they were free, they looked after each other. With the help of Bruno Gierszewski we were assigned part of an apartment on Luitpold Strasse 15C, which belonged to a German woman, the wife of an *Oberrat* (city councilman). Her husband, a Nazi officer, was now in an American prisoner-of-war camp, waiting to be rehabilitated. Their two sons who lived with her, 21-year-old Dieter and his 10-year-old brother Helmut, were very pro–American, which probably eased the strange feeling of having *Ausländer* (foreigners) sharing their apartment. We (Mother, Sonya, Misha and I) were given two rooms; Sergey Ivanovich Nekrasov, his wife Anastasiya Nikolayevna, and son Paul all occupied a single room; and an unmarried young German woman refugee occupied the very small room that used to be the maid's room when the Jaehle family was still together before and during the war.

There was one bathroom (just a toilet and a small sink) for all us refugees. Frau Jaehle and her sons used the master bathroom, which included a tub. To bathe, we had to go into town to use the public bathhouse and although it was clean and warm, it was not very convenient and sometimes the wait was quite long. We had to bring our own towels and soap. The fee was quite reasonable, but nevertheless we did not, or could not, use the bathhouse as frequently as we would have liked; therefore, we had to use the little sink or take a sponge bath in our bedroom, which I shared with Sonya and Misha (Mother slept on a sofa in the "living room"). Paul, an intelligent, but unsociable, carefree, and sometimes spiteful youngster, constantly doing things that annoyed all of us and for which he was frequently reprimanded by his stern father, very often used the little sink to wash his muddy boots, leaving the bathroom dirty and flooded. Frau Jaehle could not abide Paul, and although as time went by she got used to having us around, she showed her dislike for Paul and he did his utmost to spite her. After Paul and his parents emigrated to the United States, Paul became a successful electrical engineer, married, and fathered two children. He established very warm relations with the Shlykovs and my family. At the Jaehle house the three families used the kitchen stove by taking turns at their assigned time. The young tenant ate where she worked, using the kitchen only to boil some water. After a while, especially after Frau Jaehle was able to help us strike a deal with a butcher friend, she even began to like us. The deal amounted to exchanging our beautiful oxen for meat. Since the butcher had a working farm in addition to his store in town, he agreed to take our beloved oxen to his farm to do some plowing, etc. In exchange, he agreed to give Frau Jaehle and us so many pounds of various meats and sausages. We would come with a slip to his store as often as needed, and each time he would make a subtraction from the total amount that we had bartered for. It was no wonder that this deal made Frau Jaehle and her children happy. She not only did not have to pay for all the meat, but she was supplied with products that few of her German friends could even dream of. I visited my oxen friends at the farm and kept making sure that the butcher was keeping his promise never to slaughter our animal friends. They were kept clean and happy—what better reward to give them for having saved our lives!

In the basement, the Jaehle family had a substantial supply of liquor. One day, Frau Jaehle came to ask us if we perhaps knew why her supply was slowly being depleted. Knowing that Misha liked to have guests and parties (which she herself sometimes attended), she must have thought that it was Misha who was helping himself to the stored bottles. But it turned out that Dieter, her older son, was the guilty one, who finally, although reluctantly, confessed to the thievery, after which we all were relieved, as we all silently suspected our fellow refugees of the tippling.

13

Back to School

Shortly after we settled at 15C Luitpold Strasse, I enrolled in the newly formed Polish *gimnazjum* (high school) at the displaced persons camp in the outskirts of the city, which was run by the *kompanja wartownicza*, a guard company formed immediately after the end of the war employing displaced Polish persons to do guard duty for the American authorities. Before and during the war, the site and its brick barracks were used by the German army. The Polish guards wore uniforms and had several offices throughout the DP camp. We, like the rest of the refugees, were also eligible for camp housing, but since we had been assigned a portion of the Jaehle apartment, we preferred to be living independently outside the camp. We forwent all the camp privileges, but gladly exchanged our German black bread ration (*Bauernbrot*) for the camp's delicious white bread baked by the American army. To this day I wonder why, if the American army could produce such delicious, wholesome bread, there is now no bakery to be found to match their product. Many Poles found jobs at the Army facilities. One of my girlfriends, Dzidka, had a part-time job baking doughnuts at one of the American mess halls. She was allowed to take leftover doughnuts and the fat that they were baked in. She shared this with her schoolmates and often I would bring some home with me. The fat was usable, but had a sweet taste to it.

Although living on the economy was to some extent a privilege, for me it was a hardship to live in town, primarily because every day I had to walk quite a long distance to school. Part of the walk was through an isolated area with buildings that served as storage, or were partly abandoned. I often took this short cut to the camp, until one day a man, who was hiding behind one of the empty buildings, suddenly jumped out and exposed himself as I was passing. Frightened, knowing that there was no one else in sight, I started to run. He tried to catch up with me, but when I screamed, he stopped. I could not help turning around to see if he was still running after me. He shouted obscenities and continued exposing himself. There were no more short cuts for me, unless a group of us were walking together. From then on, very often, if I had to go home after classes, I invariably would talk one or two friends to come with me into town. Walking alone was quite boring, but with friends it was always fun. Irka, who did not have the heart to say no to my pleas, was the best one. Sometimes, she would walk with me as far as our house, have tea and cake with us, and then I had to walk her halfway back. That was the usual deal. Another drawback to living in town was that nearly all of my friends lived in the camp, and because of that I felt that I was missing out on comradeship. The only two friends beside myself who lived in town were Rozia (daughter of the Polish Jew who had helped us when we arrived in Regensburg) and Nina Polanska, who was a Belorussian refugee living with her mother. Now and then I would stay at the school dormitory for a night, or several nights in a row if there was a school function planned. I liked staying there and being part of the togetherness. On those occasions I would be assigned a kitchen duty, like the rest of the dormies, which amounted to helping with the cooking, preparing meals, serving food, or cleaning up. It was no hardship partaking in the different chores; even washing dishes seemed like fun. Being an outsider at the dorm, one inconvenience was that I had to share a bed with one of my girlfriends. They would draw lots to see who would be the "lucky" one to end up with me for the night. On one of these occasions, while I was sharing a bed with Hanka (Kwiatkowska), a roommate of Dzidka, I became sick. I had a very high fever and noticed that my big toe had doubled in size. It was throbbing and a red line was visible along my leg. I suffered through the night, as I did not want to wake my friends. Hanka, whose nickname was *Djabel* (Devil), was a naturally curly brunette, with two jet-black eyes like two pieces of coal and she had the temper, well, of a devil, thus her nickname. If I had told her what pain I was in, she would most likely have laughed it off and told me to go back to sleep and tell her about it in the morning. At daybreak my friends realized how serious it was and they rushed me to the dispensary of the hospital run by the United Nations Relief and Rehabilitation Administration (UNRRA). Hanka's first words to me were, "Why didn't you speak up sooner?" Once at the hospital I found out that I had blood poisoning coming from the infected toe. They did surgery and I was hospitalized for about a week. Mother was told why I did not show up at home. When she came for a visit she brought a friend, a Russian man who wanted to marry her, whom I despised. I was very disappointed that she had brought along someone I disliked, which somehow spoiled the visit. Speaking of visitors, I was simply flooded with visits by different friends and teachers who dropped in on me between classes, or before and after school. I was a celebrity!

The dormitories were separate, with male students in one building and female in another. The dining and recreation halls were coed. The students varied in ages. Some were adults whose education had been interrupted because they were taken by the Germans to do forced labor. Many of these were without parents or families. Some were teenagers who had survived the war but were temporarily separated from their parents. And there were those who had

ended up as refugees together with their families and were in the UNRRA camp. The last-named ones were housed in barracks for families, while single students were in dorms. Despite the fact that there was quite a gap in ages, all the students were very well behaved, never violating the regulations imposed by the *gimnazjum* authorities. Teachers for the various classes were carefully picked from professional teachers among the refugees. An ex-teacher who had qualified in a subject while still in Poland taught each subject. There was a Polish priest teaching religious studies and teachers for biology, chemistry, Latin, zoology, math, art, music, foreign language, etc. The classes started after the dorm breakfast, with a recess at noon, after which classes resumed until three or four in the afternoon. There was lots of homework and the teachers, although quite friendly, were very demanding. During strawberry season, I always brought to the school large baskets full of freshly picked strawberries. If not for any other special virtues, I was certainly popular because of the strawberries, which were otherwise not to be had at the camp.

In addition to attending Polish *gimnazjum*, I arranged to take private piano lessons. The German lady who lived above us on Luitpold Strasse was more than willing to let me use her piano for lessons with the German music teacher, as well for daily practice. She charged a small fee, but I always obliged her with some sausages or meat from our butcher friend. The drawback was that the room in which the piano stood was not heated, so in cold weather I had to wear gloves without fingers and a coat in order to keep warm. The arrangement was not very stimulating, to say the least. I had a hard time squeezing my music lessons into my already very busy daily schedule, because during my free time I was on call to do all sorts of errands for Misha's different businesses.

Nina Polanska first enrolled into a Belorussian school, but since the school had only lower grades, she transferred into the Polish school. Paul Nekrasov, however, and many other sons and daughters of Russian refugees were in a Russian school, which was formed in a manner similar to the Polish one. The Russian community was quite large, but most of the refugees lived in town.

14

Obshchina

Soon after our arrival in Regensburg, we were told of a *Russkaya obshchina* (Russian community center), which was housed in that city in a rented German *Gasthaus* (restaurant) at Silberne Gasse 17. There, several Russian women ran a *stolovaya* (dining hall), charging minimal prices for hardy, tasty home-cooked meals. At the *obshchina* one could not only eat one's favorite lunch or dinner, but also meet one's countrymen. Like the Polish community at the camp, there at the *obshchina* Russian refugees would hang around, hoping to meet a lost friend or make a new contact. They were of different ages and walks of life. Misha, in particular, visited the center daily, not so much to eat meals, since he had the best cooking at home, but to discuss and plan activities for the stranded Russian community. There were two priests, Father Vasiliy and Father Fiodor. These two clergymen were in constant disharmony and competition, and Misha very often tried to calm down their disagreements and disputes for the sake of the parishioners. Sometime later, a third priest by the name of Starikov was ordained. As a personal gift at Father Starikov's ordainment, Misha gave him a sterling silver cross. It so happened that when we moved to Santa Barbara in 1973, we discovered that Father Starikov, after emigrating to the United States, had settled in Santa Barbara where he founded the Russian Orthodox Church on Castillo Street. Unfortunately, he died just before we arrived in California.

The *obshchina* was a haven during those difficult times for those without a country and without a family. Poetry readings, concerts, and children's plays were staged during the evenings. All holiday celebrations, weddings, and even *trapezas* (funeral receptions) took place there. It was there that one day a young Russian ex-soldier (actually a deserter) joined in singing Russian songs. He had a most beautiful lyric tenor voice. It was as clear as a bell! His very sentimental rendition of Russian gypsy songs was astounding and we all would not let him stop singing. To our surprise, in addition to gypsy songs, he knew many of the old White Russian prerevolutionary melodies that brought back nostalgic memories to many former White Russians like Misha. He also sang, unfamiliar to many, Soviet war songs, which differed quite a bit from the

Members of the Russian Community Center, Regensburg, Germany, gathered for a *trapeza* (post-funeral repast), 1948.

upbeat, peppy White Russian ones. The Soviet songs were very melodic, but full of sadness and sorrows, almost heartbreaking. Through them one could picture the lonely life of a young Soviet army soldier. One song followed another and the requests were endless! He was happy to oblige and was ecstatic to be so warmly received. At last he felt at home among his own! After this evening and in later meetings, Misha was so impressed with this young man's voice and his innocent boyish personality that he very seriously tried to convince Sonya to adopt this young and lonely soldier. Misha, in the same way that Sonya felt about Stepan, our wagon helper, saw in this lad the image of their lost son Igor. They missed their beloved son so terribly and suspected that the worst fate had befallen him, so much that they were hoping to find another son that they could call their own. Although Sonya was very tempted to agree, she kept putting off the decision, and so the adoption never happened.

For several years, the *obshchina* served us all as a warm place to spend many interesting hours in good and stimulating company. Especially during cold winter days, quite a few people found a refuge there from unheated rooms or apartments. The place was not only warm and full of delicious kitchen aromas, but it was cozy and lively. Misha became friends with quite a few people that he met there, and as usual opened his heart and hospitable house to them. Because Misha needed more room to entertain his friends, our stay at Luitpold Strasse 15C, despite pretty good arrangements with the Jaehle family, came to an end. After our move to larger quarters, we kept in touch with

Seated, left to right: unidentified, Aleksander Filatiev, the Rev. Vasiliy, Gen. Popov, the Rev. Feodor Mikhailov, unidentified, Kirshanov (fnu), Vsevolod Zabolotny. Standing, left to right: Aleksander Feodorovich Mikhailov, unidentified, unidentified, unidentified, Mikhail Shlykov, Viktor Sergeyevich Kobylin.

our landlords and they continued to draw on our meat credit from the butcher. The Nekrasovs moved out as well, as they, too, had found a better setup. I am sure that Frau Jaehle rejoiced not to have Paul around. Eventually, Herr Jaehle was let go from the American camp and the family was once more together and without tenants.

15

"Save Me, Tante Luzie!"

In our new, larger requisitioned quarters, with a kitchen of our own, we were able not only to spread ourselves out a little, but Sonya and Misha could entertain in the style to which they were accustomed. Our new place was a rather pretentious villa at Weissenburg Strasse 11, which had once belonged to the *Oberbürgermeister* (mayor) of Regensburg. It was a two-story house with an attic and a basement and a small garden in the backyard. Our family was assigned two bedrooms, a large living room, a powder room (toilet and sink), and kitchen, all on the ground floor. Two other, small bedrooms on each end of the long hall were assigned to an elderly couple, Herr and Frau Opat, German Jewish refugees from Oberschlesien. The Wolf family was already occupying the upper floor. This family consisted of Walter, a German Jew, his Polish-Ukrainian wife Eugenia ("Genia"), their five-year-old daughter Kristina, and their young German au pair Emmi Bursik, who was about fifteen years old. My association with little "Kristl" was exceptionally warm. From the very beginning she called me *Tante Luzie*. She would make just any simple excuse in order to be where I was. She was ready to help with anything that I was occupied with. I took her for walks, played games with her, and babysat her whenever her parents would go out. If it was in the evening, I would read to her endless children's books until she would finally persuade me to stay with her upstairs overnight. When she asked for something, it was hard to turn her down. She was an adorable child, full of charm, and very bright for her age. Her golden-blond hair, beautiful smile and her very big eyes made her look very coquettish. She used her charm to get out of being in trouble. Very often we would hear her mother scolding her, then Kristl would come running down the stairs calling: *Tante Luzie, Tante Luzie, Muttie wird mich hauen! Rette mich, Tante Luzie!* ("Mummy wants to spank me. Save me, Aunt Lucy!"). Once with me, she would beg me to hide her from her mom. Gena, sometimes with a *Kochlöffel* (cooking ladle), primarily for effect, would follow Krista down the stairs. Often, seeing her little one hiding behind me, and hearing her whisper to me, "Tell Mummy that Krista ran away," her mother could not keep from laughing. Krista was the apple of her father's eye. She could do no wrong and he never disciplined her; on the contrary, he would undo whatever punishment her mother applied.

The bathroom, which was upstairs between the Wolfs' kitchen and the hall, had no door but only a curtain to serve for privacy. It was at their and our disposal. The Opats preferred to take their baths in town in a public bathhouse. In addition to their large kitchen, the Wolfs had a good-sized living room, a small study, and a large bedroom. Off the living room they also had a huge open deck overlooking our small garden. It was on this deck that the Wolfs liked to entertain their many friends on warm days. Since there was no door to the bathroom, it was very awkward to take a bath without the assurance that someone wouldn't barge in on you. I was a frequent scapegoat and an easy target for pranks. If I wanted to take a bath and did not want to go to a public bathhouse, I had to put up with the jokes that were played on me. One such incident comes to mind, when, on a Saturday, thinking that I would be able to take a quick bath while the Wolfs were out, I began my bath when all of a sudden, not only did the Wolfs come home early, but a whole bunch of their friends followed them in for coffee and freshly baked *Kuchen* by their *Hausmädchen* Emmi. Once they heard that I was taking a bath in the almost unprotected area, the "fun" began! Their friends threatened to barge in with me still in the tub. Since my protests were ignored, I covered myself with a towel, still wet with soap and dripping all over the floor, and ran down the stairway, followed by gales of laughter. Bringing friends home for coffee and cake after a walk or an outing was a ritual for the Wolf family. There were several families, which, like Walter, came from the same area of Sudetenland. Most of them were Jewish, or one of the marriage partners was Jewish. Soon after the end of the war, almost all of them were able to get into some kind of business. One of them, Dr. Beran, was a dentist, and one Rosenkrantz started an import company dealing with salt water and importing conserved fish from the north of Germany to Regensburg. And one that especially comes to mind was Herr Brode, who was the live wire of the group. He was not only a practical jokester but was also the best teller of funny anecdotes. One of his practical jokes, kind of an innocent one, I will never forget. Once, while his very young nephew was taking a bath, Uncle Brode, looking at the naked boy, teased him and said, "If you won't be good, Uncle Brode will bite your little pee-pee off!" The boy took his uncle seriously and promised to be good. Soon after that warning, Brode came with the little nephew to visit the Wolfs. It being a hot summer day, Gena drew a cool bath for the visiting boy and her little daughter Kristl. Both children hopped into the bathtub and when the boy looked at the naked Kristl, he started to cry and called out, pointing at Kristl, "Poor Kristl, Uncle Brode bit her pee-pee off!" The grown-ups rushed to the bathroom on hearing the boy cry. He just kept shouting, "Uncle Brode bit it off." The frightened boy had to be given an anatomy lesson before he could calm down. The Wolfs and their guests almost split their sides laughing!

They all met somewhere regularly, but it seemed that their favorite place to gather was at the Wolfs' apartment, perhaps because Gena was the best cook and pastry maker.

Downstairs, in the front bedroom, which was occupied by Mother and me, there was a small coal fireplace, a bed that we shared, a table where I did my homework and sat with my various tutors, a couple of chairs, and a huge wardrobe with a storage space above it. Facing the street, our bedroom window served our dog Trolli and Mickey the kitten as an observation post. In order to economize on fuel, we all congregated in the living room, which had a potbelly stove (with a long exhaust pipe stretching out to a hole cut out in the window) that was on nonstop during cold weather. Meanwhile, our bedroom would be freezing. Water in a glass left overnight would freeze solid! One day we were in a hurry to go out. Mother quickly brought in her laundry from the garden and placed it on the bed. Before doing that, she had tried to find the cat to put it outside and scolded it for not coming out of hiding. Being in a hurry, she decided to let the cat stay until our return. When we returned and opened the door, the kitten rushed out in a hurry. We socialized some more in the living room, and then eventually went back to our bedroom to retire. As she was tired and sleepy, Mother picked up the laundry she had left on the bed, planning to put it on the chair, to be folded the next day. Once her hands were inserted into the laundry bundle, consisting mostly of her stockings and underwear, she screamed as if she were hurt, followed by many swear words. It turned out that the cat had taken its revenge for being scolded and locked up. It had deposited a big, stinky mess in Mother's clean laundry. It was a job to clean, and then to air the room properly (there were no deodorizers back then!), before we could retire. No matter how we cleaned, the smell was with us for many days. It was fortunate that the cat had run out before Mother had discovered her mischief. It would have been murder on the spot, I am sure.

Another disaster soon followed the above incident. During the summer, we would pick various berries of the season and, using clean beer bottles with hermetic closures, we would fill the bottles with the berries mixed with sugar. Then, each bottle would be placed for storage on top of the wardrobe in our bedroom. Once they were ready as preserves, we used the delicious berries in making blintzes, quiches, and the like. One time, for some reason, our way of preserving the fresh berries did not work, either because we used too much sugar or because the closures on the bottles were not strong enough. While Mother and I were out of our room we heard a loud bang. We rushed into the bedroom and saw a huge splash of burgundy red all over the wall. Then came another bang accompanied by a splash of blue all over the room. One by one the bottles kept exploding. We were amazed that all the bottles had almost simultaneously reached their fermentation peaks, when they would explode, one after the other, like the firing of artillery loaded with real ammunition.

The room looked as if artist Jackson Pollock had created a masterpiece. We carefully scraped the berries off the walls, floors, and the ceiling, but the whole room had to be repainted! So much for our brilliant method of preserving and storing fruit!

I continued to walk to the camp to attend classes, and stayed at the school until the camp was disbanded. Once the *gimnazium* was dissolved, many of the unemployed teachers, who did not want to move with the camp, but preferred to stay in Regensburg, offered to give private lessons to their former students, who, like me, wished to finish their high school curriculum but were unable to go to a school in another area. For example, my friend Irka Ozimek Guzinska moved up north with her family when the DP camp in Regensburg no longer could house them, and she enrolled in a high school at the new camp in Kefertal. Other friends transferred to other locations, some returned to Poland, and some began applying for immigration to countries that had opened their doors to the vast numbers of displaced persons. Once again, close friends one by one started to disappear. Luckily, the transition from *gimnazium* to private lessons was immediate, so there was hardly any time lost. On the contrary, the few teachers who became my sole instructors kept me so busy that I was able to finish the whole program in a relatively short time. It was as if we had revolving doors; no sooner did one teacher leave than another was there. It was very hard to cope with the intense school program while helping Misha in his three different businesses. Eventually, I had to forgo my piano lessons, and I had practically no time to be with friends. With constant guests and daily house chores to tend to, there was hardly any time for anything else.

One of my many chores was the responsibility of doing the family laundry in the large basement, which we shared with the Wolfs and the Opats. There we also stored the coal and briquettes for our potbelly stove, as well as our potatoes and vegetables. There was a large basin with a washboard, a huge kettle to boil the laundry white and a very old-fashioned wringer, which one had to crank. Sonya, or sometimes Mother, helped me with larger pieces like tablecloths, sheets, and blankets. Once the washing and wringing was done, I took it to the attic to be dried. We almost never used the garden to dry the laundry; even in the summer we preferred the attic. Most of the laundry had to be ironed, so while doing it, I would keep repeating and memorizing new words in English or Spanish.

Most of the cooking was done by Sonya, but I did the grocery shopping. Occasionally, Mother would help Sonya, especially when company was expected. At these times Misha would insist that I clean the house, set the table, and decorate the food plates. He always maintained that Sonya and Mother were "not much good as housekeepers, because when they are through with cleaning, one can't tell the difference." My few home economic lessons back in Warsaw, for which I always received 5s (equivalent to As), came in handy now. Anything that needed patching, mending, darning (especially

Misha's socks!), or catching runs in our stockings was done by me. (To catch runs, I used a very small hook, similar to a crocheting hook, except that this one had a movable arm, which was attached to the end of the hook. I would insert the open hook into the last stitch of the run, close the hook, and pull it through the next stitch. Doing stitches one by one, depending on how long the run, was a tedious job, to say the least.) As careless a dresser as was Misha, he nevertheless noticed immediately who had darned his sock. Sonya did the job by over-sewing the existing hole, which usually gave Misha a blister on his foot, whereas I did the job in the correct way, using a fine needle and a darning ball, thus keeping Misha blister-free and happy. In general, Sonya was an indifferent housekeeper and left those duties to others, preferring to concentrate on her specialties, cooking and baking, at which she was superb. I should add that doing the dishes was my responsibility as well. Now, when I recollect all the different chores I had to perform, I can hardly believe it. After all, the days had only so many hours, but housekeeping was an endless task, and so much of it was my responsibility. There was never a free moment. One luxury I was allowed was a weekly visit to the local beauty salon for a shampoo, set, and manicure. But even then it was not a 100 percent relaxing time: while under the dryer I would be catching up on school homework.

Once I had the high school program behind me, I enrolled briefly at a local *Dolmetscher Schule* (interpreter school). It was sheer hell! To study a foreign language (English) using another foreign language (German) was double trouble. Almost from day one they insisted we read an article from *The London Times* and translate it orally into German. Fortunately, at this point my spoken German was almost fluent, which made things a bit easier, but despite that, the speed of the instructions, homework, and other assignments made it next to impossible for me to keep up, but somehow I did. Many native German students were dropping out almost daily, so I was proud that, being a foreigner, I was able to last through two semesters. I finally left the *dolmetscher schule*, not because I couldn't keep up, but because my many duties for Misha's various enterprises were rapidly growing and, at the same time, our chances to immigrate to Argentina had become quite promising, so I decided to start learning Spanish. Actually, in a way the excuses I had for leaving the course were a noble way out, since I dreaded the pressures of the interpreter school, rather than enjoying them. Once more the ship of my education shifted course. I found a very capable Spanish-speaking German instructor and once more, in my "spare time," I undertook the new challenge. Oddly enough, it never occurred either to Misha, Sonya, or Mother to take some lessons of the language of their future country-to-be. After all, they were in their forties, still in their prime years. The responsibility was exclusively mine, as if I was to be their translator/interpreter for life. In any case, the instructor was a very intelligent, elegant man, a former German officer, who came still dressed in his green uniform, minus insignia. He made the lessons fun and interesting, although at times, because I had had no time to do the homework, embarrassing. When I was obviously not prepared for the lesson, he politely always found a reason for a compliment, to keep things running smoothly. No sooner had I reached the level of thinking in Spanish, rather than translating from German into Spanish, I was forced to terminate our lessons, because of a major shift in our immigration possibilities. Misha, Sonya, Mother and I had also applied together for visas to the United States. Misha wrote on his application that his occupation specialty was meat production, and because there was a sponsor in the U.S. who needed someone with meat production knowledge, it became apparent that they would be leaving for the U.S., and sooner than expected. Mother and I did not wish to leave for Argentina (at this point our visas for Argentina had already been granted) without the Shlykovs. We decided to wait for American visas. Knowing that we would most likely follow the Shlykovs to America rather than leave for Argentina, I quit taking lessons in Spanish, and quickly switched back to English. This time I found an older German teacher of British English, who also spoke some Russian, which made the family happy. He lived in a rented, unheated room in town and when he came to our relatively warm place (more later about the relatively warm place) and was served Russian specialties and hot tea, he often forgot what the mission of the visit was. He would indulge in Russian conversation with anyone, whoever was present, and reminisce about the old Russian times (I do not remember what his actual connection with Russian culture was) while I watched his huge nose slowly thaw out from its previously half-frozen state, the nose lightly dripping with each swallow of hot tea with plenty of lemon. Coming from his cold room, and then from the freezing street, he was bundled up to his nose. Wearing a rather old-looking, heavy, long coat that had seen better days, with a fur collar, a huge fur hat with ear muffs, heavy leather mittens, and a long scarf, he looked rather grotesque. Once inside, one by one he removed his outer layers of clothing, displaying his rather thin bent-over frame. Despite all this, he had the bearing of an aristocrat, a typical character from a Gogol novel. Finally, after lengthy socializing, mostly in Russian, he would remember that we ought to have our English lesson. I liked him as a person as well as a teacher. He made the grammar rules quite clear, despite the many exceptions. One thing I could barely stand, however, was when he illustrated the pronunciation of the article "the." He would put his huge tongue between his horse-sized teeth and, facing me, would push the "the" sound out together with a mist of spittle. I tried very hard to pronounce this sound right in order not to have him demonstrate it to me. Sometimes, unfortunately, I did not succeed.

While taking almost daily English lessons, I was also enrolled at the health department of the United Nations Relief and Rehabilitation Administration in a course of first aid. From early childhood it has been my dream to study medicine—someday. The older I got, the further away I seemed to get from my dream. Taking this rather intense course, I thought, might be a good beginning toward achieving my goal. After completion of the course, my interest in medicine grew even stronger. While at the health department I received a lot of compliments for having good comprehension in this field and encouragement for the future. My thoughts at this point were to immigrate, and as soon as possible, apply to a college and eventually get into a medical school. As time went by, it was apparent that one of my dreams was not meant to come true.

A few months before our immigration I passed a test of the Preparatory Commission for the International Refugee Organization certifying me as an Interpreter, Second Class, in Russian, Polish, German and English. This helped me land a job, which was offered to me by Capt. Edward Shock of the Criminal Investigation Division (CID). It amounted to clerical duties. He said it would give me firsthand exposure to "real English." An American Army jeep came for me every day at eight in the morning. The job was rather easy, I was able to eat at their cafeteria, and I received a small pay in script, which at the time was the occupational currency. Also, thanks to Capt. Shock, I was able to purchase some small items at the post exchange (PX). I no longer had to ask my friend Nina, who had an American boyfriend (whom she later married), for things that he could buy which were only available (like nylons) at the PX. Unfortunately, the job did not last long. The time for our departure came earlier than expected. I had to quit my army job in order to take care of packing and the liquidating of the apartment.

16

Live Fish and Dead Bones

King Ludwig the First of Bavaria wanted to create a place to honor distinguished Germans, so he had Walhalla (*Valhalla*), modeled on the Parthenon in Athens, built high above the Danube (*Donau*) between Donaustauf and Sulzbach, about 40 kilometers from Regensburg. This unusual monument takes its name from the Nordic mythological resting place for warriors' souls. Walhalla was completed on October 18, 1842. At the opening ceremony 160 people were honored (represented by 96 busts and 64 plaques). The temple has 358 steps, spread out in three massive sections, and 52 columns surround the magnificent structure. A huge portal leads into Walhalla; the outer side of the door is plated with bronze and the inner side is maple wood with insets. The temple's interior, which is made of nine different colors of marble, is filled with rows of busts, twelve marble chairs and eight marble pedestals, and large friezes that tell the history of Germany. This majestic hall today honors about 187 people, but curiously enough only ten are women. Among the honorees are Mozart, Haydn, Beethoven, Strauss, Brahms, Wagner, Bach, Handel, Kant, Schiller, Dürer, Goethe, Kepler, Stifter, Paracelsus, Copernicus, Martin Luther, Roentgen, Einstein, Leibniz, Bismarck, Adenauer, and many more. At the time we were living in Regensburg, the interior of this majestic historical monument was closed to the general public, but the grounds were open. Students, local residents and visitors came from time to time to be closer to nature and to have a picnic lunch on the steps while admiring the gorgeous views, or to stretch out a blanket on the lush grass below and take an afternoon snooze. We were told of the priceless treasures inside, but could only use our imaginations as to what the interior really looked like.

There was an excursion boat that traveled between Regensburg and Walhalla on the river Danube. Many of our local friends would join us on these pleasure trips. Frequent companions also were the two boys, one five and one three years-old, of the Woodberrys (our American neighbors whose father was an army captain stationed in Regensburg), as well as Olga and Alex Ulbrich (the latter was Misha's secretary). Also tagging along were the Ulbrichs' white bulldog, Jerry, and our rambunctious Trolli (meaning "the true one"), an eleven-month-old German shepherd that we acquired when we moved into the Weissenburg Strasse house. Having my first pet, Trolli, along on the trips on the river was for me always more fun. Jerry, being an older, overweight, and somewhat grouchy dog, eventually learned to tolerate Trollie's unruly behavior. The following incident, only one of many, comes vividly to mind. During one of our boat trips to Walhalla, we were just approaching the dock when our mischievous dog, seeing a huge flock of geese on the banks of the river, suddenly jumped off the boat into the river and took off after the geese. We, still on board, called, whistled and shouted, but he paid no attention. Geese were flying in the air, Trolli was running around like a mad dog, and feathers were flying all over! The German passengers were outraged. No German-owned dog would do such a thing! Finally, when we got off the boat, our dog, half dead from exhaustion, calmed down and we caught him and put him on a leash. There were many other trips to Walhalla, but none so embarrassing.

While visiting Walhalla and the surrounding villages, we discovered that there was a carp hatchery nearby. We bought a few carp and brought them home. That gave Misha one of his brilliant ideas. Why not go to the village more often, buy more carp, and bring them to the city to sell to the Jewish community? On his next visit to Khalka's eatery, he suggested to the owner that we ("we" was Misha's favorite expression, when the operation was to be executed by others, rather than by him) would supply the fish for her restaurant. The word spread as quickly as the wind that Shlykov was in the fresh fish business. No sooner had we made one trial delivery of live carp, than the demand became so great that Misha began sending his truck and Ovchinnikov (the Russian driver), and often me as well, to fetch a substantial amount of fish, in order to fill the many orders. To satisfy the requirements of the Jewish restaurant and those of private customers, the fish had to be delivered while still alive, so the fish had to be transported from the hatchery in barrels filled with water. Then we would take them to a huge tub in the basement of our house, weigh them, and wrap them in newspapers, the only available wrapping material. Mother and I would then carry the still-wriggling fish, packed individually for each order, to our prospective customers. Some deliveries were nearby, some far away. Since most German houses had no elevators, we often, already breathless from walking and carrying our loads in knitted shopping bags so that the fish had air to breathe(!), had to struggle with the wiggling carp up several flights of stairs. Many buyers would look under the fish's gills to make sure the fish was not only fresh, but also alive. This carp enterprise continued for quite some time. It was rather profitable, and Misha liked to say that "we" were doing it with our own labor force. And because of this enterprise, our Polish and Russian friends were never short of fish on their tables. Needless to say, by now you probably can guess who was in charge of scaling and cleaning the fish we used for our family. Considering all the meat products we were getting from the local butcher in exchange for the oxen, all the fish we needed from our fish enterprise, and fresh white bread from the camp, we were living not like the average displaced persons, but almost like foreign dignitaries!

Some time had elapsed since our first carp delivery, and Misha continued to have time on his hands. For him, to run only one business was not satisfying. Therefore, as usual, to help his thinking, he would sit in an armchair, looking up into the ceiling and whistling (unfortunately not in tune) and in no time a new idea would be born. He would excitedly present his new idea to "his women" (Sonya, Liza and me) and then set to work on it immediately. That is how the bone business came to be. Whenever we would go to get our meat or *Wurst* (sausages) he thought to himself, "What does the butcher do with the extra bones?" Many of the good bones were sold to the Germans for cooking soups, but what happened to the rest? Once we found out that the butcher did not use those that were not good enough to sell, we offered to take the surplus off the butcher's hands. We already had a truck and driver, so we periodically would load the bones onto our truck, then deliver and sell them to a soap factory in the outskirts of Regensburg. And so another moneymaking operation was underway!

At a social gathering with Herr Rosenkrantz, he told us he could supply us with salt-water and canned and marinated fish, which he regularly had delivered to his warehouse at the railroad depot. All we needed to expand our fish business was a store in an area with good foot traffic, preferably in the center of town. Misha thought that was a splendid idea! Off "we" (meaning I) went to look for a store that would have the right potential. I found a little store around the corner from the *Dom* (cathedral). Now we needed a few display cases to hold and display our products, a cash register, a counter, and a few other essentials, to be able to call it a fish market. Shortly after the store was nicely equipped, Misha hired a lulu of a saleswoman, a Russian woman who lived with her daughter and mother. Little did he realize that having her as an employee was as good as having no help at all. She was constantly making mistakes in orders, weight, and money. Also little did I know what I was getting into! I was told to "help out" in the beginning. But actually, my helping amounted to having a full-time job in my "spare" time. In order to get the fish from the railroad depot, I had to be there with the truck and the driver almost at dawn! Before that, it was my responsibility to prepare the list of the day's requirements: how much of each fish, how many cans, whether marinated or smoked, etc., all of which had to be weighed, counted, signed and later paid for. Once loaded and delivered to the store, we had to unload everything, place it in designated areas, and price everything, by which time a huge line would be outside waiting for the doors to open. Often, Irina, our saleslady, would be late, since she had a daughter and a helpless mother to settle for the day before she could leave the house for the store. Our boss, Misha, would appear around noon, "to check the cash register." Mother did not participate in this operation, and Sonya was busy at home, cooking for the hordes of steady guests that Misha was constantly inviting. For most of the time, I did all the functions described above. Did I forget to mention that our saleslady spoke very little German, so she would look helplessly at me for help whenever she could not comprehend an order. Once the fish was sold out, I would quickly put out a sign *Bis Morgen* (Closed 'til tomorrow), quickly clean up, and lock the door, hoping that there was still time left to run home for my next language lesson.

Although Alex Ulbrich was a paid secretary, Misha preferred my assistance when it came to business deals. He often found it a struggle dealing via his secretary Alex, despite the fact that Alex's German was as fluent as was his Russian. The two men differed a lot in business mentality. Ulbrich was lacking in imagination and in the business attitude that Misha, probably from early childhood, possessed. Alex often would refuse to translate Misha's ideas into German, stubbornly insisting that nothing would come of a given idea. Sometimes, Misha had to hold back his anger and disapproval of Alex's reluctance to fulfill his assignment. Occasionally, when I was present at a meeting to close a business transaction, I would witness Alex's misinterpretation of Misha's thoughts to a prospective German businessman. It seemed that Alex Ulbrich did not appreciate that he had a good income and did not have to worry about what he and Olga would eat the next day, as did so many refugees.

A couple of times Misha tried to start a business with Walter Wolf, more for Walter's sake than for his own profit, but nothing came of it. At this time Walter was already an alcoholic and a poor businessman. Misha made money and spent freely, making no restrictions whatsoever in his lifestyle. He invested in jewelry and gold coins, which he acquired via Rozia's father, who at that time dealt in gold. Fortunately, Misha invested at an opportune time, leaving a minimal amount of liquid cash on hand, just enough to pay the bills, so to speak. We realized how good his timing was when, for the first time since the end of the war, Misha and Sonya decided to take a trip to southern Bavaria. They invited me to come along (more for the usefulness of having a translator, rather than for my company). No sooner had we settled into a nice hotel when, the next day or the day after, a money reform was announced, which reduced the value of money so drastically that we returned to Regensburg immediately. So much for our outing!

I hope that what I have written about my life, especially the four years in Regensburg, does not make me sound cynical, which was not my intention. Although it was hard at my reasonably young age to have had to take care of this and that, to get schooling in a sometimes haphazard fashion, and having to be in several places at the same time, I did not feel sorry for myself, but rather felt proud of the fact that I was trustworthy. Even though often underappreciated, I was still happy-go-lucky and, I think it's fair to say, a good

Uncle Misha and I in Regensburg, ready to go on another of his business-seeking jaunts, 1948.

sport. From the time Mother and I joined the Shlykovs in Kleine Maria Zell it was clear that my uncle Misha was becoming my surrogate parent, my mentor for life. He was a strict disciplinarian, who often intimidated me with his self-righteous, sometimes unfounded demands and restrictions. On occasion he made belittling comments, by which he tried to "keep me in line." Sonya, my aunt, had very little to say, but, whenever she could, would usually side with me. Mother, on the other hand, always sided with her brother-in-law and when conflicts between me and Misha arose would defend him by saying: He has only good intentions and your welfare at heart. Often I felt rejected, hurt, and helpless, but I was quick to forgive and glad to see the conflict put aside. Why I suffered so from his demanding nature and still loved and respected him might be a good question for a psychologist. Fortunately, my relationship with him changed dramatically once I married. He finally began treating me with respect and admiration, and even had words of praise for me. All in all, there were many good sides to life in Regensburg, some fun times, and most of all lots of firsthand education about what life is all about. Perhaps one can say that I went through the school of hard knocks and still came out whole.

17

"Quanta la Gusta"

While living in Regensburg, I had most of my fun when I could spend time among my friends at school or while staying in the dorm. Since the camp was on the outskirts of the city, oftentimes we, a group of several girls and sometimes a few boys, would take long walks into the country. While walking we talked or tried to memorize Latin verses, or sang Polish scout songs. Sometimes we would take a blanket or two and, under a tree on the lush, grassy meadow, have an improvised picnic, often including strawberries I had brought from town. On our field trips, we regularly passed farmhouses and fields with grazing horses and cows. There were many geese along the road and they always tried to attack us. I do not know why, but they seemed to dislike girls especially. Boys almost always were left alone; maybe they preferred to pinch our bare legs rather than the long pants the boys wore. There were at least two lonely horses that invariably were waiting for us along a barbed-wire fence. I remembered my horse Kashtan from Brest, which liked sugar lumps, so I always had a few lumps for our new friends. They drooled while licking the sugar from my hand, but it did not bother me much, since it felt rather nice to know that they enjoyed the treat. Sometimes during warm evenings we would have a kind of camp-out set up on the school grounds, but without a bon-fire, which was not allowed. We sang, danced and played games. On occasions a few students acted out plays. I was never one of them, as I was quite shy and felt I had no talent for acting.

As soon as the performance of an opera was announced in the newly opened theater, Sonya and I were among the first to buy tickets for the opening night. On our very first visit to the theater, unfortunately, we did not check how long the performance would be and forgot that a curfew was still in force. It being our first such show since Warsaw times, we greatly enjoyed the opera, *The Barber of Seville.* It was well staged, the music was great, and the audience went wild in appreciation. We left the theater singing and feeling simply ecstatic! What a treat it was, we felt alive and happy. The crowds soon dispersed, just a few dozen people were still walking about, but soon the two of us ended up all by ourselves on a deserted *Gasse* (street). We quickly realized why the streets were completely empty: it was because of the curfew. Then out of nowhere a covered police wagon, sounding a loud siren, appeared. A couple of policemen with rifles jumped off the wagon, surrounded us, and ordered us to board the police van. We were frightened out of our wits! It felt no different from the way the Nazi occupying forces had been treating us during the war. This was exactly how the frequent Nazi *lapanki* (street roundups) were executed all over Poland. Once we had seated ourselves on one of the two benches inside the covered and locked van, Sonya, more than I, became petrified when she realized that we were among a whole bunch of German prostitutes. They sat quietly, apparently feeling no pain or shame. On the contrary, they seemed amused when they saw that the two of us had now become part of their group. They were being transported to a police station for a venereal checkup and to be charged with prostitution. We tried in vain to convince the policemen that we were simply returning home after a theater performance. Since we were caught not far from our house, I asked them, unsuccessfully, to stop at Weissenburg Strasse to verify that we indeed lived there and were not the streetwalkers they took us for. Fortunately, however, the policeman behind the counter double-checked our identity documents and asked if someone could come to verify who we were. And so, in the middle of the night, Misha and Wolf came to bail us out. Of course, Misha did not fail to use this opportunity to admonish us, saying, "It served you right," when all we wanted was to have some diversion from our daily chores and work.

Another pastime that comes to mind were the wrestling matches often held in the city. Initially they were of no interest, until several matches were advertised about contests between a German and a Polish wrestler. Once Gena Wolf, being very Polish in spirit and soul, heard that a countryman was going to try to beat a German fellow, she absolutely had to attend the match. Since Walter was not interested in seeing the match, she talked me into going with her. We went and I must say it was quite a scary experience. There were mostly Germans in the audience, but the very few Poles (we and some Poles who had come from the camp) made so much noise, shouting and cheering, that it made the Germans around us very angry. Gena would not sit still; she especially reacted, screaming wildly, whenever it appeared that the Pole was losing. Shouting as loud as she could, she insisted that the German was cheating or was not observing the rules. Her booing was nonstop. Needless to say, I was very embarrassed. I accompanied Gena to just a couple of these matches, but then I swore to her and to myself, "Never again!"

On one of the many Danube boat trips to Walhalla, in addition to our regulars, we took with us the two little Woodberry boys who lived across from us, and also Krista Wolf and her nanny Emi. The trip was fun as usual and we returned home later than expected, making Capt. and Mrs. Woodberry worry as to why we had not returned before dark, but I delivered their boys home "without a scratch," very happy, and full of stories to tell their parents.

A few days later, a mysterious letter arrived at the Woodberrys' home addressed, "To the Nanny of the two American Boys." It apparently was meant for me, although I was not their nanny, but simply did the parents a favor now and then by keeping the boys either at our house or going over to babysit them at their house when the parents had a function to go to. The letter was given to me and it turned out to be from a young German man who had traveled on the same boat with us the previous Sunday. He wrote that he would very much like to meet me in person, that he had observed me throughout the whole trip and that I had made a great impression on him. I showed the letter to Gena, who, as usual, got very excited reading it and became very intrigued as to who this person might be. She talked me into sending an answer immediately. The two of us composed a reply. Gena's chauvinistic Polish nature did not permit her to be silent and not to emphasize in the body of the letter that I am Polish and not a German. She said that once the admirer finds out he is dealing with a Polish girl and not a German one, he will either accept the fact or will drop the idea of meeting me. "It will reveal his true character," Gena said. As soon as he received my (our) reply, the young German showed up at my door with a huge bouquet of flowers and dressed as if for an important party (I had suggested in the letter that he come for tea). Knowing the hour of his arrival, I made sure Gena would be downstairs with me, not so much to chaperone, but for moral support. The meeting went well; the very polite man told us about himself and his future plans, asking only a few questions of us. We had tea and pastries and after a while said good-bye, without any suggestions from me about meeting again. Gena was disappointed that I did not show a little more interest, but I was relieved that the meeting had ended as it did. Apparently, while on the boat and later in the village of Walhalla, I was so busy with the Woodberry kids, Krista, and Emi, as well as keeping an eye on Trolli, that I had not noticed that a young, tall, rather handsome German man was watching me. If I had noticed, Gena's curiosity with respect to the letter, more than mine, would not have taken hold of me, and I would not have extended the invitation to tea. On the other hand, I suppose, I can say it was a polite gesture on my part that didn't hurt any of us, other than perhaps leaving the fellow disappointed that I was so young.

Once, there was a school excursion by train to Bad Salzungen to see Garmisch and the underground salt mines at Berchtesgaden, Hitler's former hideaway. After we arrived in southern Bavaria, we were taken to and housed in a former army barracks, from which we made many excursions to different towns, including a trip by cable-car to the *Zugspitz*, the highest mountain in Germany. There we spent one whole day hiking, picnicking, and sunbathing in the bright mountain sun. Most of the girls, and I was one of them, were determined to get a deep suntan to show off at school. While the boys were off on another hike, we stayed behind to work on our tans. Soaking up the rays, I fell asleep and did not realize how intense the sun was until it was too

On a school outing, dressed for a trip through the underground salt mines at Bercht-esgaden, Bavaria. I am seated next to last, 1947.

late. When I awoke, I not only was as red as a lobster, but I had to be rushed to an army dispensary to be treated for sunstroke. Back in the barracks, I was as sick as a dog, with a terrible headache, vomiting, and burning all over. While the rest of the group continued sightseeing, I stayed put until our departure back to Regensburg. So much for my first outing after war's end.

Most Sundays, like almost every other day, were spent with family friends, who usually came for early dinner. Dinners were quite elaborate, and it seems there were always occasions, if not real, then fabricated by Misha, that called for a celebration. As he used to say, "We have plenty of fish, and fish like to drink!" which, of course, meant alcoholic beverages. And so they drank, ate, and drank some more! But, I must say, they seldom over-drank. After coffee and a nice dessert, it was time to work off the calories by going for a long walk. Sometimes there were just a couple of friends, but more often there would be as many as a dozen. And, as the Europeans do when walking, most of them, men and women alike, would go arm-in-arm. One would choose a partner and, after a while, change the partner if the conversation was becoming boring. A favorite destination almost always was a distant cemetery. It had a parklike setting and we were allowed to bring our dog Trolli, and the Ulbrichs would drag along Jerry as well, who was slow and became tired easily. Once at the cemetery we always ended up at the grave of Olga Filatiev's husband, who was the first of our circle of friends to have passed away. It was like a reunion for her, and she'd say she "was glad that her husband had so much company." After the cemetery visit, or a long walk to some other place, we would slowly return home, one by one losing members of our Sunday company as they returned to their respective homes. One or two people of the group would occasionally come back with us to our place. In most cases it would be our frequent (almost daily) visitor Georg Lomov, as well as Dr. Nikolay Proskuriakov and his brother Alexander.

Speaking of walks, I also took some with just my friends, usually including Nina Polanska, who lived just around the corner from us and was a very frequent drop-in visitor. (Since at the time in Regensburg very few people had phones, visiting friends would simply drop in on each other.) If by chance Nina stopped by while Lomov was there, he invariably would ask her to sing, again and again, the Spanish song "Quanta la Gusta." Nina obliged every time. Whenever one of my friends came by, I would take my dog along and off we would go, even when it was raining, despite the fact that Trolli was a sissy and hated walking in the rain. To get him out, I had to bribe him with something tasty before he had time to hide and lie flat like a sack of potatoes. During the spring and summer a nice place to walk was along the river Danube, which was just a couple of blocks from our house. In the fall, as in my childhood, we would go to parks in search of chestnuts. And in the winter, while the snow was still fresh and clean, we would go sledding.

Movies were not popular with us, except that we liked to catch up on the news by going to cinemas showing primarily newsreels. Instead of movies, plays were more to our liking, even though they were in German. And, of course, we tried never to miss seeing operettas and operas whenever they were performed.

When it was announced that masses were to be said in Polish in the cathedral's side chapel, which housed the Black Madonna icon (the one drawn by Klemens Kwiatkowski), some schoolmates and I began to attend. Most of us went to church more to meet one another, rather than to pray or go to confession. The Russian community arranged their Orthodox services in a private house, which was transformed into a makeshift Russian Orthodox church (*tserkov*). They had two permanent priests, a fairly substantial, quite good choir, and the *obshchina* nearby for the *trapezas* (funeral meals). Shortly after the church was established, the first wedding to take place was that of a Russian girl and an American soldier. Soon, a few more weddings followed, and there were two or three christenings. For some reason, Misha and Sonya were popular choices for godparents. On those occasions, Misha gallantly presented each child with a golden cross, and Sonya outfitted them with made-to-order christening outfits. Later, baby carriages and baby presents followed. All in all they were very thoughtful and loving godparents. One of the first of the godchildren of Misha and Sonya was Natasha, the daughter of Alexander and

Helen Filatiev; the other was Viktor, the son of Lyudmila and Viktor Prokofiev. When only a few months old, little Viktor died unexpectedly of an acute intestinal problem.

Speaking of weddings, Sergey Padukow (my cousin), while attending Munich University where he was studying architecture, met his future wife Gerda, who was a chemistry student. After a brief courtship, they got married in the Munich Russian Orthodox church, after which Anyuta (Sergey's mother) and my mother arranged a large, fancy reception in their apartment. I had a special dress made for this occasion, as I was the main *shaferitsa* (bridesmaid). Since one of the duties of the ushers (*shafery*) is to hold a crown above the heads of the bride and groom, usually there are several ushers, so that they can relieve each other now and then. For me it was a memorable day, even though, as a Catholic, I was the only one in the party who was of a different religion. Gerda had also been of a different religion, but before the wedding she switched to the Russian Orthodox faith. I suspect that the priest never questioned Sergey as to whether or not their maid of honor is of the same faith. Both sisters, Anyuta and Liza, who were very good cooks, did their utmost to assure that the wedding feast would resemble one such as the family was used to having back in Brest, and it really was.

Shortly after Sergey and Gerda's wedding, there was a university ball to which I was also invited. Again, I had a special dress made and was eager to make the trip to Munich. Despite the fact that I had my heart set on going, Mother, but especially Misha, just would not agree to my going. Sonya tried her best to reason with them, but they would not budge. I cried my heart out, but all in vain. Misha kept teasing me by saying, "Crying is good for you, you will need to go to the bathroom less often." On the evening of the ball that I was missing, I stayed in my room, crying some more. I really felt like a Cinderella who could not attend a ball. Perhaps they didn't realize it, but I thought they were very unfair to deprive me of this joyful experience.

I had a very good friend, Halinka Horbacewicz, who I thought was the prettiest girl in the *gimnazium*. As it turned out, she was never as devoted to me as was Irka Ozimek, who, like my other girlfriends, was often annoyed by my constant praises for Halinka. Halinka was very popular with the boys and eventually settled on one, no longer having time for us girls. When the school closed, she moved with this boy (Zygmunt Wojda) and a few other classmates to a camp and school in Lauf. After she settled down, she invited me to come north for a visit. I gladly agreed to come and rushed to visit her, thinking the invitation was genuine, and that I was missed. It turned out that she was very proud of having a steady boyfriend and wanted me to see firsthand how happy she was in her new role and situation. The visit was far from what I had expected. She turned out to be a show-off, aloof, and too busy having a good time with her boyfriend. Feeling like a fifth wheel, I left for home ahead of time. A few days after I came back, she wrote me a letter explaining and apologizing for her behavior. I am not sure what exactly was in the letter, because Misha opened it, read it, and destroyed it. Afterwards he gave me a lecture for having "a girlfriend of low morals" who had a live-in boyfriend. Both Mother and he forbade me from having any further contact with her. I never heard from or saw her again.

Another girlfriend of mine was Aldona Wanatowicz, a pretty girl who was housed with a family with five young children. She always used the term *uncle* when referring to the male head of the household. We had no reason to question the authenticity of her uncle, but rumors were going around that she was having an affair with this very married man. In the beginning I rather liked her, and thought she was genuine and fun to be with. She was my bosom friend, she said. Being a bit older, more sophisticated, and as I later found out, more cunning than the other girls, she soon became the leader of our group. She had a way with the teachers and liked to flatter them and even flirt with them. She was well-read and tried to write poetry. She attributed her talents to having her "uncle" for a mentor. She used to be a very frequent visitor at our house. Our friends, who were primarily Russians, seemed to like to have conversations with her. She would speak Polish or German, they, Russian or German. One person who was able to detect phoniness in her from the first meeting was Gena Wolf, especially when the first question Aldona posed to Gena was, "What is your coat of arms? Mine is such and such." Gena and Aldona simply could not stand each other and they liked to argue, each trying to win points and proving herself right. They were like two fighting roosters, with us the spectators. In their contradictions and squabbles, sometimes on very unimportant topics, they would become aggressive to the extent of being insolent to each other. The most popular topics in their frequent debates were Polish literature and the origin of words. On most occasions, Gena obviously had the more convincing argument, so Aldona would skillfully change the subject. It seemed that every time Aldona came for a visit, she came prepared for a new debate with any one of us, but her preferred challenger was Gena Wolf. Gena, meanwhile, because she sorely disliked Aldona, was always ready for the challenge.

Toward the end of our stay in Regensburg, after the Shlykovs had left for their new country, we now had a spare room, so Mother suggested that Aldona move in with us. This was at a time when her "uncle" and his family were ready to immigrate to Australia, at which point Aldona would need to find other housing. What better offer could have come at this time! She happily accepted Mother's offer. My protests did not matter; they were never even considered. Aldona moved in with us and stayed in our apartment until we left for the U.S. Life under the same roof for me was so unpleasant with this "bosom friend" of mine that at times I was ready to run away. Knowing how highly my family thought of her, she began currying favor with Mother at every turn, flattering her and pretending to be deeply concerned for her welfare. She came between us almost constantly, pointing out to Mother my faults and shortcomings, often succeeding in convincing Mother that I was a neglectful daughter. In her opinion, it seems, the list of my faults was very long, I was a rotten daughter to my lovable mother, and so unappreciative of all the goodness that was being bestowed on me. Only Gena came to my defense, which she did whenever she could. But Aldona's act with Mother, full of meanness and poison towards me, continued. I felt relieved the moment I was on the train leaving for Bremerhaven. Some time later, Aldona was able to join her uncle's family in Sydney, Australia, after which she wrote me a couple of "sweet" letters, but I was no longer interested in her friendship. A few years later, I heard that she had contracted tuberculosis and had died while still single. Whenever I see and hear the famous aboriginal opera singer Kiri Te Kanawa I see a great resemblance between Aldona and Ms. Kanawa both in looks and in physical movement (but of course not in singing ability!).

18

A Girl's Best Friend

One of my best friends from the Regensburg times was my dog Trolli ("The True One"), which we bought from a stranger shortly after we moved to Weissenburg Strasse. Our friend from Yugoslavia, who was a doctor of veterinary medicine (and later became my stepfather for a brief time—more about this later), checked Trolli out, found him very healthy, friendly, and full of pep. The doctor estimated he was about 10 or 11 months old. He was not the usual German shepherd. He was smaller, about the size of a fox. His color was brown-black-gray and his tail resembled a fox's tail. He kept his ears straight up, never floppy. He was very alert, a finicky eater, who answered to most commands in German and later on in Russian and Polish, and he was quite obedient. As soon as we had taken him in, he felt at home and immediately showed his affection. Since most of the time he and I were together, I considered that he was my dog and I think he felt I was his mistress, although Misha often referred to him as "my dog." His large pillow was placed under a huge desk in the living/dining room, from which he could observe everyone and everything that was going on in that room where it seems most of our time was spent. This room had the only heating, a potbelly stove with a chimney pipe that extended to the outside through a hole cut out in the window overlooking the garden. The adjacent room was Sonya and Misha's bedroom, where for a time my bed stood also, until I moved into Mother's freezing bedroom, which was on the other side of the corridor. One could say Trolli had the best place in the apartment—warm, cozy, and full of company.

Misha liked to have Trolli come to him and lie down at his feet in the bedroom, but although Trolli would obediently come and lie down, as soon as Misha started to snore (and his snoring was so loud that everything around him or under him would vibrate) he would quickly sneak away. This game would go on especially when Misha had had one drink too many: Misha would call Trolli, make him lie down or even hop onto the bed, but then Misha would begin snoring, and Trolli would rush to his own bed. When Misha would notice that the dog was not there, he would call for him. Trolli, as if he felt guilty, would crawl back and lie down, until Misha would fall asleep

164

again. So it went until Sonya would put an end to the game. I guess Misha felt good knowing that the dog obeyed him, but the dog did not enjoy it. The smell of vodka did not help. Trolli wanted to be out of the bedroom as soon as he could!

The Wolfs had a feisty dog, a Spitz, by the name of Kaytek. The two dogs became the worst of enemies from their first casual meeting in the hallway. Gena had Kaytek on a leash and was on her way out for their usual outing, when Trolli sneaked out of our apartment through an open door and came to sniff his new neighbor. Kaytek did not approve of it and started to jump and bark. Trolli attacked Kaytek's throat and would not let go. Gena became hysterical, thinking Trolli was about to strangle her "little Kajtus." Hearing the screaming, barking, and cries, we all rushed out to separate the two dogs, but to no avail. I ran to the kitchen, got a pot with cold water, and poured it over the dogs and to some extent over Gena! Trolli let Kaytek loose. Both dogs were still very nervous, but Gena was in shock. From then on the dogs could not tolerate each other, even when there was quite a distance between them. Kaytek used the upstairs terrace as his recreation area. Trolli, on the other hand, had the run of the backyard.

Unfortunately, the yard wasn't enclosed with a fence and gate. There had once been a fancy wrought-iron fence and gate, but during World War II all ornamental iron gates and such were taken and melted for use in making armament for the armed forces. Therefore, Trolli had to be tied to something or be watched so that he would stay put. One day Trolli was in the garden, just minding his business, so to speak, when Kaytek, sensing his presence, started his obnoxious act of jumping up and down near the terrace railing and barking nonstop. If no one stopped him, or took Trolli in, Kaytek could go on like this forever, until he was so hoarse and exhausted that he just had to take a break. This time, he seemed more aggravated than ever over Trolli's presence in the garden. After a long spell of jumping up and down, he took one jump higher than he should have. His jump took him over the railing and he ended up on the grass below, after falling through some pyracantha bushes that were growing just under the Wolfs' terrace. I was in the garden and was surprised to see the stunned Kaytek, who must have been in quite a shock. At first, I was sure he was dead, but then I saw him begin to move and stagger around. Then, realizing that Trolli was near him and was about to approach him, Kaytek started his usual, frantic barking. By this time Gena had rushed down, shouting that one of these days her beloved Kajtus would be killed by Trolli. Kaytek not only survived the fall, but suffered no serious injuries. He did sustain some scratches from the thorns of the pyracantha bushes. On his primarily white coat, blood stains were visible here and there. Gena blamed not only Trolli, but all of us for not supervising Trolli more closely.

On one occasion I had a brilliant idea. It being a beautiful, sunny summer day, I thought it would be nice to have Trolli stay outside in the garden

Trolli, my beloved companion during our stay in Regensburg, 1947.

together with our little kitty Micky. They were the best of friends. They often slept side by side, ate from the same plate, and frequently sat together on the front windowsill, watching the world pass by. So, instead of keeping them cooped up indoors, I decided to tie them together in the garden on a rope long enough so that they could still run around and play. I usually tied them to Misha's car, or any car that happened to be parked in the driveway, or to a tree. That day, since there were no vehicles around, the first thing that came to my mind to use as an anchor was a large, empty gasoline canister. Thinking that my two friends were secure and happy being in the garden, I left them tied to the canister and returned to my chores in the house. No sooner was I inside when, all of a sudden, I could hear an extremely loud, unusual sound ("cha clank, cha clank, cha clank") coming first from the driveway and then from the street. I ran to the front window and was amazed to see Trolli running down the street, pulling the cat and the empty canister behind him. Passing cars came to a screeching halt in order to avoid hitting the two animals. What apparently happened was that Trolli, while in the yard, sensed the presence of another dog nearby, and then when he saw the dog on a leash and following his owners, he could not be stopped and ran, barking and clanking, toward the unknown dog, who now was also barking angrily. Upon seeing this scene, my first reaction was to hide behind the curtains so that no one would

**Trolli in the company of Krista Wolf and the two sons of U.S. Army Captain Wood-
berry, Regensburg, 1949.**

connect me with this embarrassing incident. At this point several people had
gathered and with obvious outrage were trying to pull away the leashed dog.
When they finally succeeded in rescuing the dog, Trolli decided to proceed,
still dragging the cat and the canister behind him, to our American neighbors,
the Woodberrys across the street. As soon as I saw that the coast was clear, I
went across to fetch my pets. When the Woodberry boys and their nanny came
out to see what the commotion and the strange noises were about, they thought
the whole event was hilarious! Hilarious it may have been, but for me it was
very embarrassing, to say the least, and I suppose it was an adventure for the
animals, especially, of course, for the poor kitty!

Our veterinary friend presumed that when Trolli was still just a puppy someone must have kicked him, someone wearing high boots, especially the kind that were worn by German army officers. Whenever he was on his leash and being taken for a walk, and a man wearing that kind of boots would be near us, Trolli would become uncontrollably angry and ready to attack. The first time it happened we realized that we could have a problem on our hands. I was walking Trolli with my friend Nina, when a German man in boots approached us from behind. As he was passing us, Trolli grabbed one of his booted legs and kept biting it. The man forcefully kicked back, so that Trolli whimpered and let go of the man's leg. Fortunately, the man did not press charges. I apologized repeatedly, while scolding Trolli, who was obviously in pain. I realized then that men in high boots were Trolli's longstanding enemies, so from then on I tried to keep him from such encounters.

Trolli, however, despite his hate for Kaytek and men in boots, was a very cheerful, playful dog that seemed never to have grown up. Another time, while I was out for a walk with him and Nina one winter day, two ladies were walking in front of us. One of them was wearing a fox skin around her shoulders. Fox skins, worn more for decoration than warmth, were very popular just after the war. This lady's fox was draped over her shoulders so that its tail was hanging down her back. As she walked the tail kept moving from side to side, looking as if it were alive and wiggling. This sight was too much for my playful dog! While Nina and I were engaged in conversation and not paying much attention, all of a sudden Trolli jumped at the lady's back, pulling down the tail together with the fox skin. The lady, holding her friend under the arm, fortunately did not lose her balance and fall, but her surprise and fright were beyond belief. She first began to shake and weep, and then she became outraged. Her friend tried to turn the situation into a joke, pointing out how funny it was. I apologized repeatedly and finally, when it was clear that the fox skin and tail had suffered no visible damage, Trolli and I were forgiven. When we described the event to our veterinary friend, he too thought it was a very funny situation and remarked, "Trolli is a unique jokester!"

That was not the first or the last example of Trolli's capricious nature. I have already mentioned the outing on the boat to Walhalla and Trolli's delight in chasing geese. There was another significant incident in Trolli's life that occurred when Misha and I and the driver Ovchinnikov were on a car trip to the fishery. After conducting our business with the fishery proprietor, we decided to have a picnic in a nearby pasture. All around the fields there were the usual farm animals grazing or resting. We three were looking forward to the chance to rest and enjoy the food we had brought for the journey and were not thinking about Trolli's mischievous behavior, especially in the presence of farm animals, so when we found a grassy, shaded spot, free of cow pancakes, we swung open the doors of the car, and you know who was the first to jump out. Of course, it was Trolli, who most likely had a plan in mind long before we stopped. He must have observed the animals while we were driving, and whereas food and a chance to rest was on our minds, "fun, fun, fun" was on his agenda! And so it began! Free after being cooped up in the car, and with a vista full of cows, geese, and chickens, he ran around as if crazy. The cows, which had been quietly digesting their fodder, got up and started to run. So did the geese and chickens, with their feathers flying in the air. Fortunately, we were the only persons in the vicinity so there were no other observers of Trolli's mad behavior. We tried to get him to settle down, called to him angrily, and then tried to bribe him with a chicken leg. But he ignored all our efforts and just kept running in circles like a wild animal. Instead of having our picnic we rushed back into the car, slammed the doors, and started to drive away. Misha ordered our driver Ovchinnikov to "give it more gas!" Almost immediately, hearing the sound of the car engine, it dawned on our animal-chasing maniac that he was being abandoned. We all eagerly watched his reactions. First, he stood still and stared in disbelief, then started to run in an attempt to catch up to the car. The faster he ran, the more Misha ordered our now frantic driver to increase the speed. The chase lasted for some time and at one point the driver pleaded with Misha to stop the car, as he was afraid the "poor" dog was getting so exhausted that he might collapse from a heart attack. But Misha, as were we all, was tired of Trolli's not obeying and he saw this as an opportunity to teach Trolli a sound lesson, so he rejected the pleas to stop or even to slow down. Finally, after a couple of miles or more of the chase, we stopped the car. Trolli quickly jumped in, his heart pounding, his tongue hanging out at full length; he was obviously thirsty and near collapse. All through the journey home he softly squealed and whimpered, as if complaining of the harsh punishment he had suffered. When at last he was safe at home, he showed no desire to eat his supper, but he drank water continuously. After that memorable outing, whenever he accompanied us on our business or pleasure trips and were ready to start the journey home after concluding our business, it took only one good whistle to bring him back to the car, where he would struggle to be the first to hop in. He wanted to be sure he wouldn't be left behind.

Trolli was from the very beginning a very finicky eater. In those days there was no dog food sold in the stores. We fed him table food, once a day giving him oatmeal that we fortified and enhanced with enticing meat gravies. After pouring out a dish of oatmeal, with a spoon we would make several grooves in the oatmeal into which we would put some meat gravy, melted fat, and the like. Making these channels, for some reason, worked better than mixing it in, and Trolli, who was a reluctant eater, would more willingly come to his meal and eat more of it. Unfortunately, he eventually learned how to pull out the "good stuff" by simply sticking his nose into the channel and sucking the gravy out. So then we would make more channels, and the game continued. We tried leaving the food without any enhancements, hoping that when he got good and hungry he would eat. It did not work. The food could stay for two days and he would not touch it. Since he was a skinny dog, our veterinary doctor friend, contrary to his usual advice in such cases, told us to treat our prince as such, or he will get sick. And so we did. He was put on a special diet with plenty of attention, love, and care. We were still getting our meat credits from the butcher, so Trolli had many juicy bones to work on, as well as the best *Wurst* (sausages) in town. He always went with me to the butcher shop where he received his own care package, in return for which he would "shake hands" with the cashier, while waggling his tail. He became a prime customer.

Sonya and Misha for their, I guess, 25th wedding anniversary were having a party and many guests were invited. Sonya as usual slaved in the kitchen for several days, cooking and baking. We went to the country to get a fresh turkey for the occasion, which would be a real treat for many of our friends, who lived, for the most part, in rented rooms, sometimes without kitchen facilities, so for them roasting a turkey was out of the question. The day of the party arrived, and I, as usual, was charged with cleaning the house, setting the tables, doing some of the baking and cooking, serving the food, and finally washing the dishes, by hand of course. As at any other Russian party, the kind that lasts for three or four hours at the dining table, there were many hors d'oeuvres, followed by soup and various kinds of fish and meats with their garnishes, all of which was to be followed by the pièce de résistance, the turkey! With one toast after another being proposed (always an excuse for having another shot of vodka), the guests savoring the various dishes, and the serving plates being replenished x number of times, the room was filled with happiness and laughter. The guests bantered and told jokes and anecdotes, many of the saltier ones told in a semi-whisper that I was not supposed to hear. Sonya and I were in and out of the kitchen. On one of her trips to the kitchen she took the turkey out of the oven and placed it on the kitchen table to cool before it could be carved, and then she returned to her guests at the dining table. When Sonya returned to the kitchen to do the carving, she gave out a loud scream. All of us in the dining room heard her, and some of us rushed to see what had happened. What we saw was a complete disaster—the beautifully roasted turkey on the white wood floor, which was slippery from being scrubbed almost daily, and Trolli pushing the bird around while taking bites of it here and there. He had somehow come into the kitchen through a door left open and seemed to be in a great hurry to devour the whole turkey, but had to jump away from the carcass now and then because the meat was still hot. He kept dragging the roasted bird all over the floor, making the clean, white surface greasy and sticky, and in the process succeeding in devouring most of the bird's meat, leaving only its scrawny skeleton. Fortunately, the turkey was no longer in its roasting pan; otherwise, more grease would have been all over the floor. With many shouts Sonya managed to rescue what was left of the turkey, but as she looked at her masterpiece, which now resembled a bird that had been worked over by many vultures, she sat down on a stool and began to cry. At first, seeing the mess that Trolli had caused, as I usually do in such circumstances, I began to laugh uncontrollably, but stopped when I saw Sonya crying. At this point Trolli had disappeared under the table. Sonya, whispering, told Misha what had happened and asked him for advice. He called for silence in the dining room and announced to the puzzled guests that, due to our dog's behavioral problems and his probable death soon, the turkey would not be served. He further explained, in a somewhat joking manner, what had occurred. Our veterinarian friend, after examining Trolli's over-extended belly, assured everyone that Trolli would survive, although he would most likely be very thirsty and would probably not eat for a couple of days. Listening to the doctor brought to my mind a visit I had made, when I was a small child, to my grandfather's country estate, where I heard him tell of his cows over-eating on wet grass, after which their bloated bellies had to be punctured to keep them from dying. Sometimes, because early intervention was essential, Grandpa, with the help of his farmhands, had to do the task himself when the veterinary doctor could not come in time. I was frantic picturing our veterinarian stabbing Trolli's belly, but, fortunately, the doctor advised us simply to do nothing and just let Trolli suffer by himself a couple of days, after which he should be all right. The party, meanwhile, continued without any further disasters and everybody had a great time, except that Sonya suffered the lost turkey and was inconsolable for the rest of the party. Trolli, of course, paid the biggest price for his gluttony. He not only had stomach upsets, but drank water constantly and took no food for a couple of days. He survived the incident, but was in the "dog house" for a long time.

Friends and visitors reacted differently to Trolli's presence. Gena Wolf, in particular, even though she was an animal lover, could not stand Trolli because she saw him as a threat to her Kaytek. She avoided him like the plague. Our veterinary friend Dr. Proskuriakov and his brother Alexander simply loved Trolli and thought of him as the smartest dog on the planet. Dr. P. often said that Trolli's mind was like a human's. Another daily visitor of ours, George Lomov, was not fond of animals and could never warm up to Trolli. One day I saw them together on the steps of our foyer, which was between two sets of stained-glass doors. Trolli happened to be there when Lomov came in. I could observe them without being seen. Trolli wanted to greet Lomov and tried to lick his gloved hand, but Lomov kept pushing Trolli away, angrily muttering, "Go away, go away!" At that moment I opened the door and Lomov, seeing me, began petting Trolli, saying, "What a good doggie, what a nice doggie," not knowing that a minute ago I had seen him pushing Trolli away. I laughed and Lomov asked, "What's so funny?" but I didn't have the heart to tell him the truth, which would have embarrassed him. Many visitors, not knowing of Trolli's finicky appetite, often brought "doggie bags" for him. He would sniff them and tear them open, leaving a mess on the floor and almost never eating his present.

He loved to play and would fetch things like a stick, a branch, or a ball, which he would place in front of my feet and wait for the object to be thrown so that he could fetch it again. One time, I had nothing to throw for him to retrieve, except for a fairly large stone, which I stupidly threw in his direction, expecting that the stone would drop on the ground beyond him, after which he would return it to me. Unfortunately, he outran the stone and was able to catch it in the air. He gave out a loud groan and dropped the stone. When I rushed to him, I saw that half of his eyetooth had broken off and the dentine and pulp were completely exposed. I was heart-broken and did not know what to do. Dr. Proskuriakov later examined him and assured me that the tooth would heal by itself and that there was nothing we needed do. After a few days Trolli had no trouble chewing on turkey bones, but I felt guilty a long time.

Maybe three times in all, Trolli played the role of Romeo in love. On these occasions, he would quietly slip out of the house. When we noticed he was missing, we would search for him for hours. When we could not find him and would return home in the evening exhausted from walking the whole neighborhood, we would be so angry at his disappearance that we did not care if he was ever found. Of course, that was only a momentary reaction. Just the thought that we might never see him again was sickening. But each time he disappeared he eventually crawled back, tired, full of guilt, and whimpering for some reason. We could not tell if he was crying out of joy or pain. It was a mystery every time that he wandered off, when we wondered where he had been for so many hours. But one day, when I went for our usual walk, the mystery was solved. A few blocks from our house there was a villa occupied by a German family. They had a little female dog. When she was in heat, our Trolli's nose quickly got the signal and his natural instincts came into action. As soon as he found an opportunity, he would sneak out through an open door or a basement window. When the owner of the little pooch saw me walking with Trolli one day, she told me that every time Trolli disappeared from our house and showed up at her house, he would stand in front of the house crying his head off. She would try to chase him away, douse him with the garden hose, threaten him one way or another, but he would not leave and would just continue crying and barking in an attempt to get into the house. At that time, there were no tags with telephone numbers on dogs' collars, so she had no way of learning whose dog it was. Tiring of this persistent Romeo's antics, she would finally coax him into the garage and keep him locked up for several hours. When she would finally let him out, he was happy just to go home. This procedure happened every time he would show up at her house. Come to think of it, she was kind not to have called the dogcatcher, but I guess dogcatchers were not popular at that time. She was a friendly person and now that she had met me, she was relieved and somewhat amused with Trolli's visits.

Trolli disappeared again a couple of times after my meeting with the owner of "Juliet," but now I knew where to find him. When I got to see my dog's girlfriend, I didn't think much of her. I thought a husky, handsome fellow like Trolli could have done better than to fall for such an insignificant little pooch. Love is blind, they say.

And so with Trolli there was never a dull moment. He amused us and sometimes angered us. He was simply a jolly good fellow, full of boundless energy, mischievous, and always unpredictable. We all loved him dearly, thinking he was the best possible dog we could have. Once when I took Trolli to a professional photographer, he was ready to pose as if he knew he would have his portrait taken, and the photos show him smiling and happy to be the star. When the fateful day came when we received our visas to immigrate to the U.S., we realized that Trolli could not come along. I began looking for a good home for him. Unfortunately, most of our friends who knew him and liked him were themselves about to immigrate or had already left. But there was one possibility, a middle-aged, childless couple, the Zabolotnys, who on many occasions, especially when Trolli was giving us a hard time, offered to adopt him, but we could never consider parting with our trouble maker even for a short time, far from giving him up entirely. Whenever the Zabolotnys appeared at our doorway, Trolli always greeted them more warmly than any other visitor. Mrs. Zabolotny would bend down to him and say, "Trolli, dear doggie, come and give your dear auntie a kiss!" Trolli in turn would lick her face all over, smearing her makeup and knocking off her hat, leaving her in disarray. The same ritual took place when the Zabolotnys were leaving. At just this time the Zabolotnys received their visas to immigrate to Argentina, and there was the possibility that the rules to move to Argentina were less strict than those of the U.S. and that they might be allowed to take Trolli along. In the meantime, while visiting our butcher, I asked him if he could not by any chance add one more of our family members to his farm on the outskirts of Regensburg, where our oxen had been happy now for several years. He knew Trolli and was very fond of our dog, so he readily agreed to take him. I kept delaying our parting with Trolli to the very last minute, silently hoping that by some magic we could take him along to America. I asked our Polish friend, Capt. Edward Shock, and our neighbor, Capt. Woodberry, for advice and possible help to get permission for Trolli to be shipped to the States, but was told that Mother and I could not possibly travel with a dog on an Army transport ship. In addition, we were going on an affidavit to a sponsor in Pennsylvania, who had vouched to give us housing and work at his house, but a dog was not part of the agreement. Misha and Sonya, who were already in the States, also could not receive a dog because they, too, were working for a family that had sponsored them. All our ideas came to nothing, so the final decision was made to leave Trolli with the best man I could find, Herr Albert Homberger of Pfaeter 141 bei Regensburg. And so, a few days before our actual departure for the camp near Bremenhaven, where U.S.-bound displaced persons underwent their final checks, including thorough medical examinations, prior to embarking for America, I made the arrangement for Herr Homberger to come by and pick up Trolli. I took my beloved dog on a leash, as if we were about to go for our regular walk. We walked a few steps away from the house and then I slipped the leash into the hand of our butcher friend, who had been waiting outside for us. Herr Homberger continued the walk, and I stayed by his side, but little by little I began falling back a few steps behind them. Finally, Trolli's suspicions were aroused. He kept looking back, pulling Herr Homberger in my direction, and getting quite excited. At this point Herr Homberger began pulling Trolli harder, at times almost dragging the poor dog, which must somehow have realized it was being betrayed. I could not watch the scene any longer. I ran back into the house and broke down in tears. What a terrible way to end the close, loving friendship we had had together! Although I knew Trolli would be in good hands, no matter how I tried to convince myself that I had done the right thing, nothing could make me feel better. It was a heartbreaking parting.

19

America Bound!

World War II came to an end, but our struggles did not end with it. While in Regensburg, we had a roof over our heads and we were provided with some guidance and help from the United Nations Relief and Rehabilitation Administration (UNRRA) and from the *Katzetstelle* (the Office for Aid to Concentration Camp Survivors); nevertheless, we did not feel comfortable in our status as refugees, or so-called "displaced persons." We were constantly being reminded of our unsettled status, and it was sometimes painful. We did not want to stay in Germany, whose government had left us with permanent scars. Therefore, when it became obvious to us that there was no returning to the heavily destroyed and now socialist Poland, or to Brest, which at this point was part of the USSR, we looked at all the possible avenues for emigration. For those of us who had become stranded in Germany after the end of the war, it was a very hard decision to make to leave Europe, perhaps for good, and to start a new life from the beginning in any of the few countries that would accept post-war refugees. Some of our relatives were still in Brest and the beloved patriarch of the family, my grandfather, was at an age that he needed help. Misha's brother Ivan had settled in the outskirts of Warsaw, the younger brother Vladimir, in Olsztyn. Their sisters were presumed to be somewhere in the Soviet Union. Still unaccounted for were my two cousins, Arkady Padukow and Igor Shlykov. Mother was pressured by her friend Bruno Gutkiewicz to return "home," i.e., to Poland, apparently with the thought that he and she would marry there. The Padukows, having finally reunited with Sergey in the French Zone of divided Germany, later moved to Munich, where Sergey began his studies. The four of them, Nikolay, Anna, Sergey and Gerda, applied for immigration on their own, but at a later date than we did. The four of us, Misha, Sonya, Mother and I, had filed applications at the Argentinean and United States consulates, thinking that whichever country first offered us visas would be the country we would go to. Many of our Regensburg compatriots, one by one, were leaving for Venezuela, Argentina, Australia, Canada, Ethiopia, and a very few for the U.S. Misha and Sonya were the first ones in our family to receive their visas, destination Philadelphia, Pennsylvania.

Most refugees had to wait for sponsorships, which usually came through the intervention of various church organizations. In Misha and Sonya's case, Church World Service sent the owner of a meat products factory in Philadelphia Misha's application, which stated that his occupation in Poland had been as a meat production factory owner. This was how the various services matched refugees seeking sponsorships from prospective sponsors. Soon the Shlykovs packed up their belongings and left for the port in Bremerhaven, and, after a quick medical checkup at an UNRRA hospital facility, boarded an army ship bound for New York. Shortly after their departure, Mother and I were offered visas for Argentina, but we declined them, as we did not want to be separated from Misha and Sonya and were hoping sooner or later to follow them to America. So we remained at the Weissenburg Strasse apartment, trusting that a sponsor would be found for us also or even that, as before, the Shlykovs would bail us out as soon as they settled down in Philadelphia.

A few months after the Shlykovs' departure, Mother and I were informed that a sponsor had been found in, of all places, Nazareth, Pennsylvania. Mother and I thought it was a happy omen to be going to a "holy place." The future sponsor, we were told, was the owner of a nylon stockings and panty hose manufacturing plant, who was in need of a governess and a housekeeper for his family. The Church World Service representative convinced us that this would be a very suitable sponsorship for us. He also pointed out to us that "it is fortunate that you will be going to Pennsylvania, where your family is residing already. You are two lucky people, how can you refuse such an opportunity?" Eager as we were to be reunited with Sonya and Misha, we did not think twice, and accepted the affidavit. We were further promised that we would be picked up by our sponsors in New York City and driven to our new home in Nazareth, where we would be given room and board and a small salary. Of course, for a displaced person the offer sounded good, considering that finally we would be out of Germany, could eventually join our relatives, and would be able to settle down once and for all in a country of vast opportunities. Through the local UNRRA office, arrangements were made for us to go to Bremerhaven. In a very short time we were packed and ready to close up our chapter on Regensburg. Several friends were also assigned the same departure date, including Victor Prokofiev and his wife Lyudmilla (who was visibly pregnant), a newly married couple (Ina and her husband, whose name I don't recall), and Kurcjusz Olszewski and his son. We said good-bye to my friend Nina, to Aldona, who stayed behind in our apartment until her departure for Australia, and to the Wolfs, George Lomov, and Dr. Nikolay Proskuriakov, whom Mother had been married to for a few days. The latter was hoping that the divorce wouldn't take place and that by adopting me, he and his younger brother Alexander would get the chance to emigrate to the U.S. He was older than Mother and, as a single man, had a very slim chance of receiving a visa. Later on, he managed to leave for Ethiopia, for a veterinarian's position at Haile

Selassie's palace in Addis Ababa. His brother Sasha landed in Australia, where he later married. A year earlier my friend Irka had already left her camp in Kefertal and had emigrated to Montreal, Canada, followed soon after by her mother, stepfather and brother. In Canada Irka met her future husband, Marian Guzinski.

With just two suitcases, we arrived by train at the International Refugee Organization Transit Camp Grohn (a DP camp in Bremerhaven) where all prospective émigrés were housed in a former German army barracks and where we passed through various formal procedures and extensive medical screening. The medical screening was so thorough, in fact, that several of the refugees were not able to pass the screening and were compelled to return to another UNRRA camp, find shelter and a livelihood on their own, or return to their country of origin. When we arrived at the transit camp, it was so full of prospective émigrés that there was a shortage of housing and food, and the medical offices had endless queues. Mother and I preferred to rent a room in town and every morning walk to the camp for processing. We passed all the procedures with flying colors and faster than others, because we happened to run into Gena Wolf's friend (Genek Hurko's older brother) who was in charge of the medical screenings, and, with the help of his Hungarian friend Dr. Zoltan Agardy, he was able to push our case quite a bit forward. Finally, on May 19, 1949, we were able to board the huge Army ship, U.S. Army Transport General Harry Taylor. Little did we know that a long and difficult journey was ahead of us and that the crossing we were facing would be a stormy one! One of our baggage checks, which I still have, has the passenger number 262 (if it belonged to Mother, then my passenger number must have been either 261 or 263).

Once all the 877 displaced persons were aboard, we were assigned to one of many enormous cabins. A very large shower room with multiple sinks served for one's grooming. If you wanted some privacy you could only have it in the toilet stall. As soon as we were acquainted with our assigned quarters and the layout of the huge ship, we all, hungry and anxious, ran up to the location from which we could smell the overpowering aromas of food being cooked. The distance from our cabin to the dining facility was very long. There were endless stairways with metal steps, causing terribly loud noises from the many feet that were running back and forth on them. People were in such a hurry that in the narrow passages they would literally stumble over each other. Everyone was in a hurry to get there first! Once there, we could see through its open door that the vast dining hall was meant to accommodate possibly all of the 877 people in one sitting. The hot tables, with an unbelievable assortment of food, were tended by sailors standing side by side in a row behind the tables and eager to help feed the very hungry passengers. We were indeed hungry, as for the last few days at the camp food was almost nonexistent. Apparently, the camp had not been prepared for so many people to arrive at the same time

My mother, Elizabeth, and I boarding a train in Regensburg to take us to Bremer-haven and emigration to the U.S., May 1949.

from different parts of Germany. We were encouraged by the friendly sailors to eat as much as we wanted and to take whatever we wished. Many did just that. No sooner was the ship in the very choppy waters of the English Channel and later in the open sea, when the mess hall had only a few passengers in line getting the marvelous food. People were getting seasick, their knees were buckling under them from weakness, and they often got lost and stranded in the narrow, long corridors and stairways leading to the dining hall. Unable to communicate with the helpful sailors, many were at a loss as to what to do. For many who were able to get to the hall, although their eyes could eat all they saw, their stomachs were too sick to allow it. Mother and I were constantly

BAGGAGE CHECK № 608

IRO Emigration from Transit Camp **Grohn**
Ship: **USAT "General Taylor"**
From: **Bremerhaven** to: **New York (USA)**
Sailing Date: **May 19ᵗʰ 1949**   262
For Passenger Number: ....

Baggage claim check from our historic voyage to a new country, 1949.

reminded by our friend Olszewski not to eat anything other than bread, but to drink plenty of liquids, especially orange juice. Maybe his was the best advice we received, inasmuch as we were among the very few who did not suffer from violent seasickness. In addition to not over-eating in the dining room, there was another thing I think helped me survive the ten-day-long voyage and remain in pretty good shape: the huge cabin we were assigned to was all the way down the several decks of the ship, where the rolling of the ship was less noticeable. In the upper cabins, which were given to the elderly and people like our friend Lyudmila, who was pregnant, one could feel more strongly the rolling and pitching of the ship, and the smell of vomit was simply horrible. On those decks, it seemed, everyone was violently sick! Staying inside, with the children crying, the people moaning or swearing, and with the massive cabin doors constantly swaying to and fro and slamming with a loud bang, was for me next to impossible. Therefore, during rough seas, I chose to sit on the open deck on a small bench in a niche that protected me from the sea breeze and from the splashing of the waves, which at times came higher than the deck. In addition to being in the fresh air, I had some warmth as well, as the niche was near a boiler or engine of some sort and the escaping steam was warm and constant. My catnaps were often disturbed by the sound of the throbbing engine, which was unbelievably noisy, as the machinery worked nonstop from the hour of departure until the time of our arrival in the New York harbor. Nevertheless, I sat there day after day and sometimes I would even doze off at night. During the day I would see the ship leap up toward the sky and then fall back with a crashing sound into the ocean. Occasionally, sitting peacefully alone, imagining what my future homeland might bring, I would be awakened from my dreams by the loud, unexpected sound of the ship's horn. Now and then I would go down for some bread and water, but later when the sea was calmer and less rocky, I started to take a light selection from the hot table. The days just dragged on, most of them cloudy, rainy, or cold. But we were glad to be able to stroll on the different decks, use the library, play cards, or meet with fellow travelers, reminiscing about our colorful pasts and revealing our dreams and hopes for the near future. Among our group that met daily, there was a Hungarian, Dr. Rosenzweig, with his wife, their grown daughter, and son Oskar, a fresh graduate of medical school. Their destination was Davenport, Iowa: they even had an address, 720 E. Locust Street (or 220 Lexington, I'm not sure now). We vowed to meet with our new friends once we all settled in our new homeland, but unfortunately only very few kept their promises.

Throughout the journey the sailors were extremely helpful, friendly and accommodating. The news was delivered to us via English and German language bulletins printed on board by a small news staff. We knew what was happening on the ship, in the sea before us, and in the country that little by little we were getting closer and closer to. I saved one of these bulletins in German, which is dated May 28, 1949. Among the various news items, the bulletin states that our ship by that day's end would reach New York, thus bringing 877 displaced persons to their new homeland; that the passengers forwarded a thank-you letter to the captain, and upon landing would send a telegram to President Truman, to the Congress, and to the chairman of the Displaced Persons Commission, expressing their thanks for all that was done for them. The bulletin ends with the following announcement: "To-morrow, Sunday, breakfast will be served not at 7, but at 5 A.M. It's not a joke!"

May 28, 1949, was a very exciting day for all of us. We could not wait for land to appear on the horizon and to see the Statue of Liberty, which everyone was talking about. The sailors were pointing out the direction in which the statue should be visible. "It is so big, you won't be able to miss it! A miraculous sight!" they said, and we all kept running to the different decks to get the best, firsthand glimpse of the Grand Lady of Freedom. At last we were approaching the New York Harbor. Most passengers had recovered from their violent ordeal with seasickness, and although still quite weak from being dehydrated, most were happy, just thinking that we were almost *there*! As if on command, people started to get busy collecting their stuff and packing. The excitement was unbelievable! Quite a few prematurely congregated on stairways, causing jams, as they wanted to be first to disembark. Then out of the blue, the excitement and joy of finally arriving was quickly dampened by a strange rumor that spread faster than lightning: "We are not going to disembark, but instead we are going to be returned back to Germany!" From then all hell broke loose! All you could hear were the frantic cries, "We are being returned to Germany!" Some of the passengers, hearing the rumor, recalled the forced return to the Soviet Union of the Cossacks in 1945 at Lienz. Others spoke of the ill-fated journey of the St. Louis ship with 937 Jewish refugees aboard that left Germany before World War II, bound for freedom from Nazi rule, which was refused entry to Cuba, or Florida, so the ship returned to Europe. That journey was later known as the "Voyage of the Damned." After checking with the crew of the SS Gen. Harry Taylor, we were assured that no such thing would happen, that we will get off the ship and be free to go wherever we wished. What apparently started the rumor was the fact that the captain had been informed that upon arrival in the New York harbor, the passengers would have to stay aboard for another day because, it being Memorial Day weekend, the custom offices would be closed, so that there would be no one to process the refugees. Somehow that information filtered down to some of the passengers in a twisted form, leading to a drastic misinterpretation of the reason for the delay in disembarkation. It took quite an effort by the crew to calm the nearly rioting passengers, who were rapidly being caught up in the confusion, despair and anger. Their cries muffled the loudspeakers that conveyed clarification and assurances. Everywhere on the ship you could see the white-clad sailors walking among the passengers, trying to spread the correct, good news. Some passengers did not understand what the good hearted, joyful sailors were saying, but their big grins helped to convey their message. Finally, things got back to normal. And after spotting in the distance the beautiful Statue of Liberty and watching the magnificent, breathtaking skyline of New York appear in front of our eyes, we could only hear "Ohs" and "Ahs," and the fear of being returned to Germany was no longer on people's minds.

Rather than unpack again, most of us were content to sit on our packed bundles of meager belongings, ready to wait out that extra day on the ship. Everybody relaxed and the worries subsided. While waiting, we could watch the bustle of New York City and the speeding cars on the elevated highway. The street noise was overwhelming! We were anxious to take off once the "gates of heaven" would open. Although the sea was pretty calm the closer we came to the U.S., our ravenous appetites did not return. I guess we all had *Reise Fieber* (the excitement of traveling) and food at this moment was not on our minds. All we could think of was to get ashore and keep going. But, under the surface, there was still the great uneasiness of not knowing what the immediate future would bring for each of us. It was worrisome and frightening.

20

Nazareth

And so, finally, after a long and tiresome journey, the U.S. Army Transport General Harry Tayler brought us safely into the New York harbor. There was unbelievable commotion of almost chaotic proportions. People were extremely impatient to get going, even though they didn't exactly know where or what they were going to. Several tables with representatives of different organizations were set up to help us all locate and meet face-to-face with our waiting sponsors. There were signs posted showing where to go to collect our suitcases. People were running to and fro like chickens with their heads cut off. There was so much excitement that no matter how the immigration authorities tried to be efficient, there was no way they could speed up their efforts, due to the mass of confused refugees who could not cope with the emotion of finally stepping off onto American soil. It seemed the wait to be processed and to get the final OK to depart in the care of one's sponsor was endless. In the late afternoon we at last met Mr. Walter K., his wife Corinne, and their oldest daughter. The younger four children had stayed at home, waiting for our arrival. It was the sponsors' second trip to the harbor. They, like many of the other sponsors, were not aware that our debarkation would be delayed because of the Memorial Day holiday and had made a trip in vain the previous day. After exchanging a few pleasantries, Mother and I, together with our two suitcases, were guided to their waiting car. Once in their very comfortable Cadillac, we were showered nonstop with questions. The teenager daughter, who sat with us in the back seat, was especially curious about us, as if we had arrived not from civilized Europe, but from another planet. Despite her interrogation, she was very warm, polite, and funny at times in her own way, doing her utmost to relieve the cloud of tension that was hanging over Mother and me. We swiftly left the city and entered a very long tunnel, which to us seemed an unbelievable technological achievement. When told that we are actually under the river, not only could we not believe it, we became frightened. Once out of the long tube, we both gave silent sighs of relief. What little we could see, while speeding through various little towns and over highways and side roads, was quite impressive. Our friendly young co-traveler told us the names of the different sights as we passed them. At last, quite exhausted by the trip and the excitement, we arrived at the doors of a rather large southern-type mansion, which was to be our new home in America. I still remember the address on N. New Street, Nazareth, Pennsylvania.

We were overwhelmed by the welcome we received from the four children who had stayed behind. They could not wait to show us to our room, which was next door to theirs. Mother and I were so tired we were about to collapse. We just could not answer any more questions. When the children left us alone, we did not unpack or think of eating anything but simply lay down to rest. Our emotional state was very mixed. On the one hand we were very happy to have the trip over with and behind us. On the other hand, we were in a kind of shock, anticipating that our stay in this house was not going to be a happy picnic. Soon, from the very beginning, we realized that indeed the start in our new homeland would not be an easy one, but that it would be still another in the series of challenges we had been facing. Despite the fact that their city bears the Holy Land's name of Nazareth and is within a stone's throw of another holy-sounding place named Bethlehem, our sojourn with the sponsor family turned out to be not "holy" at all. In fact, the few weeks we spent in Nazareth were more like being in purgatory!

We were up every day at dawn, in order to have breakfast ready for the five school children and for their father, who each morning before eight left for the nylon plant which he owned and supervised. After that, we had to cope with Mrs. K., who turned out to be somewhat emotionally unstable and on tranquilizers. She tended to stay in bed longer than anyone else. When she appeared, she would tell Mother (via me) what she had to do each day. The list became longer every day, with new chores added for Mother as well as for me. While the children were at school, I helped Mother in carrying out her load of duties such as cooking meals three times a day, cleaning the whole house daily and once a week thoroughly, doing laundry, ironing, etc. When, one by one, the children returned from school, I had to supervise them, help them with their homework, and keep them reasonably quiet so as not to upset their hysterical mother. After the family had eaten the dinner we served them, Mother and I would get to eat the leftovers. Mrs. K. was not just frugal, she was a very stingy woman. She objected to our having even an extra slice of bread. Both milk and baked goods were delivered to the house, and we were emphatically told that they had to last until the next delivery. Mr. K., who seemed to realize what a good deal he had with these two hardworking refugees, would often try to tone down his wife's demands and complaints. But his efforts in this respect rarely brought any improvement. He even tried to get us together with some Polish-speaking people in town, to help ease the difficulties and loneliness of our life. The children, however, were very attentive, kind, and obedient. They liked me especially, as they saw in me a genuine buddy of theirs. They often would speak of their affection for me and ask for my assurance that I will *never ever* leave them. Unfortunately, the affection of the children did not compensate for the miserable life we were living. The worst thing, perhaps, was the fact that, in this millionaire's house, with Mrs. K. checking on how much we were eating, Mother and I were constantly hungry. We outlined our grievances to a Church World Service representative, who, instead of being sympathetic, defended our sponsors, and reminded us that we had made a commitment to stay with them and that we should be thankful they had helped us get out of Germany.

After the meeting with the CWS representative, a month passed in much the same way in our life in Nazareth. It was midsummer and the 4th of July was approaching. We negotiated with our sponsors to get the long holiday weekend off in order to take a bus to see Sonya and Misha, who by this time were out of their commitment to the owner of the meat products company in Philadelphia, and were now living in the Russian resort called Rova Farms in Cassville, New Jersey, operating a little restaurant there. Very reluctantly the sponsors agreed to let us have some time off, but they insisted that we should be back the day after the holiday. For the trip to Cassville we packed just a few essentials, enough to last us through the long weekend. If I remember correctly, all that we carried fit in one shopping bag. After all, at this point, we really intended to return, as we felt committed to our agreement to stay at least a year with the sponsors, in order to pay off our debt to them for their help in bringing us to the U.S.

21

Little Russia, New Jersey

Although Nazareth is not a long distance from Cassville, New Jersey, the bus trip seemed endless. Under normal circumstances, riding on a bus that stops at various quaint little towns would have been an interesting sightseeing trip, but for us the trip was a drag. We wanted to see Sonya and Misha as soon as possible, without any unnecessary delays. Finally, however, the tearful, happy, long-awaited reunion took place. No sooner had we finished embracing than we were told by Misha that he and Sonya were extremely busy both in the kitchen and in the dining room of their small restaurant, which was full of guests. It was obvious they did not have time to hear about our life in Nazareth, to commiserate with us, or to tell us about their experiences in the U.S. Sonya quickly returned to the preparation of orders that Misha received from the various guests. Misha, on the other hand, seeing an opportunity to get out of his waiter's duties, despite my objections and reluctance, persuaded me to help Sonya bring the meals to the guests. He told me, "I will bring the orders to the steps of the dining room and you will then place them in front of the guests; there's nothing to it!" Rather than argue and create a scene, as had happened many times in the past, I accepted my new duties under Misha's wing— or should I say I fell once more into his trap. One of the first dishes served, which happened to be Russian cutlets, I brought to an Air Force major named Chester, who, I later learned, was a frequent guest at this "mish mash" restaurant, along with the others in a group of military personnel who were spending part of the summer in this Russian community to perfect their knowledge of the Russian language. After a few orders were served in the fashion that Misha proposed, he disappeared, and instead started to mingle with the guests, leaving Sonya and me to do the whole job. Mother as well was circulating among the guests, taking notes of their advice and making connections. Looking back at this experience, I have to admit that Misha indirectly played the role of a cupid, affecting the rest of my life.

Once the dinner rush hour slowed down, the guests having retired to their rooms, and Chester and his group having left for their hotel, Mother and I helped Sonya with the dishes and the cleanup. Misha, as usual, continued

My future husband, Chester Radlo, in Lakewood, New Jersey, 1949.

to entertain the few guests who remained and were eager to talk. Finally, quite exhausted by now, we were able to hear the Shlykovs' tale of their arrival in the U.S. After they had left Regensburg and had arrived in Philadelphia, their stay with their sponsors was pretty brief, but much pleasanter than our stay in Nazareth. They were sponsored by Rainbow Farms Meat Products, owned by George Hilgenberg at Richboro, Pennsylvania (telephone, Churchville 370). From day one their very outgoing host realized that Misha was not a butcher and not a person suitable for manual labor. He told him that he did not expect him to work in the factory; instead Misha would help Sonya in her housekeeping and cooking duties. For example, he suggested that Misha could do the housecleaning and vacuuming, prepare cocktails for himself and his sponsor, and accompany his sponsor here and there, whenever Mr. Hilgenberg wanted him to come along, which turned out to be fairly often. The sponsors, being of German descent, were extremely pleased with Sonya's repertoire of European cooking. Misha soon was getting all his favorite meals, in addition to daily cocktails with the man of the house. As far as his cleaning duties were concerned, it was a different story. Sonya relied on Misha's help, but did not check on how he was performing such duties as vacuuming. One day she came into a room that

Misha was in the process of sweeping. She caught him red-handed, holding up a carpet with one hand and sweeping crumbs and dust under it. She was outraged! She exclaimed, "Mikhail!" (when angry she called him Mikhail, rather than Misha). "You are abusing people's generosity and we will be fired, ending up on the street, if you continue housekeeping in this manner!" Misha laughed and told Sonya not to worry. After all, he told her, being with him she never found herself living on the streets in Poland or Germany and now in America.

This convenient arrangement, both for the Shlykovs and their sponsors, continued for a time, but eventually Misha began feeling bored with his idle life. After hearing of a large Russian community nearby (in Cassville, New Jersey), Misha suggested to his American friend that he check out the place as a possible customer base. I really cannot picture their conversations, as Misha did not speak English, and the other did not speak Russian. Perhaps Misha's very limited German, plus the host's vivid imagination and the many cocktails they enjoyed together helped them to communicate. And so the good-hearted sponsor went along with the idea about the Russian community. It turned out to be a fairly large resort area with a substantial lake. It included a huge recreation building with a large hall for dancing, a restaurant, a bar, and a hall for holding meetings, weddings, or *trapezas* (post-funeral meals). On the grounds of the resort there was also a small church. Another Russian Orthodox church, which could hold a large congregation, was just down the road from the recreation center. There was a swimming area on the lake and all around it there were cabins and boats for rent. There was a small library full of Russian books, a country store, and an ice-cream parlor. In the woods all around the resort there were little houses (*dachas*), mostly owned by Russian émigrés. Many of the owners of the larger houses rented out rooms for the many vacationers who came, mostly from hot and humid New York. Many of the visitors had shares in this Rova Farms resort, which was established many years ago by a mutual insurance company. After getting a good sense of this strictly Russian village, Misha right away saw an opportunity for a business. He immediately suggested to his American sponsor that he lend him one of his delivery trucks, so that he could take the German's meat products from his plant, and offer them for sale among the Russians in Cassville and the nearby communities. In addition to the area of Rova Farms, quite a few Russians lived in the surrounding little towns, tending chicken farms, and in Lakewood, where another Russian Orthodox church served a fairly large local and out-of-town congregation. Thus Misha was on his way to becoming an American businessman. He got his driver's license and a truck full of *Wurst*, and off he went. While Misha played at being a door-to-door salesman, Sonya remained at the Higenbergs' until they could afford to leave Richboro and part with their hosts. For many years afterwards, the Shlykovs continued to praise the very decent and tolerant Germans of Philadelphia, who had made their start in their newly acquired homeland relatively easy.

Soon one thing led to another. During one of his trips to the Russian community, Misha met another very good-hearted man, this time a Russian, a recently divorced, very laid-back man who was happy to be in a small rental business that brought him a small but decent income in return for very little effort. In no time Misha and Shaitaroff became friends and partners. "Yasha," as everyone called him, continued his tourist business of renting rooms and cabins on his property, and Misha, subleasing from him the kitchen and dining room, opened a restaurant there, while in his spare time he helped manage the rental of rooms whenever Yasha was not there. In return for the latter duty Misha and Sonya had the free use of one of the rooms, sharing a bath with other guests. On many occasions Misha played the role of hotel manager, showing guests to their rooms. Some Russians, even though speaking in Russian, would mix in English words, which often confused Misha as to what exactly they were asking about. For instance, a frequent misunderstanding took place when someone asked Misha to show "the closet." Misha would open the door to a toilet. But when they insisted again on seeing "the closet," Misha would get annoyed; he kept showing them the toilet, and they kept on asking to see it. Finally, someone told him that the Russian word *klozet* means toilet, but the English word closet refers to a place to hang one's clothes. Watching some of the *Fawlty Towers* episodes on television reminds me of my uncle, the part-time room clerk.

During our short weekend stay with the Shlykovs, it was decided that we should relocate and leave the K.—— household, no matter what the consequences. And then Mother found another direction to go in.

Chester and the other Russian language students belonged to a group that was run by a Russian native, Mr. Mansvetov. The men in the group were mostly recent graduates of the U.S. Army's famous language school of Monterey, California. They were brought to Cassville to perfect their spoken Russian. One lady in the group was the wife of a diplomat, who was in Washington preparing to depart for a new assignment in Moscow, under Ambassador George Kennon, their good friend. Mrs. Taquey suggested to Mother that she should come back with her to Washington, D.C., to stay with the Taqueys, so that Mrs. Taquey could perfect her Russian. Mother, without hesitation, gladly agreed, and in a few days the two of them departed for Washington, leaving me behind. At this point Mother was not concerned as to how I would settle with the sponsors, leaving me to take care of that unpleasant task by myself. When Chester, whom I'd gotten to know over the course of the long weekend, heard of my predicament, he offered to drive me to Nazareth. During the drive I was a nervous wreck, dreading to think of what the outcome might be once I got to face our sponsors. Chester tried to calm my fears, assuring me that the sponsors could not harm me in any way. Although they had helped bring us to the U.S., he said, they had no right to treat us as slaves. Finally, we arrived and my nervousness was at its height as I entered the house alone, without Mother. Chester stayed in the car, ready to come rescue me in case I was threatened in any way. When Mr. K. learned of our intentions of leaving his household, he did not spare any words to express his outrage. I felt like a little kid being harshly reprimanded by this burly man who was over six feet tall and must have weighed at least 250 pounds. In addition to his husky build, his eyes underlined by dark circles seemed to be even angrier than usual. Despite my attempts to justify our decision, he kept shouting at me and threatening to take legal action against us. I ran upstairs to our room, quickly gathered our meager possessions, stripped the bed of its sheets and tidied up the rest of the room and bathroom. I shook like a leaf throughout my hasty efforts of packing and cleaning, all while still hearing Mr. K.'s outbursts from below. I was scared almost out of my wits at the thought of what might happen when I finally came down and made for the door. I was afraid of finding the doors locked shut and of my being trapped. At this moment I recalled that Chester was waiting outside, ready to come to my rescue if needed, and that gave me courage. I rushed down and quickly ran outside to put my bundles into Chester's car, hoping that he would just start the car and keep going. But Mr. K. had an after-thought and requested that I reimburse him for the 20 dollars he had spent on the trip bringing us from New York Harbor to Nazareth. I was penniless at this moment and very embarrassed that I had to ask Chester to lend me the $20. He wrote out a check, which I gave to Mr. K. I thanked him, nevertheless, for all they had done for us and expressed my regrets at having to leave so suddenly. Then I left the house as quickly as I could, without turning back in order not to hear any more of Mr. K.'s angry comments. At last, in the car with my guardian angel, all my problems in Nazareth were behind me, as we drove peacefully back to Cassville!

For the rest of the summer the Shlykovs continued their restaurant business, while Mother was enjoying her stay at the Taqueys. It was at the Taqueys' house that she met George Kennon, who was just about to return to Moscow to serve as the U.S. ambassador to the USSR. Because he was taking his family with him, he invited Mother to come along as a member of his household, so that she could help them all with the Russian language (Mr. Kennon was the only one in the family who spoke fluent Russian). Although Mother was quite tempted to take the position, she was afraid of possible problems with the Soviet authorities, and so she declined the offer. Meanwhile, Chester and his fellow students were busy following Mr. Mansvetov around, meeting various residents of the little village, speaking Russian almost exclusively, and absorbing as much of the Russian language as they could. As for me, in addition to helping Sonya and Misha in their restaurant, I obtained a part-time job at the resort's ice cream parlor. During my brief employment there, Chester must have put on several pounds, eating the generously packed ice cream cones I served him, while he waited around for me to finish my shift. A low point during my stay at the Shaitaroff's house was the day I became very feverish and had severe pains in the joints and especially in one of my knees, which had become swollen to twice its normal size. When my fever reached 104°+F, Chester persuaded me to see a doctor. The closest doctor was in Lakewood, a few miles away. The doctor informed me that I was having a bout with rheumatic fever!

As soon as I got back on my feet, the time came for my new and dear friend to leave for his new assignment at West Point. Another officer of the group, Maj. Walter Guletski, also left for West Point, and the other students went on to their respective places of assignment. The usually lively place, bustling with vacationers, began to look and sound like a ghost village. My stay with the Shlykovs was a real drag. We waited endlessly for the occasional guest who came either to spend the night or for a quick meal at the restaurant. Some locals continued to show up at odd hours, but they came mostly to socialize with my chatty and by this time very popular uncle, rather than to give us their business. I continued to hang around the restaurant, just in case guests came by, and was assured by Misha that they still needed me. Although they usually got by very well without any knowledge of English whatsoever, there were times that indeed I was needed to translate, to do the shopping, or to rent rooms. In between my restaurant hours I was at the ice-cream parlor, dishing out ice cream for the very few people that came by. There, too, business was down to a minimum. Having a lot of time on my hands gave me a chance to think about what I should do with myself next, and I realized that the choices were slim. In order to attend any kind of school or find a better, more stimulating job, Cassville was obviously not the place to be looking. I felt stuck and couldn't find any hope for improvement, at least for the time being. In spite of the gloomy outlook and the loneliness, my greatest joy of the day was a daily, long walk to the post office in hopes of collecting a letter from my dearest. As soon as I approached the door, the lady postmaster greeted me with a friendly smile, which to me was a signal that there was a letter for me c/o General Delivery (there was no house delivery in Cassville at the time). Occasionally, though, she was not smiling when I approached, which for me was a bad omen. If indeed there was nothing for me, she tried to soften my very obvious disappointment by suggesting various reasons why the letter hadn't arrived, such as that "the mail delivery was slow or late that day, because the recent holiday had fowled up everything." Sometimes, not having any explanation, she would just give me some cheerful words of support. Nevertheless, I would return to my cubby-hole crushed and saddened. But often, the next day, two letters would be waiting, making up for the one that wasn't there the day before! I must add that I never missed a day sending a letter. Sometimes, I would post one before Saturday's mail pick-up, so that Chester would find a letter from me Monday early in the morning. Now, what was in those letters, of course, is a secret, all I can say is that they were very warm, tender and full of love. They became like the water and air in my isolated life. They sustained my existence and gave me hope for the future. There were quite a few of them, which if combined could fill a lovely book. For me the weekends were the happiest of all, as Chester would arrive early on Saturday, or even quite late on Friday, and leave back for West Point late on Sunday. During his visits, as there was not much to do in the sleepy village, we listened and even danced to many popular Russian romances played on old 78 rpm records spinning on an ancient Victrola. It was then that we discovered that we could whistle rather well as a duet. Other activities included eating Sonya's delicious meals, going shopping for the restaurant, or taking the Shlykovs on different errands. Weather permitting, the four of us would drive to one of the many beaches, not so much for the swimming, but for our favorite Philly cheese-steak sandwiches. As usual, the happy moments flew by quickly and Sunday evening's parting came faster than we wished. After saying good-bye, Chester had to fight traffic and sleepiness (one time he did fall asleep during one of those return trips, but awakened on the opposite side of the road unharmed), and I spent several hours waiting in anticipation of Chester's person-to-person telephone call, confirming his safe arrival. In those days he lived first at the Thayer Hotel in West Point and then in the bachelor officers' quarters with a pay-phone in the hallway. Chester's commuting and my trips to the post office continued for several months.

When most of the vacationers left Cassville following the long Labor Day weekend, the restaurant business slowed almost completely. Misha was idle once more—but not for long. He learned that in Lakewood there was an elderly Russian man who wanted to sell his small chicken farm, including a little shack that served as his home. The property was not overly expensive, but on the other hand the Shlykovs had not been able to save enough for a down payment. Chester agreed to lend Misha two thousand dollars to help cover the deposit on the property. However, Misha was going to need more money in order to reactivate the neglected farm. It so happened that during the summer a friend from Regensburg times, Sergey Konstantinovich Shebalin, with his relatives the Filatievs and their long-lost friends from Sergey's youth, the Kozlowskis, had come to Cassville for a visit. Earlier, the Kozlowskis had helped Sergey Shebalin reestablish contact with other friends, including the famous pilot Sikorski and Mr. and Mrs. Tomann, who were now living in the New York area and occasionally visited Cassville and Lakewood. In a short time Sergey introduced his friends the Tomanns to Misha and Sonya. Mrs. Tomann showed a particular interest in Misha's plans for the future, so now that Misha was in need of capital to get his farm going, he turned to the very sympathetic Mrs. Tomann for a loan, offering to let her hold all of the Shlykovs' jewelry until the loan was paid off, which Misha was able to do a couple of years later. Once again Misha was in business, this time raising young chicks and keeping the grown chickens for their valuable egg-laying abilities. The sale of the property went through very quickly and the Shlykovs moved into the very primitive house, consisting of one small room with outdoor plumbing! Renovation of the chicken coops was the first priority, followed by the purchase and delivery of some 3,000 just days-old chicks. Misha and especially Sonya soon realized how much work was in store for them in the near future, but at least they felt they were now on their own and the future held some promise.

22

Work in the City

Inasmuch as Mother rejected the Taqueys' offer as well as Mr. Kennon's offer to move temporarily to Moscow, she returned to Lakewood, and shortly thereafter she and I took Mrs. Shaitaroff's suggestion to move to Brooklyn, where Mrs. Shaitaroff had an apartment on Schermerhorn Street. Almost the next day after our relocation, we were offered a job at Barton's candy factory. Mr. Klein, one of the brothers who were co-owners of Barton's, a factory that made chocolates based on recipes they had brought from Poland, wished to employ me as governess for his children, but remembering my recent unpleasant experience with the sponsors in Nazareth and their children, I declined. Mr. Klein was disappointed, but he still hired me, along with Mother, to work at his plant instead. Mother was one of the workers who made the chocolates, that is, she tended a machine that stamped out the confections. I was one of a group of people sitting at a large round table that had holes ringed with stiff bristles. In front of each of us there was a tray of freshly made chocolates and a stack of square papers in various colors. My task was as follows: first, with my right hand, I put a colored wrapper on top of the brush and hole, after which I placed a piece of chocolate on the wrapper. Then, with my right middle finger, I had to push the chocolate gently through the hole. As soon as the chocolate in the wrapper went through, I quickly retrieved it under the table with my left hand and folded the paper so that the chocolate was now enclosed within the wrapper. Chocolates of differing shapes and flavors had to be wrapped in papers designated for them. The wrapped chocolates were placed on a slowly moving conveyer belt. At the conveyer, several women in a row would neatly place each type of chocolate into its appropriate slot in the moving boxes. This last procedure was well demonstrated, in a very comical way, on the *I Love Lucy* show when Lucy and Ethel were tending the fast-moving chocolate conveyer. This work was done primarily by women; men were employed mostly in mixing the ingredients that went into making chocolates. We were told that while at work we could eat all the candy we wished, but none was to be taken out of the plant. Like most other new workers, we nibbled a lot while we worked, until we eventually could not stand the taste any more. Obviously, the owners knew human nature. This would have been a perfect job for Chester, who has a very sweet tooth; he would have had a field day ... at least for a while. During the Christmas holiday Mr. Klein put me to work at one of the Barton's stores at the corner of 42nd Street and Fifth Avenue, and I received a small raise. In the meantime, Mother had left the factory for a better-paying job sewing leather belts and similar items (she had never previously operated a sewing machine) in the shady district known as the Bowery, which was full of drunks and homeless people. I stayed at my job at Barton's candy store through the period of the Christmas rush, after which I quit Barton's when the prospect of a more satisfying job appeared. I'll describe that later, but first I want to show how one's memory is not always reliable.

When we were still living at Mrs. Shaitaroff's apartment, on an evening when I happened to be in a very sad mood, feeling unhappy about the lack of progress in my life, two of our relatives showed up. They were Nina Lukashuk, Mother's cousin, and her daughter Lyalya (*Lyalya* is a diminutive form of Yelena), who was about one month younger than I. Seeing how dejected I was, with Mother's coaching they tried their utmost to console me. I became more upset and simply refused to talk to them. Otherwise, the visit was uneventful and I lost contact with them, although Mother continued to see them from time to time. Many years later, when Chester and I were living and working for the government in Washington, D.C., a friend of Lyalya's called me asking if I could help her in getting a job at my place of work. She identified herself as a friend of Helen Messner (Lyalya's married name) but I, not recognizing this name and forgetting that the name Helen is the English version of the Russian name Yelena, told the caller that I didn't know anyone by the name of Helen Messner and that I was not able to help her. Many years later, at a family gathering when I again met Lyalya, she reminded me of our first meeting in Mrs. Shaitaroff's apartment and of the unfortunate call of her friend to me in Washington, D.C. Only then did I realize what had actually occurred thirty or so years earlier. Fortunately, I was able to clarify the matter and mend my cousin's hard feelings. After that, we saw each other now and then, mostly in New Jersey, although the Messners visited us in Santa Barbara on several occasions. We promised many times to visit them in Sea Cliff, New York, but somehow we never made it to their house. I corresponded with Lyalya until her death in 1993. It is a relief to be able to say that, although it took over thirty years, our "spat" was resolved in time so that we could become good friends.

Also, just about the time when we lived in Brooklyn, I had an offer of a scholarship to attend a college. It would have been a golden chance to begin fulfilling my dream of studying medicine. Unfortunately, I could not accept the offer because the Shlykovs, trying to establish their chicken farm, were in constant debt and were in need of continuous financial support. Both Mother's and my wages went almost exclusively toward paying off their farm debts, which were steadily increasing rather than becoming smaller, with no relief in sight. Hoping to find more satisfying employment, Mother and I decided to leave Brooklyn and move to Manhattan. Mother kept her job at the leather company, but I quit my job at Barton's and took a new job with the Design Registration Bureau of the National Federation of Textiles, Inc., which was at 389 Fifth Avenue, a classy location between 35th and 36th streets in New York City. The job was pleasant and rather well paid. As soon as I was hired I went through a crash orientation course explaining what the Design Registration Bureau was all about. Each textile manufacturer, before producing any material that contained a design pattern, was obliged by law to submit to the bureau a small sample of the newly designed fabric. The sample had to be large enough to include a repeat of the design. Once the sample was received, it was first classified according to what kind of a design it was, e.g., floral, geometrical, etc. Then one of us would go to an appropriate file that contained thousands of previously registered designs in that classification. Floral compositions that featured commonly used images, such as roses or other flowers, required an extra thorough search to find possible matching designs. Very close matches were pulled out for several of us to judge how close the proposed design was to existing materials already on the market. If the proposed design was substantially different from any other design, we would pass it and give it a new patent number, allowing the manufacturer to print the design in question. If, on the other hand, it was obvious to us that it was a copy, we would reject it. If the proposed design resembled very closely some previous design the new sample would go to an expert who used a special device that measured elements within the repeated pattern, including colors. If it turned out that the difference was not substantial, it was rejected. Sometimes the manufacturer would not agree with our decision, insisting that his design was indeed unique. In such cases the dispute had to be decided in court. On the other hand, if he made some significant changes, we would pass it. Most of us developed an eye for the various designs and could tell almost immediately if the new design had been copied from some other manufacturer's design. Occasionally, when a textile plant wished to use a design in question immediately, we would oblige it by expediting the search and the approval or rejection decision. To do this it was often necessary to work overtime. Working overtime was not only profitable, but also fun. Only a few of us were allowed to stay after regular working hours, so those of us that did stay became closer friends, rather than just coworkers. When we stayed late, we ordered dinner from a deli across the street. The overtime sessions also helped me to improve my English, but it still was some time before I realized how the word *whipped* is pronounced, as I often ordered apple pie with "wiped" cream. Although the rest of the offices, including those of the executives, were closed, none of us took advantage of the extra freedom; on the contrary, we seemed to accomplish much more than during the daytime, and were able to reduce backlogs considerably. One of my coworkers was Viola Mercer, sister of the famous singer Johnny Mercer. She lived in Ossening, New York, and commuted to work every day. The drawback of working late was getting from the office to the Lexington Avenue subway through mostly deserted streets, and then in the dark having to walk the short distance from 79th and Lexington over to Second Avenue, where our new apartment was located. If Chester was able to get away from West Point in time to reach New York before I left the office, he would pick me up and drive me to our apartment, where Mother was waiting for us with a nice dinner. The first dinner I prepared for Chester occurred one evening when we arrived at the apartment before Mother came home from work. Like the first meal of Russian cutlets I served Chester in Cassville, this time, as you have probably guessed, the entrée was again Russian cutlets, but this time à la Lucy. I wonder if they were really as delicious as he said they were.

While living in New York City, Mother and I depended primarily on subways as our means of transportation. Sometimes, especially during clear, sunny days, we might take buses. We never opted for taxis, though. Riding during rush hour on the subway, when only standing room was available most of the time, I learned to read the newspaper the way the New Yorkers did, folding it into a third of its width, which made it possible to read without disturbing fellow commuters. Many people, without newspapers of their own, would steal a glimpse of the headlines by reading over someone's shoulder. Riding the subway and bus systems in New York, we soon began to feel like real New Yorkers.

One of the very memorable days I can recall from my time at the design bureau was the day when General Douglas MacArthur was given a hero's welcome in Manhattan. Only New York City is capable of welcoming a hero in such grand style. Knowing that there would be a ticker-tape parade passing by right under our windows, we all were busy on the days before the parade shredding scrap paper and unwanted copies of designs and also making handmade confetti with a hole puncher. The morning of the parade saw very little work done. Everyone was standing by at the many windows overlooking Fifth Avenue so as not to miss the motorcade when it passed our area. When we finally spotted the open limousines approaching, all hell broke loose! With radios at full volume and sounding noisemakers of various sorts, we shouted our greetings to the general and his wife, who sat in the back seat of a limousine that had its top down and were graciously waving not only to the crowds that had lined the streets but also to the many who were reaching out of windows and balconies. Just as the moving car approached our building, we dumped out all of our shredded papers and homemade confetti. Seeing it shower down onto the crowds and the cars below was, for me, an unforgettable sight. I could not help but worry as to who in the world would have to clean up this unholy mess. My worry was short-lived, however, as almost immediately after the parade had passed by, a very efficient cleaning crew came by in sweeper trucks, which swallowed up most of the scattered papers. As proof that I had personally watched this hero come home, I took a snapshot of him while he was exactly under our window. The picture turned out to be quite blurry because of all the ticker tape flying about; nevertheless, it still proves that I was there.

Thinking back at my three jobs up to that time, one at the labor camp, one at Barton's Candy, and the one at the design registration bureau, all three jobs were similar in nature in that each involved large quantities of items and making choices or decisions about them. At the labor camp I was assigned to check for faulty bullets and eliminating defective ones. At Barton's, I was checking chocolates to assure they were perfect before wrapping them in different colored papers. And finally, at the design registration bureau, my job was to check incoming fabric designs against existing ones in the files and making the final decision to pass and register the new designs or to reject them. As you can imagine, each of these jobs making choices required, on my part, a great deal of patience and endurance. A couple of years later there was another job, fortunately only for one day, also having to do with great volume, which took place at the Shlykovs' farm, where I had to help with the inoculation of over 3,000 chickens. It was not a joyful experience, which I will describe in the next chapter. And then there was still another *special* job, one of many I did for the government, where with the aid of a computer I had to consolidate thousands and thousands of foreign document files. You would be amazed to know how many ways in various languages a name like Khruschev can be spelled! All these similar jobs, mostly performed by women like me, leads me to wonder if women possess more patience and endurance to perform meticulous duties, involving volumes of materials and making decisions about them, than do men—?

23

1528 Second Avenue, New York City

When I started to work at the design registration bureau we were no longer renting a room at Mrs. Shaitaroff's, because rather than in a separate bedroom as she had promised she had us sleep on a sofa in the living room. We had reestablished contact with the Filatiev-Shebalin family at just the time when they needed to sublease a room in their newly rented apartment at 1528 Second Avenue, just around the corner from East 79th Street in Manhattan. It was another pretty classy address, but "one should not judge a book by its cover." The location was actually quite good, as it was an easy distance to the subway, which we took to go to and from work. The living arrangement was another story. The apartment consisted of four bedrooms, a dining room, kitchen, and one bathroom. It was on the third floor of a building without an elevator. The ground floor was occupied by a busy Hungarian restaurant that featured a daily orchestra, which mostly played typical Gypsy melodies that ranged from soft and soulful to loud and wild. The restaurant was open seven days a week and upstairs we could tell, even through closed windows, what was being prepared in their kitchen. The smell of fried onions, paprika, and goulash was constant! Above the restaurant there was a large area used for storage. And above that, on the third floor, was our apartment. Leaving for work in the early morning, or returning home after having worked long hours of overtime was particularly unpleasant. One would have to step over one or a couple of drunken men sleeping on the second landing. The encounters with the drunks were so frequent that we got to the point that we stopped complaining to the police and simply accepted the situation as unavoidable. The drunks were actually rather quiet, as they were asleep most of the time, but if they happened to be awake, they had a friendly greeting for us.

As soon as you entered the apartment there was a horseshoe-shaped corridor from which there was an access to every room. The first and the closest bedroom from the entry, across from the kitchen, was ours. Next, there was a very tiny room occupied by Mrs. Olga Fedorovna Filatiev, mother of Alexander

Aleksandrovich ("Sasha"), and her little kitty. Then came a dining room with a large skylight, and then Sergey Konstantinovich Shebalin's bedroom, followed by a huge bedroom (formerly the living room), which was used by Sasha and Helen (Yelena Sergeyevna) Filatiev and their two small children, Natasha, who was born in Regensburg, and Misha, born in New York City. These last two bedrooms had views of the very busy and noisy Second Avenue. A year or so later, after several years of separation from the rest of the family, Sergey's wife Emilia Andreyevna and their teenage daughter Natasha arrived from Yugoslavia. There was a certain harmony among all of us, despite the fact that Olga, who was always grouchy and argumentative, and Sergey, who also was grumpy and impatient, were not very friendly with each other. Most of the frequent arguments between them were based on questions of discipline and jealousy of the attention of the grandchildren. In general, however, conditions in the apartment were tolerable; even the sharing of the kitchen was acceptable. We all tried to take turns preparing food, so that one would not interfere with someone else's activity. The worst problem in this communal arrangement, of course, was access to the only bathroom.

Olga Filatiev had an easy job as a housekeeper for a Russian painter, Mr. Sorin. I say easy, because after she tidied up his place she was free to play his grand piano or paint water colors, which in particular her employer encouraged her to do. Whenever she would finish a small painting (usually of roses or other flowers) her mentor would critique it and sometimes even improve it himself. As I have said, her husband Aleksander died while we were all still living in Regensburg. Sasha, their only son, who had been an officer in the Yugoslav army prior to their escape to Germany, upon arrival in New York, got a job at the Firestone Tire Company, as did his father-in-law, Sergey. The latter worked on the night shift. Both Mother and I worked full-time, I often until late at night. The only persons in the apartment during the day were Helen Filatiev and her two children, so access to the lone bathroom was not a problem. At daybreak, however, it was a different matter; there was always a line of impatient people. Since this was the only bathroom facility serving so many users, the toilet, in particular, often became stopped up. Plumber's visits to our apartment were quite frequent. On one occasion, when it was our turn to clean the kitchen and the bathroom, Mother decided to do the work on Sunday when all of the others were not at home. After mopping the floors, she forgot to take a rag out of the pail and poured the dirty water together with the rag into the toilet, and flushed the toilet. The large rag got stuck somewhere below, causing the water to overflow, quickly spilling all over the floor! As it was Sunday we could not reach a plumber, so Mother decided to do the job herself. Using just a household wrench, she managed to dismantle the toilet bowl, quickly retrieve the rag, and reset the toilet. Sure enough, the toilet was working properly again. I must add that whenever a handyman would come to repair this or that, Mother never failed to watch him, staring intently at his every action. You can imagine how annoying this was to the poor repair-men. On this day, however, her curiosity paid off. Remembering what plumbers do when they tackle a stopped-up toilet, she was able to fix the problem not only without anyone's help, but she also saved quite a bit of money not hav-ing to hire a plumber, of all days, on a Sunday.

Our bedroom looked out on a fire escape and nearby roofs full of laun-dry lines. Since the Filatievs' children were still in their diapers, Helen washed them daily as well as the other clothing by hand in the bathtub, and then through our bedroom window she would hang out the entire wash to dry. We did our laundry once a week, usually choosing a moment when the other mem-bers of our commune were out of the apartment. The laundry line, which was attached to a pulley so it could be pulled back and forth, extended out to a pole (I guess it was a telephone pole), which appeared to be in the middle of nowhere. It was not a pretty view at all for Mother and me to see out of our bedroom window. There was no room in our tiny bedroom for a second bed, so once again I had to share a double bed with Mother. Once Mrs. Shebalin and Natasha joined us the apartment became quite crowded, but soon there-after Mrs. Shebalin managed to get a job and Natasha began attending school, so all in all it was a tolerable situation. Mrs. Shebalin, whom we called Emilia Andreyevna, was a very quiet, tolerant, and agreeable lady. From day one, Mother and I became very fond of her. In the beginning, it was hard for her to get used to having her husband under the same roof, never mind in the same room, and constantly under her feet, especially on the weekends. They had been separated by the war for many years. He, together with their older daugh-ter and her husband, escaped from Yugoslavia to Germany, while his wife and the younger daughter stayed behind. The years of separation had changed the personalities of husband and wife, so it was no wonder that the new period of adjustment was so hard on both of them. Fortunately, she found a job work-ing days, whereas he worked at night, so they ended up seeing very little of each other. Shortly after Emilia Andreyevna's arrival in New York, her favorite screen idol James Dean was killed. The tragic news affected her very much and she was in deep mourning for days. Her husband was fit to be tied, not being able to understand why a mature woman would feel and suffer so over some actor's death. The more he fussed, the more she grew angry with him. Finally, they just stopped talking to each other. Later, when they resumed talking, they argued almost nonstop. Poor Helen, who loved both of her par-ents, had constantly to referee and try to keep peace in the family. Despite their differences they stayed together for many more years, until the death of Sergey Konstantinovich in San Francisco.

In addition to helping the Shlykovs' farm business, we also had a com-mitment to help Anyuta (Mother's oldest sister) and her husband Nikolay ("Kolya" as we all called him) who were still in Munich waiting for their visas to the U.S. Their son, my cousin Sergey, was at that time attending the University of Karlsruhe, studying for an architect's diploma. Married and the father of a baby son, he also needed a financial boost. Every Saturday Mother and I would go to the local A&P store to do our weekly grocery shopping, at which time we would also buy, depending on our finances, five or ten one-pound packages of coffee plus items such as cocoa, tea, and so on. Loaded down with our heavy grocery bags, we walked the several blocks back to our apartment and then wrestled the heavy load up three flights of stairs. Once we unpacked and sorted out everything, we repacked the coffee, cocoa, tea, and other items into several packages, weighing each package so that it would not exceed the allowed poundage for a shipment by mail to Karlsruhe or Munich. Then, with our load of several bundles, each packed to just under the allowed weight and wrapped in heavy brown paper or cloth and tied with strong string, we trudged to the nearby post office, where, on Saturdays, the long wait in line was always exhausting. What a way to spend our free Saturdays! Once the care packages would arrive in Germany, where there were still severe shortages of almost everything, but especially coffee and tea, Sergey or his parents would leave whatever they needed for themselves and sell the extra goods with a nice profit. The additional income allowed them to survive and pay the rent.

To escape from our crowded housing we often took a trip to the beach at Coney Island with Chester in his brand-new, green Chevrolet convertible, or paid a visit to the cool, but not so pleasantly smelling countryside, i.e., the Shykovs' farm. For me, the latter outing was often more of an added burden rather than the relaxation I hoped for. Although their little shack was soon enlarged by the addition of a bedroom and an outdoor shower, whenever Mother and I decided to stay overnight, the sleeping accommodations were still haphazard. Also, as soon as I showed up at the door, I was literally whisked off into town to interpret for Misha at the different offices he had dealings with. It seemed that all his problems and misunderstandings just piled up, waiting for my arrival to help solve them. But once the office visits and other matters were taken care of and the business part of our visit was out of the way, the rest of the visit was spent eating Sonya's delicious goodies and socializing with the constant visitors that came by. It was as if the Shlykovs' house, as tiny as it was, had revolving doors, judging from the number of people that regularly came by to partake of Misha and Sonya's very generous hospitality.

After the young chicks grew to the point that they had become layers, a new chore was added to the Shlykovs' duties: the eggs had to be collected, washed, sorted according to their size, and placed in cartons, ready to be picked up by an egg dealer. The washing and sorting of the eggs reminds me of a funny incident that took place a few years later. Carrie, our younger daughter, must have been three or four, when we came to the farm for a visit. Carrie, as usual, ran to the chicken coop to admire the little birdies. She found Sonya being busy preparing cartons of eggs for the dealer. Just watching the procedure wasn't enough for our inquisitive young child, so she asked if she

could help. Sonya showed her how to place the eggs by size into the corre-
sponding cartons and Carrie proceeded with the task. Sonya, not paying attention to how Carrie was doing her job, didn't notice that Carrie, rather than
placing the eggs gently into the trays, was casually throwing each egg she han-
dled into its carton. When Sonya eventually noticed what was going on, there
were already quite a few smashed eggs in the cartons. Thanks to Carrie's "help,"
lunch for all of us consisted of double and triple portions of scrambled eggs,
accompanied by lots of laughter. Even Shaytan and Murat, the Shlykovs' trusty
shepherd dogs, had a great lunch, licking up the broken eggs that could not
be salvaged from the egg cartons. Periodically, the chicken coops had to be
cleaned of stinking chicken manure, which was shoveled onto wheelbarrows
and then dumped behind the coops onto a pile resembling a compost pile.
Other duties included providing feed for the constantly nibbling chickens,
washing their water containers, and refilling them with fresh water. The temperature in the coops had to be regulated carefully because if neglected, the
consequences could be disastrous. One of Misha's almost daily responsibilities was the effort to hunt down and destroy the fat rats that were constantly
preying on the young chicks. A loaded rifle stood at the ready at the chicken
coop's entrance, just in case Misha spied a rat whenever he entered the coops.
Normally, on our visits to the farm I was never asked to help in the chores
involving the chickens, but one day, much later, after the farm had been in
operation for some time, I was faced with a surprise when Chester and I and
little Ellie, who was about five months old at the time, came up from Washington for a weekend visit. This particular day had been earmarked by the local
veterinarian for small pox vaccination of the Shlykovs' chickens, which numbered over 3,000. The veterinarian was to be assisted by the Shlykovs' farm
hand, a Russian Cossack named Anton. Being a typical Cossack, Anton drank
a lot, although by his agreement with the Shlykovs he was allowed to drink
only after his work was done. On the day of the vaccination it turned out that
Anton had drunk so much vodka the previous evening and had such a hang-
over that he could not stand on his feet and was in no shape to help with the
fast-moving task that was to take place under the doctor's supervision. Again,
I found myself in the wrong place at the wrong time! Misha didn't ask Chester
to help. I guess he felt he couldn't ask a major to help in such undignified work,
so as usual he begged me to lend a helping hand. Chester remained in charge
of Ellie while I became a member of the crew, in Misha's words, "our own
labor force." The doctor, Sonya and I took our strategic places at the main
chicken coop and we were ready to go. Sonya, who was dependable and a good
sport in such situations, was inside the huge chicken coop, catching chickens
and one by one handing them to me as I stood in the doorway to an adjoin-
ing coop. Once I was handed a chicken, I had to stretch its wing for the vet,
who was standing there ready to vaccinate it. He immediately gave the chicken
a shot and then I released the screaming bird into the empty coop. And so it

went—feathers flying, chickens struggling to escape and squawking at the top of their lungs, and the heat in the rooms becoming almost scorching, despite the fans going at full blast. When I finally emerged out of the coop I could barely breathe. I had fine feathers everywhere, in my hair, nose, eyes and mouth! When I saw Chester with Ellie and a very relaxed Misha sitting peacefully in the living room, I could have burst into tears! Why me, I thought. Why do I always end up with miserable assignments like that? So that I can put another job description in my long list of "kooky" jobs?! Recalling now that horrible day, it is hard to believe that the three of us were able to accomplish the job. Until this day, after that memorable, once-in-a-lifetime experience, I am surprised that I can stand to even look at chickens, never mind eat one!

About this time, the older Padukows were given visas permitting them to immigrate to the U.S. The long delay was due to the fact that uncle Kolya had a hard time convincing the UNRRA medical commission that he was in good health. When the commission examined the mandatory X-rays of his lungs, they discovered that only a small portion of one lung was visible. The rest of the X-ray showed only a big dark spot, which was due to the fact that, many years before, in about 1924, during a struggle with tuberculosis, all of one lung and part of the other were surgically removed. He finally managed, after several interviews and follow-up exams, to convince the commission that, despite having only part of one lung, he was quite healthy and so was given permission to leave Germany for good. Their Jewish sponsors in the U.S. were the owners of a small kosher chicken processing plant in Lakewood. As soon as the Padukows arrived, Kolya began his new job, feeding and taking care of a small flock of chickens, a vocation that he previously had probably never imagined in his wildest dreams. The Padukows stayed briefly with the Shlykovs and then moved to a rented hut, which was on another small chicken farm almost across the road from the Shlykov's farm. In return for housing, Aunt Anyuta agreed to collect eggs and pack them into boxes. Shortly after they moved into the hut, they learned of a small chicken farm being sold without a house, but the property had a little shack similar to that of the Shlykovs. Since the Padukows, like the Shlykovs, brought various pieces of jewelry with them, they also were able to obtain a loan, using their jewelry as collateral, in order to purchase this property. As soon as the purchase became final they moved into their own place and began operating their own chicken farm. Kolya continued to work at the kosher place to supplement his income, but eventually he had to quit that job as Anyuta could not alone cope with the daily farm chores.

A year or so later, Sergey finished the University of Karlsruhe and was able to immigrate with his wife and now two children to the U.S. He came directly to Lakewood to join his parents. Almost immediately he found an architectural job in New York City, to which he had a daily commute. As soon as he was able to save some money, he designed his own house to be built on his parents' property. In no time, it seemed, the house was standing in front of the shack, and the family was now all together, happy and with a bright future ahead. Shortly thereafter, Sergey passed the New Jersey State board examinations for architects, and with his resume showing he had worked in New York getting his American experience, he eventually received his architect's license and was able to begin working independently, thus considerably increasing his income.

Now, whenever we all came together, as we often did, for a family gathering at either the Padukows' or the Shlykovs' farm, it was a big group. Often we talked and reminisced of the old times at Grandfather's estate in Brest. Both Misha and Kolya became very active in the Russian church. Kolya founded and taught Russian at the church's Sunday school, which became quite popular among local children as well as children coming from as far away as New York. Misha was a strong stimulus for all sorts of church and social activities. For many years both Kolya and Misha were on the church's board of directors. Because of Misha's input and hard work, there was always something going on in the Russian community. The three sisters (Mother, Sonya and Anyuta) also actively participated in the church, joining the *Sestrichestvo* (Sisterhood). One of Mother's duties was selling candles, calendars, icons, and similar items at the counter within the church during masses. She was known to be very accurate with money, so she was entrusted with the accounting responsibilities after each collection. She also was in charge of money being collected for different functions, among which in particular were collections for the priest's birthday, name-day, and family baby showers (there were five boys in the priest's family and later there were many grandchildren's showers as well). But most of all the sisters were known for their culinary talents and their willingness to work in planning, organizing, and cooking for the various parties and commemorative meals (*trapezas*), typically preparing up to a hundred pounds of fish for a given function. Misha was also responsible for initiating and organizing many patriotic events at the parish hall. There were children's performances, poetry readings, concerts, and dances. He eventually gathered enough historical material to establish a small Russian war museum.

There was no Russian person in Lakewood who could not recognize the name Mikhail Vasil'yevich Shlykov. He was a first-rate organizer. Perhaps he was good at that because, after having been in military service in his youth, his second passion became the theater and its literature. He often commented that if he were rich and did not have to worry about making money, there was nothing that would have been closer to his heart than to be an impresario. He loved to tell jokes and anecdotes and to recite poetry, for which he had an amazing memory. His repertoire was endless, and he was able to keep his audiences spellbound. One of the poems that he recited and acted out so well I can still recall vividly: *Na Cherdake* ("In the Attic"). We heard it over and over again, and were moved by it every time. Misha himself would be so moved by the story that by the time he came to the end he would have tears in his eyes. I once asked Misha to record his recitation of this poem, which he did, but in time unfortunately the tape warped and then disintegrated. I have also tried to locate a copy of this poem, but to no avail, which is such a pity.

As soon as the Shlykovs accumulated some profits from the sale of eggs and with our weekly financial contributions, they started to work on the plans of their new house. Although there was already a small foundation just in front of the shack, they thought it was too small for Misha's dream house. He showed us a picture of the house that he was eager to copy. Once we all approved the plans, the construction started. Soon more ready cash was needed, which meant more overtime for Mother and me. The plans and the actual construction labor were done by Shlykovs' next-door Russian neighbor, Mr. Maleyev. While the house was being built, the chickens did their part by supplying them with "golden" three-yolk eggs. Sonya was now getting better help from a new Russian farmhand (after the episode with the vaccination of the chickens, Anton was fired). Misha, meanwhile, in his idle moments, kept thinking of different possibilities for making extra income. He learned of various parcels of land for sale around Lakewood and Cassville. He began buying an acre here and an acre there, in each case by using a small down payment. As soon as the escrow papers were processed and his ownership was established, he would look around for a buyer, usually resulting in a quick sale with a decent profit. Some parcels he was able to subdivide, which eventually gave him considerably higher profits, as did those lots he kept longer before selling. In this way he had a second business and more income, and as a result his house construction progressed nicely. In the meantime, Mother changed jobs for better-paying ones, in order to bring more money to the "homestead."

24

Getting to Know the Radlos

So far, most of what I have been writing has been about me, my family, and my friends, but now I think I should spend a little time retelling what I had learned of my future husband and his family, to which, very soon, I was to be joined.

From the very first day of our meeting, Chester had plenty of occasions to draw a "profile" of me and my family, since, until we married, we normally met in the presence of my relatives, whereas my assessment of his upbringing, character, and the like was based on our conversations and his infrequent recollections, stories, and anecdotes about his family. Because of his reserved nature, we seldom talked, in the early period of our relationship, about his family, his childhood years, the years spent in the service and his past in general. He always seemed very modest and never boasted about his achievements or the many talents he possesses. I, being kind of shy in those days, tried not to pry for information. In spite of my bashfulness, little by little, in my own way, I managed to get to know my future husband pretty well. Even if there had been a questionable side to his character, I would not have seen it; indeed, my initial assessment of him was expressed entirely in superlatives and in time this proved to be the correct one.

Relating these few stories and tidbits about this sweetheart of mine and his family, I am only touching the tip of the iceberg. For now, I would like to mention just a few of the many splendid qualities that are so typical of Chester, such as that he has a razor-sharp intelligence (which, I think, must have helped in his intelligence work during the war and later on in the agency), he has a keen respect for knowledge and he possesses a pungent sense of humor. He is smart, talented, honest, and sensitive to others' needs, and has been a wise counselor to many. He is something of a perfectionist and is very punctual. He is a man of strong will, generous, gentle, loving and devoted to family and friends. I'm sure I have missed many other superlatives I could use to describe Chester's character.

Whenever Chester spoke of his family you could feel the warmth, fondness and the closeness he felt toward all his family members, and especially for his mother. Many times he talked of the many hardships and the frequent moves the family had to endure because of his father's search for a better livelihood. So this is what I learned about the Radlos, mostly from Chester, but also from my own conversations with family members.

A search of the Radlo genealogy reveals that in the year A.D. 980 a monk named Anastazy Radlo was the mentor of a younger monk who after his death was canonized in 999 as Saint Wojciech (Saint Adallbert), and in the 12th century was proclaimed the patron saint of Poland. Then in 1380 a Bishop Radlo was accorded lesser nobility status and awarded a grant of several villages in the area just west of Tarnow, Poland, which accounts for the fact that several towns in that area still bear versions of the Radlo name, as does the Radlo Virgin Forest (*Puszcza Radlowska*). Ellis Island records show that Chester's father Wawrzyniec, age 19, arrived in the U.S. on the ship *Rhein*. Because his birthplace, Hubenice, at that time was in the part of partitioned Poland that belonged to Austria, his birth certificate lists Austria as his country of birth.

As Polish immigrants to America at the turn of the 19th century, like so many other immigrants who came from across the Atlantic (between 1892 and 1924 there were about twenty-two million who came from Europe), once they reached New York Harbor, they still had to pass through Ellis Island. I was recently pleased to discover that Lawrence Radlo and Julia Walek are still listed on the rosters of those processed in 1887 at the island after their journey to find freedom of religion and speech, and in hope of economic advancement. Although they made the crossing on different ships, Julia and Lawrence came from neighboring places in southern Poland. The late nineteenth century in the United States was a time of rapid economic expansion and the country was desperately in need of a powerful influx of skilled and unskilled labor and the news of what to many appeared to be a golden opportunity quickly spread throughout the world, but especially in Europe, from which many of the earlier emigrants had come. In Poland, which was still in a state of partition among its three neighbors, Russia, Germany, and Austria, the promise of political and economic independence found eager listeners, especially in the rural areas, which were suffering serious hardships. Julia was motivated chiefly by the chance to improve her lot in life, in a manner similar to that achieved by relatives who had preceded her to America. Lawrence's motivations were the same, except that he had the added incentive that he was approaching the age when he would be eligible to be drafted into the Austrian army.

After processing at Ellis Island, each of them independently made their way to relatives and mutual friends in Lowell, Massachusetts, where they met. Apparently, they soon after decided to contact other relatives who had already found shelter and employment in America, and so settled down in Fulton, New York, where after a time they were married and where their first son, Leo, was born in 1906. As most immigrants with little knowledge of English, the Radlos gravitated to locations where relatives and friends had already settled prior to their own arrival and so quickly merged into the existing Polish communities. The Polish name *Radlo* translated into English means the "colter" or cutting edge of a plow. Had Chester's father desired to translate his Polish surname (he did translate his first name of *Wawrzyniec* into Lawrence), to something more English-sounding, as many immigrants were persuaded to do, the family name might then have become "Colter." Nevertheless, despite the fact that the name as it remained is a fairly simple name, it is still quite often misspelled or mispronounced into "Radlow," "Radloff," "Radio," and so on. There is no record as to what kind of employment Lawrence found in Fulton, but Julia became the housekeeper and cook for a large boardinghouse there. She was responsible for preparing meals, doing the laundry (except for tenants' laundry, which was generally taken to an outside, usually Chinese, service), and for maintaining the cleanliness of the house. It is possible that Lawrence helped her in these duties. In early 20th-century American cities, boardinghouses were quite common; they consisted of a number of individual bedrooms, two or three shared bathrooms, and a communal dining room where all the boarders ate their morning and evening meals together, except on Sundays, when the evening meal was replaced by Sunday dinner at about one or two o'clock, i.e., after church. For Julia and Lawrence the stay in Fulton was fruitful. Not only were two more sons born there after Leo, but the hardworking couple accumulated some decent savings, which enabled them to leave the harsh winters of Fulton and move closer to Julia's sister in Woonsocket, Rhode Island, where Lawrence first took up a job in a rubber factory. It was not only hard work, but the smell of rubber was so bad that his clothing and body absorbed the potent odor. He had to disrobe in the hall and immediately take a shower, while Julia promptly washed his clothes in order to get rid of the offensive smell. Fortunately, they didn't have to endure those hard living conditions for long. Soon afterwards, they opened and ran a small bakery. The business, however, failed. Once more the family moved, this time to the west side of Pawtucket, Rhode Island. On Mineral Spring Avenue, they eventually owned and managed two houses. One of them had a public billiards parlor downstairs and a rented tenement upstairs. (Chester still remembers overheard conversations involving a woman living in the upstairs tenement, who had diabetes and often complained to friends that "my blood is turning into sugar.") The Radlo family, consisting of Lawrence and Julia and their sons Leo, Edward, and Chester, occupied the downstairs tenement of the other house, where the upstairs tenement was also rented out. For some reason, their initial stay in Pawtucket did not last long because they accepted an invitation from some of Julia's relatives to move to Utica, New York, to examine the possibility of some joint business venture. Nothing came of that possibility and in about a year the Radlos, with sons Leo, Edward, and Chester, were considering returning to Rhode Island.

This is a good point to mention that Lawrence and Julia had six sons in all. Sometime between the birth of Leo in 1906 and Edward's birth in 1913, Julia and Lawrence had three other sons who died tragically, which may explain why they were very rarely mentioned by Chester's parents and why Chester does not recall their exact given names, although the names John, Stanislaw, and Martin strike a faint chord in his memory. As often happens and will continue to happen when individuals leave their native lands to find better opportunities in other places, homesickness and nostalgia for the relatives left behind is a constant companion. Julia and Lawrence were not exceptions. Ellis Island records indicate that Lawrence made three incoming arrivals from Poland, the first upon his initial emigration in 1897 plus additional arrivals from his hometown of Hubenice, Poland, in 1907 and 1921, apparently traveling alone. He made a last trip to Poland in 1929, accompanied by Eddie, but return arrivals in such cases were no longer being monitored by Ellis Island. Julia made only one return trip to her native Poland, in 1911, when she took along her four sons to meet her parents and other relatives who had remained in her hometown of Mielec. Unfortunately, she arrived when the eastern part of Poland was in the beginning throes of a serious outbreak of scarlet fever. Almost immediately all four boys became infected with, at the time, the deadly disease. Medical service in the agricultural area where the Walek family lived was rudimentary, limited mostly to the help of a *felczer*, a kind of rural, sometimes self-taught physician's assistant. In rapid fashion the boys began dying. Chester still recalls the sadness with which his mother on only a single occasion related how in a series of four weeks one of her sons died each Friday, except for the last week when the oldest of the boys showed a marked improvement that soon led to a complete recovery. Julia had left with four sons and returned to America with only Leo. In gratitude she gave the *felczer* a gold coin that she had been meaning to leave with her parents. Following that tragedy, Julia gave birth to two more sons, Edward (Eddie) in 1913 and Chester in 1916.

Not finding anything suitable to keep the family in Utica, New York, Lawrence decided to move his family back to Rhode Island. He and Julia felt a strong connection to that state: Julia's sister lived in Woonsocket with her husband and six daughters; two of her brothers, each married and with children, had settled in Pawtucket; and Lawrence's brother Anthony had settled in nearby Central Falls, as had his sister Anna. At first Lawrence and Julia rented a house on Broad Street in Central Falls, and then they purchased a two-story house on East Street in Pawtucket. Some of Chester's childhood stories date from the East Street era, when he must have been between 6 and 8 years old and used to walk by himself to and from school, which was on Middle Street. One day he left the school through the back door rather than, as usual, through the front door and because of that became disoriented, lost and increasingly anxious. A local policeman noticed the bewildered, tearful boy and led him back to his home. Although he was now safe and sound, he was completely embarrassed and can recall his chagrin to this day.

Whenever his mother and Chester would return from a walk to Central Falls, she invariably would challenge her son to race him home up the short hill that in that area separated Central Falls from Pawtucket. Eventually, he came to realize that his mother often cheated by running more slowly up the hill than he did, so that he could be declared the winner. Another memory recalls when Chester had his tonsils taken out. All went well in his hospital stay, which included the pleasure of getting ginger ale and ice cream when he came out of anesthesia, but things took a bad turn when father and son were in the vestibule of the hospital on their way out, and all of a sudden the mixture of things in his system acted up and he vomited all over the polished floor. Another incident which he still mentions occasionally, happened when he was a little older and asked his parents to let him take lessons on the violin. His father adamantly wouldn't agree to buy the youngster a musical instrument, claiming that if he would get the violin for him "it would soon be abandoned just like he gave up on the boy scouts." He was referring to the fact that shortly after Chester joined a cub scout troop, he quit after attending a couple of sessions and participating in a parade that he found tiring and embarrassing. This Boy Scout incident somehow imprinted itself on his father's mind and he often referred to it as the years went by. Later, when Chester was beginning high school, he bought a used tenor sax with his own money and taught himself to play it, but he still regrets it was not a violin. From my talks with his parents and others who knew him in those years, Chester as a young boy was without doubt a very obedient and agreeable child. In contrast to his older brothers, he apparently never got into any trouble that would deserve stern punishment. I would describe him as being a born diplomat. He tried to help his mother with her house chores, which sometimes even included ironing the many men's handkerchiefs. As a child, like I, Chester had to wear clothes that he didn't like, in particular sailor suits, tie-up shoes, and knickers, but without much fuss—whatever his mother made him wear, he wore.

Throughout the years Chester and Eddie, only three years apart in age, were quite close; Leo was somewhat of a loner and stayed a bachelor for life. Despite the fact that Eddie was two years ahead of his younger brother when they both attended the same junior high, for some reason they shared one class together, which was Latin. Whenever the teacher posed a question and called for "Radlo" to answer, Eddie, who sat behind his brother, invariably gave him a poke, prompting Chester to volunteer to answer. After a while the teacher guessed what was going on and one day said, "When I say Radlo, I mean Eddie Radlo not Chester Radlo!" From then on Eddie had to study more and whenever the teacher called "Radlo," it was Eddie who had to answer. From the early years Chester showed an unusual capacity for learning, which was enhanced by the gift of an excellent memory. I have always been amazed by his ability to remember telephone numbers. Whenever someone gives him a telephone number, he repeats it once to verify its accuracy and then, without writing it down, will remember it for as long as it is currently needed and sometimes for long after. Due to his ability to remember things, he didn't need much time, if any, for studying. Absorbing knowledge of any kind came very easily to him, but at the same time, he tended to take his talents for granted. At Pawtucket Jr. High (sixth, seventh and eighth grades, which he attended between 1927 and 1930) and then at Pawtucket High School (1930–34) he was a straight A student, but at Brown University, because of his many outside activities, he had occasional problems keeping his grades up, especially in math, which requires a lot of attention. He frequently found many distractions. For instance, when his parents became the owners of the Diamond Hill Café in Valley Falls, Rhode Island, Chester, together with his musician friends, would play there, as well as at many weddings and different functions, until the wee hours, leaving him too exhausted to hit the books. Sometimes he would have to review his lessons on the way to his classes at Brown or make a quick study of some reference books at the library, where he would take a catnap, with his head resting on a stack of books.

While still at Brown, during the summer months in 1937, Chester together with the college dance band, traveled on a Cunard liner to Europe. In exchange for playing in the tourist and second class lounges, they earned free fare and three-man cabins in tourist class. (One of the regular members of the band was Howard Hunt of Watergate fame, who played a really good trumpet, but he missed this trip for personal reasons.) When the ship docked at Le Havre, the orchestra members had three weeks ashore to visit Paris and whatever else they wished to see until the ship sailed again from Southampton. Of course, I didn't get to hear all the details of what sights they saw in Paris, but in instances like this a woman's imagination comes in handy—after all, it is known that boys will be boys. I'm sure that, despite being on a very tight budget, they had a memorable time. On the ship the most frequently requested tune the orchestra had to play was Cole Porter's "Night and Day," but in the Rhode Island clubs the one song always asked for was "Stardust." Many years later, while on assignment in Germany, Chester was surprised to learn that a colleague at work and also a Brown graduate, Gene Burgstoller, was the sax player who replaced Chester in the dance band after Chester graduated. Gene graduated from Brown a year after Chester.

In 1938 the college dance band traveled on another cruise ship, this time to Bermuda. Their fare again was free, but this time the accommodations were better; they each got a single cabin. Once on land, the boys decided to go for a whole day's bicycle tour of the island. It must have been a remarkable outing for Chester, as he had never ridden a bike before. Once he learned to keep his balance and in order not to lose it, he held onto the handlebar so intensely that when the group returned to the ship in time to play for the after-dinner dance, his hands shook so badly that he couldn't hold a cup of coffee without spilling it. I believe this was his first and last bicycle ride, except that now he gets his daily exercise riding a stationary bike. The ride doesn't get him any-where and may be boring, but it's so much safer. Speaking of music-making, when teenager Judy Garland visited Rhode Island to sing at a country club in Cranston (it must have been a year before or after she made the movie *The Wizard of Oz*), the orchestra in which Chester was the tenor sax player played backup for her. The governor of Rhode Island proclaimed the day of her visit to the state "Judy Garland Day."

I was surprised when I heard that Chester had yet another talent in addi-tion to playing the sax; he was also drawn toward the theater. While he was still a student in Pawtucket and Providence he acted out different roles in Pol-ish plays in Polish, which were staged at the Pulaski Hall in Central Falls. In one of these plays, he was to portray a very angry man. He got so carried away with being an angry man that he threw a loaf of bread across the room. After the play, this incident was sternly criticized by many of the older spectators, who said it was sinful to mistreat food. On another occasion he played in a German play (*Das Konzert* by Georg Kaiser) presented by the German Club at Brown University. He played one of the leading characters, but since his mastery of spoken German was still rudimentary, he thinks it must have been painful for the spectators to listen to him.

During the 1939 world's fair in New York City, Chester had another less than perfect experience. He had responded to an ad for guides at the Polish pavilion and was invited to an interview to assess his knowledge of the Pol-ish language. During the conversation, when Chester was asked where he was born, he chose the wrong expression for "I was born" (*Ja sie urodzilem*); instead, he used an expression for "was born" that is normally only used when speak-ing of Jesus Christ (*On sie narodzil*). He didn't get the job. He laughs about it now, but he must have been disappointed. Since then his Polish has become quite fluent, astonishing many when they learn he is not a native of Poland.

Another incident that comes to mind from this period was when Chester, together with friends visiting from Rhode Island, Peter Kielbasa and Walter Legawiec, went one day to Harlem to hear Father Divine, at the time a famous black spiritual leader. At one point Father Divine or one of his lieutenants asked the three white boys to sit on the stage during the preaching. And so, the only white boys in the hall just sat there and listened to Father Divine's preaching for two long hours.

During World War II all three Radlo sons were deployed to different army units. Leo as a recruit to Texas, Eddie as a captain in the medical corps to Australia and New Guinea, and Chester as an infantry lieutenant to Europe. Needless to say, with their three sons in uniform, those few years were very trying times for the parents. Nevertheless, their sons' patriotism and partici-pation in the war made the parents extremely proud. All three of them were very conscientious about keeping in touch with their parents, writing letters or postcards to keep them posted and to let them know that all is well and that their parents are always being thought of. It must have been a most happy time when all three sons returned unharmed to their worried parents.

At Fort Benning, Georgia, in January 1943, after he was commissioned a 2nd Lt., Infantry, Chester received an assignment as a platoon commander in an infantry division that was forming in North Carolina, prior to being sent into combat in the Pacific theater of operations. The day before he was expecting to leave Georgia on a two-weeks' leave, following which he would go directly to the new infantry division, Chester was called into the headquarters building at Benning where he was informed that, due to his knowledge of languages, his assignment was being changed. Following his home leave, he would report to the censorship school at Fort Washington, Maryland. After completing the course in censorship, working primarily on communications in Polish, he was next assigned to a course in technical intelligence at Fort Ritchie, Maryland, which is next door to the present-day presidential retreat Camp David. He completed the six-month course with the classification of order-of-battle specialist, namely, an individual who concentrates on establishing the organization and equipment of opposing forces and, in particular, the identities and biographies of opposing commanders. After a brief tour of duty at the newly constructed Pentagon, Chester sailed for London in October 1943 on the Queen Mary, which was outfitted as a troop ship and, along with a couple more ships, was escorted by a squadron of submarines. He shared a four-bunk cabin with three war correspondents.

In London, where he was assigned to the intelligence section of General Omar Bradley's headquarters (at the time, Bradley commanded U.S. troops in the European theater; he later became the commanding general of the 12th U.S. Army Group), Chester was billeted, along with Lt. Don Levine, in a private home in Ladbroke Grove. The billet lasted only a few weeks, but it was sufficient time for Chester to get to know one of the hostess' family friends, Molly Sales, who was willing to show Chester the sights of London during his time away from work. Since the invasion of Normandy was several months in the future, Chester and Molly had plenty of time to get to know each other. In London, Chester worked mainly on collecting intelligence on the fortifications the Nazis were building along the coast of Normandy, such as hedgehogs, underwater tank obstacles, and concrete emplacements.

When he finally crossed over to France in June 1944, he worked on collecting information on enemy fuel depots, ammo dumps, and transportation junctions, pinpointing targets for tactical air forces supporting the ground troops. Much of the work involved debriefing agents, partisans, prisoners, and downed allied airmen who had escaped capture. He remained on the European mainland until December 1944, when he was assigned to a disarmament course in London, in anticipation of an early end to the war. While attending the course Chester proposed to Molly and, with General Eisenhower's permission no less, they were married in St. Mary's parish church in Hendon on December 19, 1944. On October 1, 1945, Nicholas John Lawrence Radlo came into the world and automatically became a citizen of both the United States and the United Kingdom. Later on, after he had graduated from college, Nicholas' dual citizenship gave him the idea that an ideal work arrangement for him would be to have a job that found him in the States for half the year and in the UK for the other half. He hasn't quite achieved that yet, but as a freelance journalist writing on TV and video technology, he comes to the U.S. at least once a year and sometimes more often.

Inasmuch as Chester wanted to remain in military service after the war, through a contact made at the course in London he arranged to get a transfer to the Air Division of the U.S. Forces Component for the Occupation of Austria, commanded by General Mark Clark. Chester had first to return to Bradley's headquarters, which was now in Luxemburg, where it was the unsuccessful target of the Nazis' *Vergeltungswaffe* (Revenge Weapon), known as the V-2 rocket. In London in early June, Chester had experienced the other Revenge Weapon, the V-1, known as the Flying Bomb. The V-1 was launched like a missile, but once it was aloft it was propelled by its own engine, flying horizontally, like an airplane. It flew at a very low altitude and as it passed overhead the strong putt-putt of the engine could be distinctly heard on the ground. Londoners became very alert to the sound of the V-1, being especially anxious to catch the moment when the engine's fuel supply ran out and the sound of the engine stopped. The V-1, loaded with explosives, would immediately fall to earth, causing a sizeable explosion. Chester at this time had just returned from a temporary duty assignment at Gen. Montgomery's headquarters in Portsmouth and was living in a studio apartment in Chelsea, awaiting an eventual transfer to France. Standing by an open window, he listened to the sound of a V-1 overhead, when suddenly the sound stopped. Knowing he had but a few seconds before an explosion, he quickly jumped behind a couch and an instant later heard a very loud crash nearby, accompanied by the shattering of his windows, which was the only damage incurred at his apartment. A building across the street, however, sustained major damage to its roof and walls. The V-2, being a true missile, gave no such warning. It simply dropped suddenly from a clear sky at the speed of a bullet and caused much more damage than the Flying Bomb.

Once his assignment to General Clark's command came through, Chester was pleased to learn that he was being assigned as the liaison officer in London to the British Air Ministry. A captain at the time, Chester was part of a two-man team headed by Colonel Ted Enter. When the war in Europe ended in May 1945, Colonel Enter opted to leave active duty and returned to the U.S. Soon thereafter, the London office was closed and Chester transferred to the main headquarters in Vienna; Molly was allowed to join him there, Nicholas remaining in London in the care of his grandparents.

While on home leave in Rhode Island, Chester suffered an eye infection that eventually landed him in a Pennsylvania hospital for a year until the inflammation finally subsided. Chester returned to duty, which included a year's intensive study of Russian in Monterey, to be followed by a tour of duty at West Point, teaching Russian. Leaving Nicholas in the care of his grandmother, Molly made several trips to the States during Chester's hospitalization and his tour of duty in Monterey, but each time the stay became shorter than the previous one and it became clear that Molly did not like living in the U.S. She and Chester separated in early 1949 and a while later were officially divorced.

Not having been granted custody of Nicholas, Chester and Nicholas rekindled father-son relations during a couple of visits that took place in London. But once we were settled for our tour of duty in Frankfurt, Germany, Nicholas was permitted to visit us there during his days off from school. The first visit was followed by another and then another and finally a trip was arranged for Nicholas to come for his first visit to the States, while we were there on home leave between tours of duty in Germany. During this trip he not only had a long overdue meeting with his paternal grandmother, but he also met quite a few of his Polish-American relatives, as well as my Russian relatives. By this time he also had a warm relation with my mother, who became *Babcia* to him. He must have been full of apprehensions and inner anxieties to have to face so many unknown relatives, but I'm sure, once the ice was broken, his stay in Rhode Island and New Jersey was full of new, some perhaps strange experiences, which in any case left him with plenty to write home about. If asked today, I'm sure the first thing to come to his mind about his first U.S. trip would be, "There were lots and lots of good, hearty Polish and Russian food!" I always chuckled when Nicholas, while driving around in the U.S., would spot a foreign car, especially a British one, and invariably exclaim, "Look, look, there goes a *British* car!"

Previously I described how, on the 4th of July weekend of 1949, Chester and I met at the Russian resort in Cassville, where he had come to perfect his spoken Russian and how, after he had begun his teaching duties at the military academy, he would make frequent trips to visit me and Mother in New York, and occasionally would drive down to Lakewood, New Jersey, when he knew we were there visiting my uncle and aunt on their chicken farm. On one such trip to Lakewood he asked for and received Mother's blessing that we marry. Once that important decision was made, it seemed like high time we all took a trip to Rhode Island to meet Chester's family. On Mother's advice we picked the Christmas holiday as an appropriate time for the future bride and mother-in-law to be introduced to the Radlos.

Needless to say, despite Chester's repeated assurances that "my parents will just love you," I was panic-stricken. Prior to the trip, we went to look for different Christmas gifts and I learned how hard it is to look for a gift for someone that you don't know. By the time we were finished with the shopping we were exhausted and almost broke! Chester, who is not much of a shopper, got two poinsettia plants and was happy with his quick choice. Our gifts, some small and others large, numbered at least eight (one for every member of the family). And so, we were off to Rhode Island, I to be presented for approval, so to speak, by my future parents-in-law. Once the formal introduction (in Polish) took place, from that moment on we were received and treated royally, and indeed, Chester was right, his parents seemed to like me from the very beginning. We first had a traditional Polish Christmas Eve at the parents' house and Christmas Day we spent at Eddie and Sue's house, where after dinner everybody ended up in the rec room for singing carols and dancing. I was a hit dancing with little Eddie, who at that time must have been about five years old, to the endless tune of "Rudolf the Red Nose Reindeer." Later on, I found out that no sooner had Chester's parents met Mother, they right away thought that instead of one wedding it might be nice to have still another. They had in mind that Mother, being the same age as Leo, would have been a perfect match for their oldest son. Nothing came of this matchmaking, however, since Mother had no intention of remarrying and Leo was happy being what he was, a typical bachelor, with a lifelong girlfriend who conveniently lived across the street from his parents' house. Leo at that time, while working at the café, lived with his parents, occupying the upstairs of their house. What is that saying about having one's cake and eating it, too?

The two-story Radlo house, surrounded with many deciduous trees, shrubs, and lilac bushes, was situated on a large, level mound that was slightly higher than the other buildings (café, garage, chicken coops, and garden huts) that were located on their property of several acres. One couldn't see any neighbors, except those that lived across the road (including Leo's girlfriend Emma, her mother, Emma's daughter, and later a granddaughter, all of whom lived in separate houses). Beside the Radlo house there were several tall pine trees and a flag pole on which Chester's dad would fly the American flag once or twice a year. At one point the flag pole needed to be painted and Leo volunteered to do the job, but while he was up on the ladder, which was being held by his father, his father's grip faltered when he was distracted by passing traffic. Leo fell off the ladder, breaking his leg. Mother gave Father a good talking to for being so careless, but eventually Leo's leg break healed and all was forgotten.

Next to the front of the house there were several beautiful, huge plants, which Mother always referred to as "snowball" plants (hydrangeas). To the side of the house there were steps leading down to the driveway that separated the residence from the café. There was ample parking space in the back and on the other side of the café. One entered the house through an enclosed glass porch, which was used for relaxation, street watching, and observation of those arriving or leaving the café. There were two reclining chairs, a wicker sofa used

Visiting my fiancé's parents in Valley Falls, Rhode Island. From left, me, Lawrence Radlo, Julia Radlo, Elizabeth Kucharska, 1951.

by Chester's mother for her afternoon naps, and lots of potted plants. A long window extended along the whole wall separating the porch from the small living room, which was of the same length, but a little wider than the porch. This room was the primary setting for day-to-day living, but because it was rather narrow, it didn't have much room for furniture, which consisted of a day bed/couch, a reclining chair beside which there was a table full of reference materials (dictionary, Almanac, calendar, picture albums), two smaller tables, and a television. Next to that room, behind double glass doors, there was a formal parlor, a sizeable, well-kept room with plush furniture (which eventually was given to us, but of which at present only two often-reupholstered chairs remain) and several large potted plants. This room was used primarily during the holidays or to entertain larger groups of people. Backing up to the parlor, at the rear side of the house was his father's bedroom, then his mother's bedroom, which was small, but large enough to accommodate an old-fashioned sewing machine with a foot treadle, on which I later learned (more or less) how to sew. Adjacent to Mother's bedroom was the dining room, from which a door on one side opened to the living room and an opening on the other led to the kitchen. A door at the far end of the dining room opened to a full bathroom, which always seemed to be the warmest place in the whole house. The kitchen, by today's standards, was tiny, but large enough to accommodate a large old-fashioned gas oven, which eventually was updated, and a small table. Off the kitchen there was a little pantry and steps leading to the outside, where there was a vegetable garden and a toolshed. The upstairs had several rooms with another full bath. The upstairs would have been suitable as an independent apartment, but in this case, with the exception of one large room, which was designated for winter/summer storage, the upstairs space housed Leo, and us whenever we came for a visit. The house was heated by a very efficient heating system. Originally, the furnace used coal but after a number of years the furnace was replaced by one that used oil, but the hot water radiators throughout the house remained. Sometime after Chester's father's passing, during the change of the furnace, his mother found a note written by him in Polish: *Szukaj az znajdziesz*, which translates as "Look for it, until you find it." She looked and searched, but whatever father might have hidden there, if anything, she never found "it." During the summer, the upstairs part of the house was hot, whereas in the winter it was sometimes freezing cold. After spending a very cold, but, as Leo insisted, "healthy" night, we always rushed down to bathe, dress, warm up and have a great breakfast. All in all, although the house was an old-fashioned one, at the same time, it was very cozy and the downstairs part was always toasty warm.

Between the first visit and our wedding, several trips to Rhode Island took place and each was nicer and more interesting than the previous one. In no time, I felt welcomed and at home. In addition to being able to spend time in a very warm home atmosphere, I also liked taking those trips because it enabled me to get away from the office and our cramped living quarters in the city. We often took country roads, instead of using the Connecticut and New York turnpikes, which gave me a chance to see different rural areas and quaint little New England towns. (My father-in-law, speaking of trips via the two turnpikes would say, "You don't get to see anything, just a lot of bushes.") Going east we stopped at different places to get a bite to eat or to stretch our legs. Our favorite eating places were the roadside diners that had both booths and counter seating. These were clean and simple in decor and the food was inexpensive, but wholesome. In those days I couldn't get my fill of Boston cream pies and Howard Johnson's hotdogs! On our trips back to New York, there was never a need to look for a restaurant. Chester's mom invariably packed us a picnic lunch full of surprises that would last us through the trip and would still leave enough leftovers for several days to come. Just before our departure, she would send Leo to town to buy our favorite pastries, bread and cookies, such as poppy seed or prune-butter filled strudels, *babkas*, cheesecakes, rye and dark breads and meltaways, which were cupcakes that truly melted in one's mouth! Those Leo usually bought at the famous Korb Bakery in Providence or the August Bakery in Central Falls. (Mentioning meltaways reminds me of a story of many moons ago, when Ed, prior to a trip west to see his son Eddie, bought for us a box full of Korb's meltaways. To keep their freshness, until he was ready to come south to visit us in Santa Barbara, he kept them in Eddie's refrigerator. He left Palo Alto and somehow forgot the meltaways, leaving them behind. We were disappointed and Ed was mad at himself—but his son had a feast!) Chester's mom always reminded Leo to stop at a Polish butcher shop for some kielbasas and different homemade cold cuts. Although in those days New York City had everything under the sun that one could imagine, including many favorites things from Barton's candy stores and from Babka bakery, including their delicious babkas, poppy seed cake and other European specialties, one couldn't beat some Rhode Island goodies.

Winter trips to New England were especially charming. The countryside, every inch of which would be covered with thick, white, glittering snow, looked gorgeous. While the snow was falling, the motionless trees stood in an unbelievable, absolute silence. The many tall pine trees, with their ample broad branches bent by the weight of the thick, freshly fallen snow, resembled a page from a fairy tale book. Despite the extraordinary beauty, now and then the trips were somewhat dangerous. On one such a trip (it may have been during the trip just before Christmas) just a couple of miles from Chester's house, we gently slipped off the road and ended up in a ditch. I say gently, because at that point we were only able to drive at a crawling rate of speed, we could barely clear the windshield of the fast accumulating snow, and visibility was near zero. We had to be pulled out of the ditch, and I don't recall who helped, but most likely it was a family friend from a nearby gas station. We then proceeded very carefully to Valley Falls, with our car full of poinsettias, presents, and baggage.

Our most enjoyable trips to New England, however, were in the fall, in the middle of Indian summer; when driving through this enchanting part of America one can easily get intoxicated by the endless, flaming beauty of the autumn leaves. There is such splendor in the trees, full of the brilliance of the dying leaves as they turn into the most glorious fall colors. Their branches, occasionally moved by a gentle breeze playing between them, together with the soft sunlight created shimmering shadows on the ground. The sight of those beautiful leaves dropping to the earth always filled me with a certain sense of sadness. New England's dazzling autumn spectacle is an experience never to be forgotten and I'm afraid that the nostalgia for those good old days will always be with me.

During each visit, even when short in duration and despite Chester's father's heart ailment, we always had a real fun time together. Chester's dad may not have been as frisky as in years before, when he was known as a jolly good fellow who could dance, sing, and have a few drinks; nevertheless, on our visits, he seemed to be full of life and peppy again. He liked to joke, turn sayings into jingles, and occasionally would sing a song. He even would agree to have a drink with us. (I don't remember what his favorite drink was, but Chester and his mother liked blackberry brandy, Mother preferred a highball and my drink was Rock and Rye, which, by the way, was introduced to me by my fiancé.) While Chester's father liked to entertain us, Chester's mom did what she could to keep our stomachs happy. And did she ever! Starting with a hardy breakfast, followed by a tasty lunch and then a delicious Polish-style dinner! No sooner would we settle in the living room after consuming a full evening meal, she would insist we go for a ride to a local creamery for a cabinet (a Rhode Island-style milkshake) or a similar dessert. During those or any restaurant outings, invariably there was the secret transfer of a wallet under the table. His mother insisted that Chester should pay the bill, but with money she provided. Chester's parents, especially his father, would tell us stories, not so much of the extended family, but things in general. One thing he liked to explain was how much he and Julia were proud of Chester and Eddie's careers, bragging how smart they were, how Chester helped by playing at the café in the orchestra, and how Eddie and Sue always helped out at the café during the busy days, sacrificing their free time. Unfortunately, Leo and his input into the café business was rarely mentioned or praised and I think his father generally took him for granted. The somewhat strained relations between father and son apparently dated to a time when Leo wanted to switch from high school to attend a business school, but his father would not agree. As a result, Leo failed to get a college education as did Chester and Eddie. Mother Radlo, however, had a high regard for Leo and his devotion to the family business and she would often be moved to tears when speaking of him.

The story about Eddie's decision to go into medicine and later changing his mind was described by the parents with lots of humor and laughter, as they told about an incident that took place after his mother had cut her finger while trying to decapitate a live chicken with an ax. The wound was so deep and bled so profusely that Eddie had to rush her to a nearby hospital's emergency room, where her dangling finger had to be reattached and stitched. Apparently, during the emergency treatment, the sight of the free-flowing blood gushing from his mother's finger was too much for poor Eddie to endure. He gradually became light-headed and for a moment fainted when the doctor was stitching up the wounded finger. His parents thought this incident was decisive in making Eddie switch careers from medicine to dentistry, but Chester thinks it was Eddie's difficulties handling the heavy medical curriculum at Tufts University in Boston along with commuting back to Diamond Hill. Chester's future, on the other hand, was planned by his mother, but her dream, fortunately for me, didn't materialize. She said, "With his smooth, white hands, soft spoken voice, and good manners he would make an ideal priest." But priesthood was the farthest thing from Chester's heart, no doubt to his mother's disappointment. He was more inclined toward an academic life, working in linguistics and German literature. Later on, already as Chester's wife, I found out that in the past, BL, Before Lucy, the whole family had another disappointment concerning Chester, namely, that he missed out on a good and lucrative marriage to Isabella, a Polish girl from Central Falls whose father owned the best kielbasa factory in Rhode Island. Her father thought Chester would be a good match for his daughter, who apparently also thought well of my future husband, but Chester insists he never seriously considered the idea. I wonder if Isabella ever learned that Chester and his pals always referred to her as the Kielbasa Queen! Life is full of might-have-been, but I'm glad that Chester turned down both of these golden opportunities, becoming a priest or the husband of the Kielbasa Queen. (Would that have made him the Kielbasa King?!)

In the early days of the Diamond Hill Café, when the business was booming, the Radlos featured free spaghetti Friday nights and clam bake dinners on Saturdays. Beer then was 10 cents for an eight-ounce glass, and then it was 10 cents per six-ounce glass and eventually went up to 25 cents. Because of the popularity and good business of the café, the workload was heavy. In addition to a couple of waitresses (one of them was Leo's girlfriend Emma), all members of the family had to pitch in, especially on the weekends, including Sue and Eddie serving and tending bar, and Chester playing in the orchestra once or twice a month. Sometimes Walter Legawiec would play the piano, Walter Moskwa the violin and trumpet, somebody else on drums and occasionally an accordionist would join them as well. All of the players were school buddies. At that time Eddie no longer played the trombone, so didn't participate in the orchestra. During those years Eddie attended the University of Rhode Island as a premed major. After graduating in 1934, he enrolled in the MD program at Tufts University, but later switched to dentistry. For his Rhode Island state license exam he asked Chester, who needed a tooth filling, to be his patient, warning him "not to show pain even if it should hurt." At that time the drill was activated by a foot pedal. The test went well, Chester survived the treatment, and in 1938 Eddie became a full fledged dentist. Ed and Sue married in 1941. Eddie practiced dentistry on weekdays, while Sue helped as his secretary/bookkeeper, but on weekends they were busy helping out at the café. Many years later, whenever the subject of "working in the café" came up, Sue never failed to recall that Chester was the one who put in the least time and effort into the family business, because of his frequent gigs playing with the Cameo Orchestra.

Chester remembers perhaps the only robbery incident that took place at the café. While at the house, Pa heard some noises and commotion coming from the café. He went to investigate and Chester followed him. When Pa came to the eating section of the Café he encountered a robber, who had entered through a window to steal beer. (Outside the window he had already placed one case of beer a few minutes before.) To Chester's surprise, in a second, Pa literally grabbed and picked up the robber and threw him out into the parking area.

In the '30s and '40s, there was an old-fashioned gasoline tank out front of the café. In those days, one had to pump gas in two steps, first into a transparent container and then into the customer's tank. Pa was never very happy if he saw a customer waiting at the gas pump, as he had to leave customers at the bar or in the back, get out and do the awkward pumping. The worst was when the customer would say, "Could you check the water and oil?" It made him furious. In those days the attendants usually not only pumped the gas, but checked water and oil as well—and of course, washed the windshields. I'm sure after pumping gas, checking water and oil, Pa's service was done—*fait accompli!*

Later on, when the business had dwindled down to mostly just the bar service, the hours at the café were long and boring and shared by just the three of them, Ma and Pa Radlo and Leo. The schedule usually would go somewhat like this: Father would open the business, sweep around (in and out), and replenish empty bottles with liquor and beer. Then he would open a new cask of beer and prepare the cash register to be ready for the first customer to come by. Usually, the first thirsty soul to show up would be Dupre, their freeloader tenant, who lived with his friend Jake in the woods in the back of the property in a one-room shack with a dirt floor, see-through walls, and a wood-burning stove. Even during severe winter nights they were never cold, because it seems they were kept warm with plenty of internal liquid fuel. When walking to the café, on a narrow footpath worn smooth by many years of daily trekking for the replenishment of their empty beer bottles, Dupre, who had a soft heart for Chester's mother, spotting her at the kitchen window, would greet her warmly with a friendly smile and shout out, "Hello, Ma, how are things today?" (The old-timers referred to her as Ma and Lawrence as Pa.) She, in return, very often, would call him to come and get a dish full of food. He and Jake were allowed to live on the property without cost, so they occasionally helped out doing this or that, but mostly their value to the Radlos was as a kind of extra security for the property. Despite the fact that the property was large, most of the upkeep and gardening was done by Leo, which included clipping the hedges and shrubberies and once in a while sitting on a tractor mower and having a fun ride over the grass lawns. Planting and harvesting of the vegetable garden was mostly Ma's job, while Pa tended to the care of the rabbits and chickens. In the wintertime the county snowplow helped

Leo clear snow away from the driveway and the parking lot, but cleaning the walks and steps around the house was Leo's task. The small vegetable garden, which Chester's mother tended, was right off the kitchen steps and extended to the toolshed. The garden had a variety of vegetables, but mostly essentials she needed day-to-day for her specialty dishes. In addition to early customers like Dupre and Jack, in general most of the customers were tradespeople who traveled between different jobs, stopping for a drink at lunchtime or for a social happy hour at the end of the day. If they were short of cash, they would leave something as collateral, which may have been an electrical gadget, a hammer, a shovel and the like. And this is why Chester's parents ended up with all sorts of things that customers never bothered to come back for. The shed came to look like a messy pawn shop full of junk, which now would be considered treasured antiques.

His father's usual tour of duty in the café lasted, most of the time, until early lunch. While he was working, his mother would prepare lunch for him and for Leo, if he was around and not on an errand or visiting somewhere. Then his mother would walk across the driveway to the café, leaving her husband's lunch on the kitchen table, which was facing the vegetable garden. At this point I might add that Chester's father, although he had available free dental care from his son Eddie, the dentist, almost never had the need to take advantage of that care. His teeth, as he put it, were "as strong as a horse's teeth." His perfect set of teeth (until his death, not even one cavity!) may very well have been attributable to the fact that he liked to chew on very stale, hard-as-a-rock bread; he would sometimes need a heavy knife and a hammer to cut it! Despite his love of hard bread, his wife often served him regular, fresh rye bread. Every time he reached for it, he would get annoyed and often would say, "After all these years of being married to me, she never has learned to cut the loaf through!" (I still have the small remembrance that, indeed, Chester's mother never did cut the loaf of bread all the way through, thus one had to rip the slices off.) Other than this small annoyance, Chester's father was very well fed and pleased with the cuisine he was getting from his very caring "Julcia." As much as he liked the income, he hated the responsibilities that went with running the business. He never had the patience that his wife had. Having to listen to the long, repetitious stories of the tipsy, sometimes drunk customers could drive him up the wall. Often, if not always, it irked him the most when someone happened to order a hotdog. (In the beginning they served specials, like spaghetti and meatballs, free (!), but as the years went by, the only food customers could have were hotdogs, ham sandwiches, pickled eggs and green tomatoes, and cucumber pickles.) Being annoyed, sometimes in haste, he would end up dropping the hotdog on its way to the pot with hot water or if the hotdog accidentally slipped out of the bun, he would tell us with a chuckle, "In those instances, I quickly retrieved the dog from the floor, put it in the hot water for a quick rinse and then back into the bun." Despite several negative aspects of the business, he would admit that the work was reasonably easy (compared with his first job in America, at the rubber tire factory) and the profit was quite attractive. After lunch, Lawrence would take a nap, watch some television, and wait for Julia to come and keep him company.

Most customers enjoyed their visits to the café, especially when Julia was in charge. They had more laughter and fun with her, they could spill out all their troubles, ask for advice, and more than anything else they enjoyed playing cards with her. She was a fast thinker, an eager card player, but she was also not above cheating, without actually harming anyone, since they never played for money, but just for fun. With their faculties somewhat dulled by the beer and alcohol, most of her opponents thought that she was the smartest of players and hard to beat! And whenever the three of us were playing gin rummy, if Julia noticed that Chester could use a special card in order to complete his suit, she would first peek into his hand to assess his situation and then offer him the needed card by passing it to him under the table. I pretended that I didn't notice this innocent cheating and later Chester and I had a good laugh. It was usually after lunchtime, with Julia running the business, that the monks from the Cistercian monastery, adjacent to the Radlo property, came to the back wall to buy beer. Although these monks were not allowed to speak or communicate with the outside world, nevertheless, they had a way of communicating with Julia through the opening in the wall behind the café's parking lot, through which she would pass over bottles of beer for them.

After Julia's turn, it was Leo's turn to mind the family business. Usually after breakfast he would go into town, visit with friends, have lunch, and come back in time to relieve whichever of his parents was on duty. Once at his post, he would stay there until closing time. He was liked by the frequent customers more than his father, but not liked as much as was his mother. Ma had a certain flair for making customers feel at home and that she understood their needs. They simply adored her! At closing time, Leo would lock up the café and turn the day's cash over to father, at which point Lawrence would proceed to his little secretary desk, which was in the dining room, count the money, and make a note in a journal of all the day's receipts, payment, and profits. Then the three of them would gather at the dining table for a simple evening meal, after which Ma and Pa, often joined by Leo, would settle down to watch the news on TV, followed by some favorite program. Whenever a commercial for the really cheap Virginia Dare wine came on, Pa promptly would repeat the famous jingle "Virginia Dare, you can't compare!" and chuckle afterwards. Pa liked to make wisecracks in the style of Bob Hope. To Julia's invariable embarrassment, one of his favorite replies to someone's question "Where did you and Julia go on your honeymoon?" was, "Upstairs, room six!" Ma loved the Milton Berle program, although she never got his name right, usually calling him "Marton Burke." Lawrence's favorite leisure-time activity, other than TV, was paging through the Almanac. He was fascinated with the different topics covered in the book and he was able to memorize numerous facts that he later recounted in daily discussions.

Once a week, on Wednesdays, since that was Eddie's day off from his practice, after the family shopping and other chores scheduled for that day were out of the way, Eddie, Sue, and their children Marian and little Eddie would come by for an afternoon visit. On those days, Julia always had a lunch of favorite Polish specialties ready for them. If she decided this would be a *pierogi* day, even though she was always an early riser, this day would find her at the crack of dawn preparing her specialties. She had to start early since she knew appetites would be great and each of the visitors had a different favorite. Little Eddie liked *pierogis* filled with prune butter, Sue preferred them with cabbage, and Marion, if I remember correctly, hoped the dumplings would have a sweet cheese filling that goes so well with a garnish of sour cream. Ed was not particular, he just loved and devoured all of them! Sometimes there were *golabki* (cabbage rolls), which they ate with gusto and also took home with them for the next day's lunch or dinner. Julia not only treated them with Polish favorites, but with things like lasagna or spaghetti and meatballs that were part of her repertoire as well. All in all she was an excellent cook. I secretly envied Ed and his family for the fact that, in addition to the various holiday dinners when the whole family would gather, every Wednesday meant a family luncheon and a real feast, that's for sure!

Chester's maternal grandparents, Wojciech and Marija Walek, had seven children: Julia, Zofia, Stefania, Michal, Ignacy, John and Antoni. His paternal grandparents, Franciszek and Katarzyna Radlo had nine children: Wawrzyniec (known in the U.S. as Lawrence), Marcin, Antoni, Teresa, Maria, Julia, Agata, Walenty and Anna. Julia and Lawrence had many close as well as distant relatives in and about Rhode Island. At first, there were many family gatherings, reunions and simple drop-in visits, but as each nucleus of the Radlo/Walek family grew larger with years, the gatherings tended to consist mostly of immediate family, rather than extended family relatives. A few close relatives that come to mind who played a significant role in Chester's life (and later in my life as well) were Uncle Anthony (Tony) and Aunt Victoria (*Stryjenka, Stryjencia* and also called *Viktusia*) Radlo and their four children: Bridget (Bertha) and her daughter Mary Jane, Adam, Genevieve (known as "Jennie") and her children Claudia, Dennis and Betty, and Robert (Bobby); and Aunt Anna Haczynska and her daughter Angie. There were several brothers and sisters on Julia's side and their children who often exchanged visits with the Radlos, namely, Uncle Michael and his children Joseph (Joe), Francis (Frank), Raymond (Ray), Mary, Valerie and Genevieve Walek, as well as the Zajac sisters—Michaline, Wanda, Mary, Josephine, Celia, and Stella. I must add, that without exception, every member of both sides of the family, as soon as they met me, readily adopted me as one of their own. Perhaps they were pleased that I spoke their language and could relate to their culture, but no matter what played its role in our warm relations, it left me a winner. Most relatives, once they moved to Rhode Island, settled there for life. Since we moved around quite a bit, it was we who did the visiting, at which time we would hop from house to house to say hello. Thus, every trip to Chester's hometown was filled to the brim with all sorts of reunions. Despite the fact that the few days we spent were quite hectic, a trip to Rhode Island always left us full of wonderful, warm memories.

25

Elizabeth Kucharska, My Mother

As memories float back in later years, it seems that only our version comes into view. Someone else may remember the same event—the history of one's life or a simple story of the past—but in a different way. In this case, my recollections of the past and my mother's recollections are matching up quite closely. Of course, this doesn't mean she would agree with me (or would people that know her well) about how I will try to portray her and primarily describe her character. If one were to analyze why and how men were so prominent in her life, one could associate it with the fact that due to the loss of her mother at the very young age of three, her father solely was responsible for caring for his often sickly daughter and for her upbringing. He wouldn't leave any stone unturned to give her everything, anything she desired. She not only was the apple of her father's eye, but she was her older brothers' favorite as well. While attending school, being frail, it was the boys who showered her with kindness and help if needed. From her early days, she was treated like a little princess who could do no wrong. Because of the preferential treatment, she became not too popular with her sisters. They eventually became jealous of her. In no time a real fairy-tale life had developed.

By the time she became a teenager, she possessed great beauty. She was very different from her other five sisters. In addition to being beautiful, she also had an inborn charisma and charm, which her siblings, to some extent, were lacking. Her soft, dreamy cornflower-blue eyes were set in her beautiful features, which seemed as if chiseled in marble; her face had a lovely sculptured bone structure, the chin line firm and almost square. (Chester often pointed out to me with some regret, "Why couldn't you inherit your mother's chin?") Very erect, with great posture, she carried her nice frame—not too skinny or fat, not too tall or too short—just right. Her long-fingered hands resembled those of a pianist. She had an assertive gait, but at the same time quite feminine. I, and others, saw a strong resemblance in her to Carole Lombard and Greta Garbo (although Garbo's eyes were deeply set, whereas

Mother's were very prominent and very expressive). Because she had a smooth, wrinkle-free complexion that she was so anxious to maintain, she was seldom found laughing. Even when happy she would produce nothing more than a "Mona Lisa smile." Thus she was teased, especially by her oldest brother-in-law who would say, "You never laugh and are reluctant to smile, because you're afraid to end up with premature wrinkles!" Although he had teased her endlessly, in later years, he would always remind her and emphasize the fact: "If you want to stay wrinkle-free, eat yogurt everyday." He did what he advised and when he died at 90, his complexion was smooth and indeed, wrinkle-free. At the age of one hundred, Mother's face showed just a very few lines, much less than mine! Speaking of Uncle Kolya, being the oldest of the clan (after his father-in-law, my grandfather), he often exercised his authority over his very young sisters-in-law, and the girls were not only annoyed with his discipline, but at times resented him a lot.

My mother's character was quite complicated. Although from early age and throughout the years Mother was given lots of attention and was surrounded with affection, love and security, she always seemed to be melancholy and somewhat insecure. In later years, while very helpful and devoted to her family and friends, she felt unappreciated, persecuted and often felt self-pity for being an underdog, burdened with the fate she had to cope with throughout her life. She was a born worrier. If she didn't have a reason to worry, she would find one and would dwell on it. She was very determined, persistent to the extent of being very stubborn. Her most common response was, "No, I don't want," "No, I can't" or something similar of a negative nature. She was a very, very strong-willed woman, like the rock of Gibraltar, hard to be convinced of things, very set in her ways, and very independent. Sometimes it seemed that she felt that her way is the only and the very best way and there is no question about it. Only her father, her husband and her brother-in-law Misha had any influence on her or the power to "bend" her. If she had been more flexible and could have drifted with the tide rather than constantly swim against it, I'm sure her life, as well the lives of those around her, would have been much easier. *But*, despite the negative streaks in her character, the many positive ones take precedence. With aristocratic behavior, but at the same time, many funny—some strange even—habits made her, even at the age of one hundred plus, a unique and fascinating woman.

As long as I can remember, Mother was always infatuated with cemeteries, cemeteries of any country or of any religion. After her mother's premature death, as a very young child, especially when she felt blue, on the way from school she would stop at the grave of her mother (whom she hardly knew, but felt very close to in spirit) to share her day's problems or disappointments. Being there, she tried to get some consolation in telling her mother her troubles, crying out, "Why did you have to leave me?" and after a good cry, she would return home in a somewhat more cheerful mood. While strolling through different cemeteries she liked to visit familiar or even forgotten burial sites. Having an inborn curiosity and an inquisitive nature toward life and death, she would read the inscriptions on the different tombstones and would examine the attached photographs. Collecting clues in this way, she could come up with an interesting story about each deceased person. Sometimes, sitting on a little bench or just resting on a relative's grave, in the shadow of trees, with a cool breeze flowing by, the silence gave her a sense of peace and tranquility. No matter which or whose grave she visited, she tended it—cleaning the markers, dusting off the leaves, weeding all around and watering the planted bushes or flowers. She had a soft spot in her heart and felt sorry for abandoned graves. To those, on subsequent visits, she brought fresh flowers. All in all, she found a great comfort being among the tombs of the departed. To get to far away cemeteries it often took a planned expedition for the visits. Sometimes, after dinner, when guests were ready to leave, she would convince them to take a long walk, take a trolley or a car with her to see "what's new at the cemetery." Once agreed, she and her friends ended up in a nice outing. She couldn't understand why in America, especially in California, there are more and more markers in cemeteries, rather then headstones. "Why should people walk all over them?" she'd ask. "After all, it is disrespectful of those that rest beneath those markers." Whenever we visited cemeteries in New Jersey, where most of her relatives are buried, such as the Woodlawn Cemetery in Lakewood, where Sonya and Misha are buried and Mother herself was to be buried, or the Russian Church Cemetery in Jackson, where the Padukows are buried, Mother would go from one grave site to another and point out to us the graves of her many friends and acquaintances. She knew who was who and what the person had died of, and a story of each person would follow. And just as in her daily dreams, where she often visited among the dead, she felt very comfortable with the departed at cemeteries. In addition to frequent visits to their graves, she used to devote a great deal of her thoughts to the departed, ordering *panikhidas (remembrance masses)*, burning memorial candles, and remembering them all in her daily prayers. She did it all in a very normal, habitual manner. It was part of her daily routine. She often remarked that she was leading a double life—with the living ones and with those that have departed, some many, many years ago. Curiously, the strong connection with the departed, her frequent visits to cemeteries, frequent bouts of feeling sorry for herself and the many sad moments during her whole life didn't prevent her from enjoying life and being happy.

Until recently, Mother's past romantic involvements were kept by her in secret. Although all of us knew about them, she never liked to discuss them and felt almost shy or even embarrassed when someone would tease her or bring them up in conversation. There were two things that she preferred not to talk about or to be reminded of—how many suitors she had had and how many of her bones she had broken in her long life. There were at least twenty of the latter misfortunes. One of them occurred shortly after she and Father married and were being driven through the Bialowieska Forest in the insurance clinic's newly acquired "Ansaldo" convertible. With the top down and only the supporting ribs of the cloth top between them and the sky, the chauffeur, going at a good clip, failed to slow down for a big dip in the road. Both passengers in the rear seat bounced up, with Mother hitting her face against the support rod, breaking her nose. They quickly returned to the clinic, where one of the doctors reset the nose perfectly. Another time Mother was out shopping in Warsaw and was traveling in a very crowded streetcar, one of those with a "dashboard" at each end, so that at the end destination, instead of turning the trolley around, the operator took his driving instruments and simply attached them at the other end. Because of the commotion this maneuver caused, plus the addition of more passengers boarding the trolley, Mother was squashed into the iron dashboard and at one point heard a loud crunch and felt a sharp pain in her rib cage. It turned out she had broken two ribs.

As time passed, and when she had reached what seemed to be the summit of her life, and to some extent even when she had reached her hundredth year, almost any chat with Mother would bring to light some of her happy memories of childhood, but foremost were the times when she was young, beautiful, and so desired by many men. Her fondest and most vivid recollections were those of growing up at her father's estate and of life in the country. The hidden, treasured stories, one by one, finally began to be revealed and told with pleasure and a faint smile.

Her first "real" infatuation took place when she was about seventeen, after finishing high school. She was asked to join her oldest sister and sick husband and their young son in San Remo, Italy. Since she had the duty of helping to take care of the toddler while his mother was preoccupied with her tuberculosis-stricken husband, Liza (my mother) would often take her little nephew along for walks or go shopping at nearby stores and the like. The two of them were often seen throughout the neighborhood. One day, Sergey fell and got hurt quite badly. To the rescue came a very handsome man. Almost every such story Mother started with the description: "He was a very handsome man." Short, fat or bald men had not even a slight chance with Mother. This "handsome man" happened to be a military man, Major Scardemalia, M.D., the son of the storekeepers where Mother frequently shopped. After this rather serious accident, Dr. Scardemalia became very attentive. He started to invite Liza out and eventually became very much in love with her, and Mother had great fun enjoying all the attention she was getting. Despite the fact that she was not Italian, the major's parents adored Mother and when their son's love and willingness to marry this young girl became clear, they tried to put some pressure not only on their "future daughter-in-law," but on her sister and her husband, who they thought had a great influence on Mother's decisions. The romance continued until the once very sick brother-in-law was cured by the

Italian sun and dry climate. When the time came to part, and apparently the parting was very dramatic, the major couldn't believe that he had not won Mother's heart and love. He wrote letters to her for a while, but as for Mother, it was out of sight, out of heart. Nevertheless, curiously enough, many years later when Chester and I, while stationed in Germany, took mother along on a trip to Italy and visited San Remo, she insisted on trying to locate the places where she and the Padukows had stayed and where she had met Major Scardemalia. To her considerable disappointment we couldn't find either.

Sometime after she and the Padukows returned from Italy, one of the two sons of *Batyushaka* (Father) Znosko tried to court Mother. She liked him a lot, but their friendship, which didn't go beyond that since he was a theology student, never progressed. Mother's comment was, "Marrying him I would have become *Matushka* (wife of a priest). For the life of me, I can't imagine myself being a wife, of all people, of a priest!" Frankly, I can't either.

With her personal attractions, youth, and graceful manners she was in her element amid the social swirl of parties, balls, receptions, dinners and informal picnics. All her life she loved to be fashionably dressed (she loved kooky and unusual hats) and especially loved formal dress. Her first whirl in the society spotlight (similar to a coming-out party) took place when she attended a fashionable ball at the officer's club (*kasyno*) at the *polygon* (training camp) near Brest and the family estate. After the first ball, many followed, at which she was usually considered the best-dressed young lady, "the belle of many a ball." Her formal gowns (she never wore the same one again) were made of satin, tulle or silk, in different colors, but her favorite ones were in black or white, with puffed sleeves and flounces, which rated highly, invariably taking first prize in the Best Gown competition. It was during these balls that Mother met many "handsome" men, who automatically sought her attention and, after a short courtship, her hand. But being flirtatious, charming, radiant and gracious, marital intentions were often rebuffed.

At Marta and Ivan Shlykov's wedding, Mother met four "handsome men," Marta's two brothers, Edward and Franz, as well as a captain and a count. After the wedding, she had two marriage proposals—one from Edward and the other from Count Zaslawski (the Zaslawskis were nobility from Zaslaw near Horyn, a family of Kresy magnates *[Magnatow kresowych]* who were very influential in the first half of the 17th century, but around 1673 their power began to diminish). To everybody's surprise, the suitor Liza chose was Edward and they became engaged. Shortly after their engagement, Edward was sent on a business trip. While he was out of town, out of the blue Captain Kunkel showed up, expressing his interest in her. Liza eventually broke up with Edward, and very soon thereafter became engaged to Capt. Kunkel. While engaged to the captain, one day who should arrive to pay a visit, but the count! Seeing the count in the doorway, Mother quickly took off her engagement ring. Her haste made the ring fly off her finger, and roll down the hall. To say the least, she found the situation very embarrassing. Being confronted by her one-time suitor, she had a hard time explaining how the engagement came about, but it was obvious it didn't take place because of being in love with his rival Edward. Many years later, while already married to my father, when strolling along the famous *Ulica Piotrkowska* in Lodz, Poland, they ran into Capt. Kunkel and a colonel friend. After a brief chat, the four of them went to a restaurant for dinner. It was one of the many typical situations—three handsome men and the Queen Bee. When they were saying their good-byes, out of the blue, Capt. Kunkel asked Mother if she would like to join him the next day for horseback riding (they were accustomed to enjoy horseback riding while they were at the estate in Krasnyy Dvor and engaged to one another). Mother looked at her husband and asked, "What do you think, Felus?" (a nickname she used for Feliks). Feliks answered, "By all means," but when Mother and Father were back home, Felus spoke up: "Were you out of your mind even considering going?" Obviously, she didn't go, the subject was closed, and this was the last time Mother saw her former fiancé.

Between several more serious romances there were many cases of infatuations and just friendships, until the day Ivan Shlykov came to the estate for a visit. He brought with him a couple of his friends and a director of the future medical facility that Ivan was contracted to build. The visitor was introduced to Mother as *Pan Dyrektor* (Mr. Director) Feliks Kucharski. This was a "handsome gentleman, dressed to a T, with very charming manners and a very warm smile," thus Mother would describe her first impression of my father. The first encounter must have made an enormous impact on her, because when the visitors finally departed, she was left in a haze, but not for long. The visiting couple had inadvertently left behind their little dog. *Pan Dyrektor* was most happy to return to the estate and fetch the little pooch. From then on one visit followed another. Feliks sometimes came accompanied by Ivan, but often by himself. At that time, Mother, who was engaged, but at this point I have lost track to whom, broke off the engagement and after a courtship of six weeks Liza and Feliks were married. Mother from then on had the "title" of *Pani Dyrektorowa*. (In similar fashion, in Poland, the wife of a doctor, *Doktor*, becomes *Pani Doktorowa*. It is the same in German, the wife of *Herr Doktor* is called *Frau Doktor*.) The wedding took place at a Catholic church rather than an Orthodox *tserkov*, for which the future newlyweds needed special permission from a Catholic archbishop. Mother had to vow that she would bring up any future offspring in the Catholic rather than the Russian Orthodox faith. An elaborate reception followed with many guests attending. I never heard, but often wondered, if Mother's former suitors were present at this very happy occasion. As I have described in previous chapters, many happy events, balls, formal receptions, changes of residence and also my addition to the family followed. Needless to say, my parents' union was made in heaven. His slight seniority over her and their reciprocal tenderness made her more mature, secure

Elizabeth Romenko before her marriage to Feliks Kucharski. Brest, 1928.

and stable, and having her at his side made him the happiest fellow on Earth. They both were very proud of each other, which reflected on them throughout their marriage. The only "arguments" that I was aware of would be because she had misplaced something, like a clothes brush, or rearranged his papers when trying to make order. All in all they spent thirteen idyllic years together. Once her Felus was no longer at her side, she almost lost all zest for life. She closed her heart and it seems it never opened again. From then on she had to cope with the world around her alone.

Shortly after Mother married, Father taught her to light up a cigarette as a joke at parties, but soon, a widow at age thirty-five, she became a chain smoker, which lasted for another fifty or so years. She no longer was the life of the party, and instead, became muted as a result of the emotional scars she carried following the experiences she'd had that were tragic and devastating. At a gathering of family or friends, if she had a drink, rather than becoming relaxed and joyful, she would start crying and become inconsolable. All her bottled-up bitterness, sadness, self pity and anger would come to the surface. It broke my heart to witness every time this scene would repeat. There was not much I could have done to help her cope with her sorrow, but to be an obedient and understanding daughter and offer her consolation, which she was reluctant to accept. I managed to give her as little reason as possible to worry about me or cause anything that could displease her or make her situation worse. I became quite independent and while she was out of town, I learned how to take care of myself. I tried to avoid any confrontation between us.

Throughout the years, although there was love, devotion and a very strong bond between us, unfortunately our relationship was lacking in communication and closeness. She always had a heart of gold and a willingness to help everyone, sometimes resulting in paying a big price and feeling disappointment for her generosity. It was in Mother's nature to build a wall around herself, which prevented closeness even with people dear to her heart.

Her life after Father, during World War II, and in the postwar years after immigration was no fairy tale; it was a long struggle for survival and hard work. But despite it all, she managed to keep her head above water and from time to time she was able to enjoy herself. Coming to America, she was merely forty-three years old and as good looking as ever. Once again she was the Queen Bee at many parties, surrounded by more suitors than I can ever count. Numerous times she was asked to marry by one or the other of them. In the past, one marriage she may have considered was to Dr. Bruno Gutkiewicz in Warsaw, but because of the outcome of the uprising, it didn't take place. Her brief marriage in the displaced persons' camp, which came about due to my and the family's encouragement, was almost instantly annulled when it was discovered that the groom, Dr. Nikolay Proskuriakov, was not yet officially divorced from a previous spouse. Despite my and other family members' urgings, she never agreed or even considered marriage again. In any possible encounter, as soon as she became "threatened" with the possibility of marriage, up came the wall and the relationship was quickly over. One more instance comes to mind, when Mother, while living in New York City, had a very nice and warm friendship with a man that she thought highly of. He proposed marriage and laid out a plan for it, mentioning that soon after, they would start a family. Mother,

My mother, Elizabeth Kucharska, holding me, her newborn daughter Lucyna. Miedzychod nad Warta, Poland, May 1931.

My mother, ever beautiful, seated among a group of admirers. In foreground, left, her brother-in-law Mikhail Shlykov. Lakewood, New Jersey, 1966.

hearing that the rosy future included children, got cold feet and quickly retreated. They stayed friends, he got married to someone else, had two children, but once, when they met by chance, confessed to Mother that he regretted greatly that Mother had rejected him. Obviously, he still loved her.

In previous chapters I have described Mother's first few years in the U.S. during which she managed to get adjusted to her new life, make new friends and to participate in the lives of her sisters and in ours. She was an excellent cook and gracious hostess, doing her own cooking, housekeeping and taking care of the garden, which she continued through all the years until about the age of 96, at which time reluctantly she surrendered herself to the care of frequently changing live-in caregivers.

Having described some of the difficult and even tragic events that Mother endured during the war, I feel I should go on to describe the unusual changes that began taking place at about the time Mother passed her 100th birthday, changes that were undoubtedly connected with the trauma she endured during the war. We first noticed that her behavior was changing when as time went by she became increasingly focused on controlling her environment and she became more and more obsessed with routine matters. Getting her settled in bed for the night sometimes took over an hour. The shades on her window had to be just so, not too high or not too low. The length of the blanket overlapping each side of the bed had to be exactly the same. The clothing for the next day had to be prepared and arranged just so. "Turn the light off, no, let the light stay on!" At meals, drinks or food were always too hot or too cold. Some food she wouldn't touch, saying, "I don't want to eat anything that comes from the ground." (We had to say, for instance, that potatoes don't come from the ground, they grow on trees.) Later on, at every mealtime there would be an argument about the colors of the dishes she was served. She had to be served pureed food because she was having trouble chewing, but since pureed food didn't look attractive, she would say, "Why do you serve me compost?" But she felt comfortable eating blintzes or zucchini fritters, and often would eat these and nothing else.

Then, just before she turned 100, during a new caregiver's first night with her in her apartment, she had a frightening nightmare, during which she was screaming so loudly that the neighbors called us to find out what was happening in her apartment. Even after she awoke, the screaming from this little frail lady's lungs was unbelievable. The caregiver, not being able to quiet her down, suggested calling me. Mother replied that this would be to no avail as "Lucy is not alive, she has been killed and the German soldiers in uniforms came, and wanted to drag me out to their car stark naked. They will be back!" Fortunately, after an hour or so, and with the aid of a tranquilizer, she was able to calm down. The nightmare, which was like a replay of the time during the war when in the middle of the night Nazi soldiers came to our Warsaw apartment and took away my father, was the beginning of a persecution complex that continued to the end, the most disturbing aspect of which was the fact that Mother would not believe us when we said that she had been having a nightmare. Every other day or so she would tell us that the men had been back to see her and had told her they would be back soon to take her away. Watching Mother's newly developed personality, it never dawned on us that all these obsessions, nightmares, mistrust, suspicions and strange behavior in general are not unusual for a person like her who went through the real nightmares and horrors of both World War I and then World War II. Such behavior, it turns out, is explained in part by the normal effects of aging and senility coupled with the impact of suppressed memories due to extreme traumas suffered years earlier. In the many hours I spent talking to her about her past, she rarely wanted to discuss the hard times in her life and only would discuss her childhood and her happy prewar times. But then the cork popped out of the bottle where she kept the horror stories bottled in for so many years.

After thirty years, three sisters, Olga Liza, and Sonya, reunite in Brest, Belarus, in September, 1975. Left to right: Mikhail Vakulchik, his mother Olga Vakulchik, Olga's granddaughter Oksana, Elizabeth Kucharska, and Sonya Shlykov. Left to right, Mikhail Vakul'chik, in front of him Olga's granddaughter Oksana, Zhorzh Vakul'chik, Elizabeth Kusharska, Olga Vakul'chik and Sonya Shlykov.

It became very rare to find Mother in a sunny disposition. Just being nearly 100 years old, most likely her age alone gave her many reasons to feel unhappy. With no bright future in sight, with the loss of independence, most of her hearing, and vision in one eye, and with having to put up with numerous pains and aches, she had more than enough reasons for her moods to become even cloudier and unhappier. Earlier, not out of disrespect, but merely as a joke, I gave her a nickname, changing her name Kucharska to "Kwasniewska." Kwasniewska comes from the Polish word *kwasny*, which means sour. When she fussed, I would say, "*Pani Kwasniewska*, cheer up, things could be worse than they are!" Unfortunately, things did get worse.

In recent years, there were many scary moments and close calls, when it seemed that Mother might not make it through this or that illness, but even in those cases, her strong will and determination won over, and she quickly was able to bounce back and keep going. One could say she was a lady of nine lives. Which reminds me that Father, after learning how much she loved cats, had given her the nickname "Kota"—from the Polish word *kot* which means cat. At the sunset of her life, when her body seemed to be giving out and the tumultuous life of the past was over, it appeared to be touch and go for a while, and yet it seemed the faint light wanted to continue to burn in her, for which I was very grateful. Despite a strong disbelief that she would make it to her next birthday, on the 30th of November 2006 she became one hundred years old! At our house we had a surprise party for her with many friends that knew her through her later years. At the party she kept asking, "Am I *really* 100?" On her 100th she received greetings from still another president and first lady. In the past birthday wishes had come from Presidents Reagan, H. W. Bush, and Clinton. After the big event, her life remained the same, but with more ups and downs. The highlight of our daily visits was to watch *Who Wants to Be a Millionaire?* She liked to watch this program especially when Regis Philbin was the host. On the other hand, when Meredith Vieira was hosting the show, Mother showed impatience. Even here she demonstrated a tendency to be partial to men.

After our visits, when saying good-bye, I always approached her in order to kiss her and give her a hug. On some occasions, she would stop me and say, "It's not necessary to kiss and hug." I invariably made a joke: "Are you afraid to give me your germs or are you afraid that I may share some of mine?" Then while she was figuring out what I meant, I quickly bent down and managed to steal a kiss. Once we were outside, from her armchair at the large picture window overlooking the street, sad, without a smile she always waved good-bye and blew us a kiss. Every time I was leaving her I was paranoid that this time might be the last good-bye. Her last accident happened shortly after she had recovered from a previous one in which she was struck and knocked down by the edge of a garage door that was activated by an approaching vehicle. In that fall she sustained a fracture of the hip and pelvic bone, but eventually recovered from these injuries without surgery. Then in June of 2007, calling her caregiver and not getting a response, Mother decided to get up from her chair by the window to investigate whatever the caregiver was doing in the kitchen. She reached for her wheelchair, but the wheelchair slipped out of her grasp and she fell. At first it seemed that she was just bruised, but the next day an X-ray revealed a very bad break in the hip and a break in the forearm. In the hospital, with a surgeon standing by ready to perform surgery, once I heard the anesthesiologist's strong opinion that, due to her severe aortic stenosis, Mother would not survive this difficult procedure, I was torn apart and just could not sign a consent that would have amounted to a death sentence for my mom. The surgery was cancelled and Mother was moved to one of the best convalescent hospitals in town. Although she was bed-ridden, to the doctors' and our surprise, she was reasonably comfortable and not in great pain, needing only a small amount of medication. Her biggest problem was her negative attitude and the unhappy feeling of being, as she used to say, "trapped." Our daily visits were full of frustrations, anguish and sadness. Despite her obvious fear of death, some days she was so fed up with her situation that she wished the end would come soon to "cure" it all, but on other hand, on good days, she was hoping that with some help she would get better and could stay with us for awhile.

After four months' stay at the convalescent house, the prognosis seemed to indicate that she would not survive for much longer and the immediate future for her recovery was bleak, so she was moved to a hospice facility. Knowing her strong stamina I had the deep hope that once there, Mother's determination for life would escalate and things would improve. She took the transfer quite well and once she got settled in her private sunny room, surrounded by very loving and caring people, she became completely calm and looking very serene, and fell into a sound asleep, only to wake up the next day for a very short while, as if to "scout out" the situation. Approving what she saw, she soon fell again into a "deep sleep," which continued for six days. (I was told it looked like but was different from being in a coma.) We talked to her, but she wasn't responding. The night before her passing, just before I was saying good-night, while telling her how sad it will be without her, all of a sudden I saw one tear roll down from one of her eyes. The next morning, on the 29th of October 2007 at 8:15 she took her last breath, just a month before her 101st birthday. The angelic hospice attendants bathed her, combed her hair neatly, and tucked her in under a cheerful quilt covered with scattered rose petals. In the semi-dark room, surrounded with flickering candles and flowers, she lay looking very peaceful, serene, and as beautiful as ever.

Many times through the years she had expressed the wish that when her time would come, she would die the way Chester's mother had passed on, in her sleep, and so her wish was fulfilled. The next evening, at the Russian Orthodox church, during a very moving *panikhida* (a memorial mass that is celebrated instead of the customary American Catholic viewing and rosary at mortuaries), I placed in her coffin a portrait of her beloved Feliks, together with my final letter to her (in the past when we were apart, I used to write her daily letters). On the following day, the third day after her death, in accordance with precepts of the Russian Orthodox Church, the *odpevaniye* (funeral mass) was celebrated and Mother was then laid to rest at the Santa Barbara Cemetery. I realize and believe that her passing was unavoidable; that the time had come for her to be free from life's physical and psychological anguish and that she no longer could fight in order to be able to stay with us and be at my side as she always was. At the same time, for me, it was an unacceptable finish to our long bond over three quarters of a century.

26

Married Life Begins

The year was now 1951. Chester and I were about to marry. We picked July 7 to be the day, and I promptly gave a short notice at my place of employment. The office had already had enough warning and clues that sooner or later they would lose me to a major from West Point, whom they had heard about but had never met. The whole office, design bureau and front office combined, gave me a farewell/bridal shower party. From then on I was preoccupied with things that were close to my heart. A bright future was in front of me. Not having any close friends nearby, such as Nina Polanska and Irka Ozimek, I asked Natasha Shebalin to be my maid of honor. Despite the fact that Natasha was Russian Orthodox, the priest fortunately did not object to her taking part in our marriage ceremony. Walter Legawiec, Chester's friend, was to be the best man, and Edward (Eddie), my future brother-in-law, was going to "give me away." The wedding was to take place in St. Stanislav's Polish church on 7th Street in Manhattan, between 2nd and 3rd avenues, with a small reception afterward at our future home in West Point. Father Mikulec was asked to perform the ceremony, which in true Catholic tradition would be preceded by a confession, Chester's first since his childhood! (In Santa Barbara, about 48 years later, we were at a party where we met a visiting couple from Wisconsin, the husband an orthopedic surgeon from Poland, and his American-born wife. During our conversation we were surprised to learn that this couple had also been married at the same church, with the same priest officiating. There were just a few months separating our two weddings.)

As soon as Misha learned of my forthcoming marriage, he began making big plans on his own. He thought the ceremony and reception ought to take place in Lakewood, or better still, at Rova Farms. He was making a long list of who should be invited and so on. Once he was denied the pleasure of having the festivities take place in Lakewood or Cassville as he had planned, he became "mortally" offended and as a result refused to come to the wedding ceremony or to our small reception, and prevented Sonya from coming as well. Misha's decision really put a cloud on my sunny day. After all, both Misha and Sonya had played an important role in my childhood and later during my life with them in Regensburg. Now his refusal to be part of this important event in my life, at least by attending the church ceremony, was quite painful for me and I could not understand Misha's childlike behavior.

As the big day approached, Natasha and I had our gowns ordered and fitted. The deliveries of flowers and wedding cake were arranged. The ceremony was to take place at ten in the morning. When the big day arrived, Eddie, who was staying with his parents at a hotel on Fifth Avenue, came promptly in his car to drive me to the church. When we arrived, we were told to stay in the car and wait. The waiting time seemed to me to be an eternity; it went from minutes to half an hour to almost an hour. Needless to say, I was getting more and more nervous, worrying about the unusual delay. Upon my constant urging, Eddie kept going into the church to check out the reason for the long wait. Eddie, I later learned, had his reasons for not telling me the reason for the delay, and simply told me the delay would soon be over. I could see from his brusque manner that he, too, was getting impatient, especially with my questions. As the minutes ticked by, the tension kept building up. I could see familiar people lined up on the steps of the church waiting for the arrival of the bride. At one point it went through my mind that Chester had either become sick or at the last minute had lost his nerve. Finally, it became clear that there was a funeral in progress, which for some reason, due perhaps to lengthy eulogies, was causing the huge delay. Once the funeral service came to an end, the casket removed and the mourners having departed, we received the green light to proceed with our ceremony. At this point I was a nervous wreck. However, once I saw Chester waiting patiently at the altar, with a slight smile on his lips, I felt confident that all would be fine. As Eddie escorted me down the aisle, he also relaxed and came back to his pleasant self and kept making cheerful comments to put me at ease.

Those attending the ceremony in the large attractive church came nowhere near filling it, since, other than a handful of friends and coworkers of mine and Mother's, the only family members there were Mother, Chester's parents, brother Eddie, and his wife Sue. Eddie's children, Ed and Marion, were away at school, while Chester's brother Leo was left tending the family business in Rhode Island. But it didn't matter to me who or how many people attended; the most important thing for me at that moment was that Chester was at my side! The ceremony turned out to be quite formal and it soon became obvious that the mass would be a prolonged one. Because of the delay caused by the preceding function (the funeral), our ceremony coincided with the time when the priest normally celebrates High Mass, so that is what we were in for. As a result, the mass seemed endless, with much of it spent on our knees! Finally, we were pronounced "man and wife." The small crowd managed to shower us with congratulations and lots of rice and confetti as we left for the photography studio, located just around the corner from the church. After the official bridal pictures were taken, we quickly changed into less formal clothing and

A very happy picture of me with my husband, Major Chester F. Radlo, just after our wedding at St. Stanislaus Church, New York City, 7 July 1951.

along with other family members drove to West Point, where ahead of time Mother had arranged a mini reception. After the delicious brunch that Mother had somehow found time to prepare, plus some singing and laughter, Chester and I left the party and drove to Poughkeepsie, where we spent the weekend. We were not able to take a customary honeymoon trip, as on Monday morning Chester had classes to conduct. Several months later, however, when I was visibly pregnant, Chester and I drove up to see Niagara Falls. I was both surprised and annoyed with the fact that so many people would stare at me and then make comments to their companions. Only when Chester explained to me that Niagara Falls is known as a favorite place for honeymoons did it become clear to me why I was the object of so much attention. Chester was rather amused but I was just embarrassed. During that trip we continued on to Montreal, where we visited my bosom friend Irena Ozimek and her family. The reunion was very warm, full of chatter and a recounting of the events that had occurred since last we had seen each other in Germany. But to get back to our Poughkeepsie trip—when we returned to West Point that weekend, we found that before Mother, Chester's mother, and his sister-in-law Sue had returned to their respective homes, they'd left the house in spotless condition, with lots of delicious leftovers in the refrigerator. A few weeks later, a short notice, composed and submitted by Misha, appeared in the New York Russian newspaper, announcing our marriage.

And so I became a full-fledged lady of the house, at Quarters 153, a beautiful two-story townhouse with a long view of a manicured grassy area. Our complex consisted of five attached brick townhouses, all covered with ivy. Behind them was a row of carports. There were two entrances to the house, back and front, with a few stairs leading to each entry. In the entry hall there was a staircase leading to two bedrooms and a bath on the second floor. The upstairs bedrooms were large and airy. On the first floor there was one long, large room, which served as living and dining room. The kitchen was off the dining room. The whole house was pleasantly cool in the summer, but very cozy and warm in the winter. We furnished the house mostly with hand-me-down furniture given to us by Chester's parents, including a handsome plush-covered sofa and two easy chairs, which for years followed us around wherever we went. As soon as we settled down, Chester began giving me driving lessons. The car was an almost new, pale green Chevrolet convertible. It was great, but it did not have an automatic shift. Every evening we would go for a ride. My driving went quite well, except when I had to shift from one gear to another. It was especially embarrassing on our return home if there would be neighbors sitting outside their quarters and they would hear me make that awful screeching sound as I awkwardly shifted gears. I became so discouraged that I thought about abandoning my lessons. But Chester persevered and I finally managed to complete my "driver's ed." I eventually got my driver's license, but it was only after we had changed the Chevy for another convertible, a jet-black Pontiac. Driving this new, fully automatic car was a dream!

At West Point, Chester was assigned to the foreign language department as a Russian language instructor. Chester, at the time an Air Force major, was the only Air Force officer in the department; all the others were Army officers, except for one civilian, Mr. Maltzoff, who was a native Russian and served as an advisor on grammar and current usage. Chester's duties at the academy were satisfying and enjoyable. He had an unusual schedule: language classes were only held in the morning, while the department's instructors used the afternoon hours to correct papers, work on lesson plans, and perform occasional administrative duties, such as Officer of the Day assignments. His classes started right after breakfast, at eight. Often he walked to the building across from the hospital where the foreign language department was located, then at about noon, when the classes ended, he would walk or drive back home or I would pick him up. In the latter case we would often continue driving somewhere to go shopping or for lunch, but on Wednesdays, as a ritual, we almost always headed for New York City to see a matinee, followed by dinner at Mother's apartment. Since Chester on these occasions usually still had student papers to grade and/or a lesson plan to prepare, he often tackled these chores at Mother's place while waiting for dinner. During Chester's assignment to the foreign language department he developed friendships with the German, Spanish, Portuguese and French instructors and close personal relations with Major Michael Mirski and Major Walter Guletski, both U.S. Army officers, who were also native Russians. While Chester was teaching Russian, Major John Eisenhower, son of President Eisenhower, was teaching nearby in the English department. Shortly after I settled into my new role as a married woman I met the members of the department and their wives. One couple in particular, from Brazil, became our first friends. Lourdes and her husband, instructor of Portuguese Major Heitor De Matos, had a young son. Lourdes' mother, who came from Brazil, also lived with them. As Lourdes was an "old-timer" (they were in the last year of their three-year tour of duty at the academy), she became my daily chaperone in and around the Point. We used to go swimming in the huge pool, but could only use it after or before the cadets needed it for their training. Very often we would come too early and then had a chance to watch the cadets play or practice water polo. A few months later, when Lourdes and I each discovered that each one of us was pregnant, our swimming became more a matter of necessary exercise rather than pleasure. Lourdes had a baby boy, Jose Augusto, born on November 20, 1952; I had Ellie, born five days earlier.

Shortly after we settled down, I learned many things about the academy, in particular about the life of a cadet and what each has to go through in order finally to graduate from this fine institution. While he or she is still in high school when the dream is born of getting into West Point, a prospective cadet has to start building up his physical stamina in order to be able to face the academy's six-event physical-fitness test. He has to pass an SAT, write an essay on why he wants to become a cadet, and he has to get his teachers' recommendations. Having these in hand, the candidate must secure a nomination by a member of Congress or the Vice-President. A senator is allowed to nominate up to ten candidates per year to each of the military academies, but final approval of the nomination is the prerogative of the academy involved. Once nominated, many interviews follow in which the prospective cadet has to show a decent understanding of world affairs and military matters and that he has the moral qualities and mental outlook that will help in his eventual status as an officer in the service of his country. Once accepted, a new cadet, who for his first year is known as a "plebe," undergoes a very rigorous training. Plebes get up at 6 A.M. and often their morning duties will include cleaning bathrooms, taking out trash, delivering newspapers, helping out at the mess hall and so on. They are obliged to take "commands" from upper classmates, who can sometimes go to extremes in testing a plebe's compliance. A plebe is not allowed to talk to another plebe other than in their rooms. When approaching officers or upper classmates, he must be the first one to give a salute. Out of the blue, he may be approached and asked how many days are left before the Army-Navy game or some other such trivial question. Suffering such treatment throughout his first year, the new cadet must be able to demonstrate his ability to withstand such rigors without showing annoyance or defiance. When finally, after four years, he graduates from the military academy as a second lieutenant in the U.S. Army, he will not only have as a foundation a well-rounded education in military matters, science, and the humanities, but also the personality, composure, and strength of character that comes with meeting the numerous challenges set before him.

Now and then, one of the officers in the department was assigned as Duty Officer of the Day. On such occasions the designated officer would wear an armband indicating his status. The Officer of the Day was responsible for alerting the proper authority if something unexpected happened that he could not resolve by himself. On one occasion when Chester was the Officer of the Day it was fortunate that, in addition to the Russian language he needed for his classes, Chester was fluent in Polish. An excursion group of Poles had come up from New York to West Point specifically to visit the monument to General Tadeusz Kosciuszko. In addition to playing host to the group, Chester also made a speech to the group in Polish at the foot of the magnificent monument, in which he presented a short history lesson on the important role that the Polish hero played in the fortifications at Saratoga and West Point during the Revolutionary War.

Once there was a big, very festive ball hosted by the academy's commandant. It was my first as a married woman. We went to New York City to look for a special gown for me. I settled for one that had a full black and white striped skirt with a black velvet halter top and a large velvet shawl to cover my bare shoulders. Chester wore his blue uniform. It was great fun to attend the dinner-dance and to be swirled around the magnificent ballroom by my new husband and by several high-ranking officers. That evening I could very well picture how excited Mother must have felt attending the many balls in her youth. Just before the ball I was nervous and full of apprehension, almost ready not to go, but once we arrived and I heard the beautiful dance music played by the West Point band, I felt very much at home. The rest of the evening was full of fun, good food, and pleasant company.

We participated in office activities, picnics at the Bear Mountain picnic grounds, and boat rides on the Hudson River. We attended football games and watched cadets march for this or that occasion. Being still a novice in my new role, I was reluctant to do much official entertaining, especially because of one disastrous incident. Having been entertained on numerous occasions by our Brazilian friends (the mother and the daughter were fantastic cooks), we decided to reciprocate by impressing them with Polish cuisine. Looking through Polish cookbooks, Chester found a recipe for chicken in a sour cream sauce. It was more complicated than it sounded. I was reluctant to prepare this meal, remembering the saying, "never practice cooking on company." Chester was more optimistic with respect to our experiment's outcome. Needless to say, the chicken was dry and a big flop! Although the rest of the dinner was fine, it left me very unhappy and embarrassed. The next cooking flop took place when I prepared a hare, fortunately just for the two of us. While grocery shopping one day, knowing how fond Chester was of rabbit meat (his parents kept rabbits and often when the brood got out of proportion, some were prepared by his mother in a delicious recipe), on my insistence we bought a fairly large hare, or perhaps it was an ordinary rabbit. I had many times watched my aunt cook rabbit and thought it would be easy to prepare one on my own. Again, something went wrong—the hare not only looked ugly, but it tasted awful! I tried to explain to Chester that it did not turn out right because the hare probably was old and therefore very tough. In any case, Chester never again showed any interest in rabbit and so we've never had one since that time. I, so to speak, cured him of that taste. It was lucky we hadn't tried this recipe on friends! However, these two cooking flops did not discourage me from trying out new recipes, which I have been collecting since the time when I was preparing for my forthcoming marriage, and so I became a constant recipe clipper. At one point in the '80s, when I had assembled a large number of various cheesecake recipes, all of which we had tested and approved, we decided to put them together into a book, including an elegant foreword and a history of the types of cheese used in making cheesecake. We even sent a sample copy to a publisher. After the publisher answered that he "cannot use the material at this time," we lost enthusiasm for the project and put it aside. (I still have the unpublished copy of my *Cheesecake Symphony*, just in case.) Every day I made a point of serving something different, with the hope of pleasing my hubby, who in turn was a good sport in trying almost anything that was placed on the table. I did not use any shortcuts and everything was done as closely as possible to the directions in the sometimes complicated recipes. The same was true when I was doing the laundry. Although we used the base laundry for big items, like sheets and tablecloths (each thing had to have the last four numbers of Chester's Social Security number, either on the item with indelible ink or on a label that was sewn on), I faithfully washed most things by hand. And of course I ironed everything myself, each piece of clothing, including Chester's boxer shorts! After he switched to jockey shorts, I stopped ironing them, just folded them neatly. I was not a cleaning freak, but tried to keep the house neat and orderly. Living in our own warm, spacious place, with constant hot water, and not having to share the bathroom or the kitchen with half a dozen tenants was for me a sheer delight! In such a place I was happy to do the cooking, washing and cleaning! And I felt that Chester, being a neat person by nature, deserved to have a nice and tidy home to relax in. (I guess I should thank my mother-in-law for bringing him up the right way! He once revealed to me that, in order to help his mother in her various housekeeping chores, he sometimes even ironed his own, his father's, and his brother Leo's handkerchiefs!) Although from day one of our married life, we seemed to be almost constantly on the go, we spent many happy hours in our beautiful #153 quarters.

One day we received an announcement about various classes being offered in the evening hours, including classes in beginning Spanish and in Latin dancing. We decided to enroll in the Spanish class and attended it a few times, until I got annoyed that Chester was always doing better than I. When we sat in a circle and were called upon by the instructor for an answer, Chester always gave his answer quickly and correctly, but when my turn came, I not only had to think longer, but sometimes gave a wrong answer. I could feel Chester looking at me, and could imagine him saying, "We practiced that lesson last night, why don't you know it?" So I persuaded Chester that we quit the Spanish class and switch to the dance class, which turned out to be easier for me and at the same time more enjoyable. I no longer had to feel embarrassed and it seems to me that in this class I was quicker to learn than was Chester, although we both eventually learned to dance a nice rumba and cha-cha, as well as a passable tango.

There were many trips to and from New York City, but not always were the roads or the weather just right for covering the relatively short, but rather dangerous stretch comfortably. Nevertheless, even if it began raining cats and dogs, or a snowstorm was in the forecast, we would prefer to take the risk of driving home, rather than staying overnight in the city. A couple of such occasions come to mind when, together with Mother, we were returning to West Point late at night. One late evening, as we were relatively close to home, all of a sudden it became so foggy that we could just barely see the hood of the car, but could not see the road or its shoulders. Mother, sitting as usual in the front with us rather than in the back seat, was on pins and needles, frightened to death, because she realized that Chester was unable to see the road. She offered to get out and walk in front of the car to show Chester the way. Reluctantly we agreed, and thus she marched in the middle of the road, midway between the dividing line of the road and the right shoulder, a few steps in front of our car, leading the way. It seems she guided us a considerable stretch of road, but finally the dense fog lifted and we were on our way with Mother aboard. Later on we often joked that Mother was lucky that her son-in-law liked her and did not use the opportunity to do away with her. Another incident also happened when we again were returning home with Mother. There was such a snowstorm that not only was the visibility almost down to zero, but the ice-covered roadway was very slippery. As we struggled to keep moving at a turtle's pace, the car kept sliding and twisting, with the tires spinning in place instead of moving us forward. At one point when the latter happened and the car was making no forward progress, Chester instructed Mother and me to make forward-moving motions with our bodies to help the car keep going. I, as often happens in tense situations like this one, started to giggle uncontrollably, which made Chester angry and he told me "to stop laughing like a schoolgirl!" Easier said than done! The three of us kept pushing and pushing with our bodies as hard as we could, but the car still would not move an inch! Mother offered to get out and push, but first we both gave a strong push, while still in our seats and, to our relief, the car began moving forward. Mother was especially relieved because she was afraid that if she and I got out of the car to push it from behind that Chester wouldn't be able to stop and would continue without us, to teach us a lesson for my being silly. Until this day, when I think of this "pushing in the seat" episode, I can't help but start laughing "like a schoolgirl."

Having lost everything during the Warsaw Uprising, the end of World War II found Mother and me with very few possessions and certainly no household goods. And then when we were ready to immigrate to America, shed our refugee status, settle in a permanent place and start life anew, we didn't want to schlep extra baggage, so we even left behind some of what little we had. Thus, when I married and found I had a great place to live in, I was eager to furnish our home and make it cozy and warm. It was a blessing to have as a helper a mother who was more than happy to present us with all sorts of goodies, so that in no time our assigned house indeed was transformed into a very cozy home. On many occasions Mother would call us from New York, saying that she had bought a "treasure" for us and we ought to come to get it at once, as the store had agreed to keep it on hold for us. Since most of the purchases were made at an antique store across the street from her apartment, Mother was quite well known there and the storekeeper kept her eyes open for different things that could be of interest to her frequent customer. Mother's acquisitions often created a problem in picking them up, because parking was very limited in the vicinity of the store. An incident connected with this problem of parking comes to mind. One day, when we agreed to meet in front of the store, there was no parking to be had. Mother saw us going around and around the block in our convertible, being not able to park the car for enough time to load her latest find, a beautiful china cabinet. Waiting for us to find a parking space, she stood on the sidewalk in front of the store along with both the china cabinet and a newly acquired stand-up lamp. Finally, a car moved out of a space, so she promptly planted herself and the lamp in the middle of the empty space, trying to reserve the spot for us. But another anxious and perhaps frustrated driver drove up just before we got there. Despite Mother's gesturing that the space was taken, the rude man slowly, but steadily, inch by inch, backed into the spot, forcing Mother, with lamp in hand, to vacate the space. However, she gave up the struggle very reluctantly, almost ending up on the car's trunk. Finally, we did what New Yorkers do all the time, which is to double park, risking the possibility of getting a fat parking ticket, but this time no traffic cop came around and we were able to load our treasures and depart happily for home.

The first purchase that Mother made at this antique shop was a dinner set for 24 people of Haviland-Limoges china. The next time it was the china cabinet to accommodate this beautiful china. Then there was a flower stand, and after that the list is too long to remember all the different things she bought for us. Mother did not own an auto, as she had never learned to drive, and bringing the different things on the bus was out of the question, so it turned out that our convertible became rather handy. When we purchased a baby grand piano in New York, we were tempted to try hauling it also in our convertible, but we finally chose to have it delivered, after which our best man, Walter, came and after trying the piano out, concluded that not only was it a great-sounding instrument in a good-looking case, but it was a terrific buy as well! Although we now had a voluminous china service, neatly arranged in our elegant china cabinet, we still could not resist the good buys we found during our strolls in the nearby sleepy town of Highland Falls, such as a tea set by "Y" of Austria we saw in the window of one of the town's many antique stores. The pattern was similar to our Limoges dinner china. At that point we had all the china we could possibly need. Nevertheless, we later bought more—a Rosenthal-Sans-Souci coffee set in Frankfurt and later, in Santa Barbara, a tea set by Limoges. I'm not in the habit of bragging about my possessions, but these notes are really for my daughters, who would probably want to know where the different things they will one day inherit came from. After we got the china dinnerware we thought, what is china without good silver? We had no savings to speak of, so buying silver was definitely beyond our budget, but the temptation was greater than our common sense. We were encouraged further when we found a store in Newbourgh that gave a military 10 percent discount. So we took the plunge and bought on time, with a small down payment, a set for twelve of the *Romance of the Sea* pattern by Wallace. Our tastes already then proved to be quite similar, because we agreed independently on the pattern we preferred.

Unfortunately, at West Point, with the exception of a few dinner parties, we didn't get to entertain as much as we thought we would. Chester's family, as well as my family (with the exception of Mother, who learned how to take the bus) were too busy or too lazy to make the effort. Nina Versakos, my friend from Regensburg (who is now Nina Goloub and whom we located in Paterson, New Jersey, after a prolonged search) was our first house guest.

During our stay at West Point we spent most of the holidays either with

Chester's family in Rhode Island, with Mother in New York City, or in Lakewood with the Shlykovs. When driving to any of these places, if the weather allowed, we usually drove with the roof down. The speed limits then were relatively low and the roads were mostly free of heavy traffic. You could relax and enjoy the ride, instead of rushing to get from place to place. One time, on a hot, sunny day, while we were driving in our open car on the Connecticut Parkway, Mother was sitting in the back seat with a huge floppy Mexican sombrero hat firmly attached to her head. Almost everyone in the passing cars couldn't help but turn around with a smile to look at her, probably wondering how it was possible for the hat not to fly off. The trick was in the elastic bands she had attached to the hat, pulling them under her chin, thus at a distance they were invisible to the passengers in other cars.

All in all, our assignment at the academy was one very joyful, prolonged honeymoon! My regret until this day is that I wish I knew then what I know now! Our life at the Point would probably have been even fuller. Nevertheless, whatever improvements might have been made, those gorgeous days were a great start for the years to follow.

Shortly after I got married and left the Second Avenue apartment, Mother relocated as well. She took a sewing job at a small plant in downtown New York and rented a room in the apartment of the Chwetczuks, who had been with us in Kleine Maria Zell and later escaped with us to Bavaria. The stay at their apartment turned out to be a good thing for Mother, now that she had been abandoned by me. She had all the care and love she might need from the very warm Serafima Chwetczuk. Her husband had recently decided to change his last name to Federal. It seems he was tired of hearing his name mispronounced and having to spell it constantly. He also decided to leave Serafima and to relocate to Poland to be with a former Polish lover, so Serafima was glad to have Mother's company. Eventually, Federal parted with his mistress and returned to Serafima, who nursed him until his death after he suffered a stroke. Both Serafima and Mother occasionally got catering jobs at the Pakistani consulate, preparing food for official receptions. For them the jobs were enjoyable diversions as well as being very well paid. After each party they were allowed to take home all the leftovers, which were often enough to feed an army. After a time, however, the Shlykovs as well as the Padukows, who had recently settled near the Shlykovs, persuaded Mother to relocate to Lakewood. The Shlykovs' house, although not quite finished, had a finished basement in which Misha was able to make a comfortable "pad" for himself, so that Sonya and Mother had a little more room in the shack. Mother's new job was a few miles away outside Lakewood. It was at a small sewing establishment that produced children's coats. Later, both our daughters had beautiful coats for every occasion or season.

Misha was happy to see his favorite sister-in-law relocate and was quite willing to deliver her to and from work. While Sonya was busy cooking, Misha enjoyed conversing with Mother and discussing his numerous schemes for making money. And, of course, he was glad to have a smoking and drinking companion. When Mother came home from work and Sonya's chicken coop and household chores were done, Misha was pleased to drive them to one of the many nearby beaches in the Seaside Heights area for a snack, a stroll on the boardwalk, or a swim in the open Atlantic.

Once the two-story house was finished and furnished, Misha finally had a proper bedroom for himself, while Sonya slept on a sofa bed in the living room. On the ground floor there was also a separate dining room, bathroom and a large kitchen. Two bedrooms and a bath made up the entire second floor. The two bedrooms quickly found tenants. One was rented to Nikolay Gorin and the other, after several temporary tenants, was rented by Mr. Tokarev. Unfortunately, the house plan did not provide any room for Mother. When she realized that she would like to stay permanently in the Lakewood area, she asked the Shlykovs if they would not consider letting her add to the house an extra bedroom and bath, the construction of which she would pay for. For some reason or other, they did not agree. There was no room at the inn. Mother continued to sleep on the other sleeper sofa next to Sonya until she took a new job at a nearby resort area as a live-in companion to an elderly woman stricken by cancer. The job was relatively easy. There was a German cook, a gardener, and a chauffeur who would drive the lady of the house and Mother on various outings. Mother's patient liked to have various groups of women friends come to the house to play bridge, during which time Mother often played the role of hostess. Later on, interspersed with her frequent travels in the U.S. and abroad, many jobs followed. The jobs provided her with comfortable housing, so for the time being she didn't worry about her retirement years. Since she had always liked to live out of a suitcase, this mode of life suited her fine. She was able to have her cake and eat it, too. She was always ready and willing to join the Shlykovs in the many parties that were taking place in Lakewood. At these, beautiful as she was in those years, she was always the queen bee. Many of our photos show Mother, the only woman in the snapshot, sitting in the center surrounded by eight or more men! During those times, there were many serious suitors, primarily Russians, but there were also some Poles and even a couple of Americans. It was a happy time for Mother, who simply thrived on the attention and admiration she aroused.

When Mother finally retired, she decided to settle permanently in Lakewood, renting a small cottage on Alexander Avenue, on the same street and within walking distance of both the Shlykov's chicken farm and the property of the Padukows (her sister Aniuta and husband Kolya). Intimately involved in the lives and activities of her relatives and accepting various duties in support of the Russian Orthodox church in Lakewood, Mother felt happy and fulfilled.

In July of 1952, Chester's tour of duty at West Point having come to an end, we moved to Montgomery, Alabama, where Chester was assigned to take the senior officers command and staff course at Maxwell Air Force Base. The long drive through the pervasive summer heat of the southern states seemed to mark the end to my long and involved struggle to escape the evils of the war, as I realized the bliss of being safely in the United States, happily married, and expecting the birth of the first of my two daughters.

Appendix:
Who's Who in the Extended Romenko-Kovenko Family

Note: Around the time of World War I, family members began dropping the use of the Kovenko portion of the Romenko-Kovenko surname, except in official documents.

**Anton ROMENKO-KOVENKO (in Polish, *Romenko-Kowenko)* (dates of birth and death unknown)—my maternal great-grandfather

Nikita ROMENKO-KOVENKO (1869–March 12, 1956)—my maternal grandfather

Anastasiya Semenovna YANCHUK (*Janczuk*) (1873–March 20, 1911)—my maternal grandmother

Ustin'ya Danilovna, surname unknown (1859–1943)—Nikita's second wife; was referred to as Machekha (stepmother)

Anna KUCHARSKA-MACIOLEK (?–1936)—my paternal grandmother

Wawrzyniec MACIOLEK (?–1941)—my father's stepfather

Yelizaveta (Liza) ROMENKO-KOVENKO KUCHARSKA (Nov. 30, 1906–Oct. 29, 2007)—my mother

Feliks KUCHARSKI (June 2, 1897–Feb. 6, 1941)—my father

Lucyna Bozenna KUCHARSKA RADLO (May 16, 1931–)—me

Anna (Anyuta) ROMENKO-KOVENKO PADUKOW* (Feb. 13, 1893–May 9, 1957)—my aunt, Mother's oldest sister

Nikolay (Kolya) PADUKOW (Nov. 25, 1885–Oct. 25, 1975)—Anna's husband

Arkadyy PADUKOW (1913–Nov. 1940)—oldest son

---

*Transliteration from Russian of this surname is Padyukov, but family members living abroad preferred the modified Polish spelling Padukow.

Sergey PADUKOW (Oct. 23, 1922–Oct. 22, 1993)—youngest son

Sergey ROMENKO-KOVENKO (Sept. 13, 1893–March 28, 1978)—my uncle, Mother's oldest brother

Mariya (*Maria*) ROMENKO-KOVENKO BOGUTA (1894–1929)—my aunt, Mother's older sister

Nina BOGUTA (Feb. 1, 1912–Jan. 3, 1999)—oldest daughter

Lidya (*Lidja*) BOGUTA (June 19, 1921–)—youngest daughter

Sofiya (Sonya) ROMENKO-KOVENKO SHLYKOV (Aug. 18, 1902–Jan. 7, 1986)—my aunt, Mother's older sister

Mikhail (*Michael*) (Misha) SHLYKOV (Oct. 21, 1900–July 15, 1975)—Sonya's husband

Igor (Guga) SHLYKOV (Nov. 11, 1922–executed 1943?)—son

Yelena ROMENKO-KOVENKO DEVYATNIKOVA (1904–1928)—my aunt, Mother's older sister

Pyotr (Piotr, Petr or Petya) ROMENKO-KOVENKO (1900–1920)—my uncle, Mother's younger brother

Olga ROMENKO-KOVENKO VAKUL'CHIK (July 24, 1910–May 31, 1993)—my aunt, Mother's youngest sister

Georgiy (*Zhorzh*) VAKUL'CHIK (May 20, 1909–Dec. 3, 1990)—Olga's husband

Yuriy (Yura) VAKUL'CHIK (May 20, 1934–)—oldest son

Mikhail (Misha) VAKUL'CHIK (Nov. 15, 1941–June 1, 1971)—middle son

Aleksander (Sasha) VAKUL'CHIK (1939–1990?)—youngest son

Index

Numbers in *bold italics* indicate pages with photographs.

Agardy, Dr. Zoltan 177
Agentura Sledcza przy XIII Komisariacie, Warsaw *109*
Aleje Szucha (Gestapo HQ), Warsaw 84
Alexander the First (czar) 12
Armia Krajowa (AK) 57, 94, 104, 105
Armia Ludowa (People's Army) 105, 106, 109
Augunas, Claudia 225
Augunas, Dennis 225
Augunas, Elizabeth ("Betty") 225
Auschwitz (*Konzentrationslager Auschwitz*) 55, 75, 91–93

Babich, Ivan Kornilovich 28
Bar Pod Beczka, Brest 22
Beran, DDS 144
Bereza Kartuska 99
Biala Podlaska, Poland 60
Bialowieska Puszcza, Poland 28, 29
Bialy Dom, Warsaw 33
Bialy Palac, Brest 24
Birkenau (Brzezinka) 92
Black Madonna 134
Black Market (*Handel*) 94
Boguta, Ivan 14, 18
Boguta (Babich), Nina Ivanovna 8, 14, 18
Boguta, Leonid Ivanovich 18, 41
Boguta (Prolisko), Lidiya Ivanovna 8, 18
Boguta (Romenko-Kowenko), Mariya Nikitichna 4, 8, 10, 11, 18
Bor-Komorowski, Gen. 33, 104
Bradley, Gen. Omar 213, 214
Breitungen /Werra 119; *see also* Lager Kirchberg
Brest 6, 18, 50
Brest Pogrom 13
Brestskoye Trishinskoye Kladbishche (Brest Cemetery) 11, 18
Brode 44
Bronnaya Gora 99

Brzesc (Brest), Poland 3
Bug (river) 5, 10, 59
Bukraba, Kazimierz, Ks. 28
Buna Werke 92
Burgstoller, Gene 211
Burski-Goldenberg, Arkadiusz *107*

Chabowska, A. 32
Chabowska (Piasecka), Janina 32
Chabowska, Stefania 32
Chabowski, Stanislaw 32, 94
Church World Service 176, 184
Chwiedczuk, Boris Petrovich 119
Chwiedczuk, Gleb Petrovich 12
Chwiedczuk, Petr 119, 125
Chwiedczuk, Serafima 103, 120, 250
Cistercian Monastery (Valley Falls, R.I.) 224
Clark, Gen. Mark 214
Cukernia Paciokorskiego 75, 79
Czerwony Dwor 7; *see also* Krasnyy Dvor

De Mattos, Maj. Heitor 244
De Mattos, Lourdes 244
Design Registration Bureau of the National Federation of Textiles, Inc. 195
Devyatnikova (Romenko-Kowenko), Yelena Nikitichna 8, 10, 13–15, 19, 28, 41
Drzewiecka (Makowiecka), Nina 52, 79, 98
Durchlassschein 100, 101
Dzieci Podworza (courtyard children) 76
Dziennik Narodowy 52, 53

Eichmann, Adolf 56
Eisenhower, Gen. Dwight 214
Eisenhower, Maj. John 244
Enter, Col. Ted 214

Fahrkarte to Kleine Maria Zell *118*
Filatiev, Aleksander (Alexander, "Sasha") Aleksandrovich *142*, 198

Filatiev, Olga Fedorovna 159, 199
Filatiev, Yelena Sergeyevna ("Lena") 199
Fiodoroff, Prof. Nikolay Nikolayevich 126
Flaumenbaum (Pflaumenbaum), Roza ("Rozia") 134, 138, 153
Frank, Hans 4
Fuksman 5, 47, 99
Fuksman, Abram 5, 52, 84, 99
Fuksman, Oleg ("Oles") 83, 84

Garrison Hospital, Brest 18
General Government (*Generalna Gubernia*) 4
Generalgouvernement Kennkarte 72
Ghetto: Brest Litovsk 56, 99; Lodz 6; Treblinka 56; Tuliszkow 56; Warsaw 56, 57
Gierszewski, Bruno 134
Gimnazjum im. Traugutta, Brest 9
Goldenberg-Burski, Arkadiusz *107*
Gora Kalwaria 104
Gorin, Nikolay 251
Gorska 45
Guletski, Maj. Walter 190, 244
Gutkiewicz, Dr. Bruno 104, 111, 175
Guzinska (Ozimek), Irena 146, 161, 177, 240, 243
Guzinski, Marian 177
Gypsies 55, 91

Haczynska (Radlo), Anna 225
Haegelsparger, Joseph 129
Hajnowka, Poland 28, 30
Hilgenberg, George 186
Himmler, Heinrich, *Reichsfuhrer* SS 91
Homberger, Albert 173, 174
Horbacewicz, Halina 161
Hospice ("Sarah House," Santa Barbara) 239
Hotel Europejski, Brest 38
Hotel Rzymski, Brest 38
Hoza 19, 52, 75–84, 86
Hunt, Howard 211
Hurko, Yevgeniy ("Genek") 177

identity card (Kucharska) *106*
identity card (Sonya) *105*
invasion of Poland by Nazi Germany 3
Ivanovs (of Vyazma) 15

Jehle, Dieter 134
Jehle, Helmut 134
Jehle, Oberrat (Regensburg City Council) 134, 142
Jews in Brest, Poland 50, 51
Jews in Poland and Europe 50, 51, 55, 91–93, 119

Kaniewski 75
Kasa Chorych 89; see also *Ubezpieczalnia spoleczna*
Katyn 19

Kennon, George (Ambassador to Moscow) 188, 189, 192
Kercelak (Warsaw flea market) 57
Kielbasa, Peter 212
Kilczewska 25, 27
Kirshanov *142*
Klein (Barton's Candy Factory) 193
Kleine Maria Zell, Austria "102, *118*, 119, 120, 123
Kobylin, Viktor Sergeyevich *142*
Komorowski, Mieczyslaw ("Mitya") *40*
Korol, Dr. Igor Pavlovich 19, 20
Korol (Sosnowska), Janina 20
Korol, Mikolaj 19, 20
Korol, (Leszczynski-Trojekarow), Nelly 20
Korol, Maj. Pavel 19, 20
Korolkov, S.G. 126
Kosciuchnowka, Poland 107
Kosciuszko, Gen. Tadeusz 245
Kovelskiy Most, Brest 46
Kozlovski 191
Krasnyy Dvor 7, 10, 17, 24, 28, 48
Kresy Export Association of Agricultural Products 10
Kszeminski, Waclaw 82, 98
Kucharska, (Maciolek) Anna 32, 33, 88, *89*
Kucharska, Yelizaveta Nikitichna (Elzbieta, "Liza") 14, 16, 33, *34*, *37*, *108*, 227–251; see also Romenko-Kowenko, Yelizaveta Nikitichna
Kucharski, Feliks 28, 30, 33, 54, 88, 89, *92*, 93, 232; arrest at Hoza 19, 83, 84; Pawiak Prison 84, 85; death in Auschwitz 86, 87
Kujawa, Jan 134
Kulczynska, Anna 63
Kulczynska, Elzbieta 63, 65
Kulczynska, Emilia 63
Kulczynski, Dr. Stanislaw 63, 64
Kunkel, Capt. 231, 232
Kutno, Poland 30
Kwiatkowska, Hanka 138
Kwiatkowski, Klemens 134

Labor Camp (Lager Kirchberg) 111–119
Lager Kirchberg *Bestatigung* (verification) *116*
Lapczynska, Mariya Ivanovna 14
Lapczynska (Romenko-Kowenko), Sophia Antonovna ("Lyolya") 8, 10
Lapczynska, Yelena Ivanovna, ("Lena") see Ugrinowicz, Yelena
Lapczynski, Anton Ivanovich 14
Lapczynski, Jan ("Yoan") 8
Legawiec, Walter 212, 240
Legiony (The Polish Legions) 88
Leitao (Radlo), Marion 225
Leszczynski-Trojekarov, Miroslaw (Mira) 20
Leszczynski-Trojekarov, Prince 20
Levine, Lt. Don 213
Lipinski, Maj. Waclaw 33, *107*
Lissner, Alfred 82, 98, 115

Litzmannstadt (Lodz) 55
Lobachev, Ludmilla 24; *see also* Shlykov,
  Ludmilla
Lodz, Poland 32
Lodz Cemetery 33
Lomov, Georgiy Vasil'yevich 160, 171, 176
Lukaszhuk, Georgiy 28
Lukaszhuk (Romenko-Kowenko), Nina
  Lukyenichna 18, 194
Lutovs (of Vyazma) 14

MacArthur, Gen. Douglas 196
Maciolek (Kucharska), Anna 32, 88, *89*
Maciolek, Wawrzyniec 7, 32, 33, 88, *90*
Mainingen, Germany *118*
Makowiecka, Nina *see* Drzewiecka, Nina
Maksimowicz, Alla 52, 79, 98
Mansfetov 188, 189
Marschbefehl 102
Mazur (shoemaker) 77, 78
Mentelhof, Ludmilla 24; *see also* Shlykov,
  Ludmilla
Mercer, Viola 196
Messner (Lukashuk), Yelena Georgiyevna
  ("Lyalya," Helen) 194
*Metalenwaren-fabrik Scharfenberg & Teubert
  Gmbh*, Breitungen/Werra 112
Miedzychod nad Warta, Poland 30, 31
Mikhailov, Aleksander Feodorovich *142*
Mikhailov, Rev. Feodor 140, *142*
Mikulec, Rev. 240
Mirski, Maj. Michael 244
Montgomery, Gen. Bernard 214
Muchawiec River, Brest 10, 11, 13, 39, *39*, *40*

Nachtausweis 73
Nazarevich, Ivan 15
Nekrasov, Anastasiya Nikolayevna 135
Nekrasov, Paul Sergeyevich 135
Nekrasov, Sergey Ivanovich 135, 142
Niemierwrzycki, Kazimierz 18, *28*, *29*, 41
Nosek, Col. Edward 33, 85
Nosek, Hanka 80, 81, 85
Nowogrodzka ulitsa 43, 43, 53, 69

Olszewski, Kurcjusz 176, 179
Opat (*Herr und Frau*) 143
Operation Reinhard 56, 57
Oswiecim-Brzezinka (Auschwitz-Birkenau-
  Familienlager) 55
Ovchinnikov 151, 168
Ozarow capitulation 110
Ozimek, Irena *see* Guzinska, Irena

Pacholski, Maj. Marian 33
Paciorkowski, Mr. 77
Padukow (Romenko-Kowenko), Anna
  Nikitichna 14, 15, 18, 19, *37*, *38*, 42, 53,
  99, 203
Padukow, Arkadiy Nikolayevich 14, 15, *37*,
  38, 53, 72, 74, 175

Padukow, Georgiy Nikolayevich 15, 17
Padukow, Gerda 161, 175
Padukow, Nikolay Nikiforovich 3, 5, 8,
  13–15, 17–19, *32*, 53, 102, 175
Padukow, Sergey Nikolayevich 18, *37*, *38*,
  39, *40*, 53, 72
Padukow, Taisya Nikolayevna 15
Pawiak Prison, Warsaw) 84, 85
Pegsa (Osuchowska), Kazimiera 95
Pfeiffer, Gen. Edward ("Radwan") 33, 104,
  105, 107, *108*
Pflaumenbaum *see* Flaumenbaum
Piasecka (Chabowska), Janina *see*
  Chabowska, Janina
Piastow, Poland 68, 69
Pietkiewicz-Golownicki *Wedliniarnia* (meat
  products plant) 36
Pilsudski, Jozef, Marshal 33, 39, 88
Platek, Col. M.D. 33
Pogrom, Brest 50, 51
Polanska, Nina *36*, 138, 139, 149, 160, 168,
  240
Polesie Clinic of Medical Specialists (*Poleska
  Lecznica Lekarzy Specialistow*), Brest 19
Polesie (Marshland), Poland 10
Poligon (Training Base), Brest 24
Polish School *im. Gorskiej*, Brest 45
Popov, Gen. *142*
Poznan, Poland 63
Poznanski 63, 64
Prokofiev, Ludmilla 161, 176, 179
Prokofiev, Victor 161, 176
Proskuriakov, Aleksander 171, 177
Proskuriakov, Dr. Nikolay 111, 171, 172, 176,
  234
Pruszkow, Poland 112, 112
Puszcza Bialowieska, Poland 28, 29
Puszcza Radlowska, Poland 207

Radlo, Adam 225
Radlo, Agata 225
Radlo, Anastazy (monk) 207
Radlo, Anna 209
Radlo, Antoni (Anthony, Tony) 209, 225
Radlo, Bishop 207
Radlo, Carolyn ("Carrie") 201
Radlo, Chester 185, 188–191, 201, 206–226
Radlo, Edward J. ("Eddie") 216
Radlo, Dr. Edward Z. 208–226
Radlo (Cassels), Elizabeth ("Ellie") 202,
  244
Radlo, Franciszek 225
Radlo (Augunas), Genevieve ("Jennie") 225
Radlo, John 209
Radlo (Walek), Julia 207–226
Radlo, Katarzyna 225
Radlo, Leo 207–226
Radlo (Kucharska), Lucyna B.: birth,
  Miedzychod nad Warta 30; childhood
  memories 30, 32, 33, 52; emigration 175;
  first Holy Communion 95, 96, *96*; *Gim-*

nazjum 137, 146; piano lessons 56, 139; recreation 156–162, 164; translator's school 147; West Point, NY 240–252; work 111, 193, 195
Radlo, Marcin 225
Radlo, Maria 225
Radlo, Nicholas 214, 215
Radlo, Robert ("Bobby") 225
Radlo, Sophie ("Sue") 216–226
Radlo, Stanislaw 209
Radlo, Teresa 225
Radlo, Victoria ("Viktusia," "Stryjecia") 225
Radlo, Walenty 225
Radlo, Wawrzyniec 207, 225–226
Radwan (pseudonym) *see* Pfeiffer, Edward
Rainbow Farms Meat Products 186
Rajpold, Roman 5, 52, 53, 78, 80, 98, 108
Rajpold, Ziuta 78, 79
Raubel (Shlykov), Irina 27
Regensburg (bombing by Allies) 117
Regional Hospital No. IX, Brest 18
Ribbentrop-Molotov Agreement 6
Romenko-Kowenko (Yanchuk, Janchuk), Anastasiya Semenovna 8, 10, 11
Romenko-Kowenko, Anna Nikitichna ("Anyuta") *see* Padukov, Anna Nikitichna
Romenko-Kowenko, Anna Nikolayevna 10
Romenko-Kowenko, Anton 7, 18
Romenko-Kowenko, Fiokla Nikitichna 10
Romenko-Kowenko, Luka Nikolayevich 10, 18, *37*
Romenko-Kowenko, Mariya Nikitichna *see* Boguta, Mariya Nikitichna
Romenko-Kowenko, Nikita Antonovich 8, 10, 11, 13–17, 19, *37*, 38, 47–49, 53, 175
Romenko-Kowenko, Nikolay Antonovich 10
Romenko-Kowenko, Nina Lukyenichna *see* Lukashuk, Nina Lukyenichna
Romenko-Kowenko, Olga Nikitichna *see* Vakul'chik, Olga Nikitichna
Romenko-Kowenko, Prokop Antonovich 10, Romenko-Kowenko, Pyotr Nikitich 8, 10, 14, 17, 18, *42*
Romenko-Kowenko, Sergey Nikitich 3, 8, 10, 14, 17, 18, *42*, 48
Romenko-Kowenko, Sophia Antonovna ("Lyolya") *see* Lapczynska, Sophia Antonovna
Romenko-Kowenko, Sophia Nikitichna ("Sonya") 8, 10, 13, 14, 15, *28*, 45, 46; *see also* Shlykov, Sophia Nikitichna
Romenko-Kowenko, Tatyana 7
Romenko-Kowenko, Ustin'ya Danilovna ("Machekha") 11, 12, 14, 19, 38
Romenko-Kowenko, Vasiliy Antonovich 10, 13
Romenko-Kowenko, Yekaterina Lukyenichna ("Katya") 18
Romenko-Kowenko, Yelena Nikitichna ("Lena") *see* Devyatnikova, Yelena Nikitichna
Romenko-Kowenko, Yelizaveta Nikitichna 8, 10, 12, 14–16, 18, 24, *27*, *28*, *38*, *44*, *46*; *see also* Kucharska, Elizabeth
Romenko-Kowenko, Yevgeniya Nikolayena 10
Rosenkrantz 144, 152
Rosenzweig, Dr. 180
Rosinska (Tloczko) ("Dusia") 4, 9
Rosinska, Krystyna 4, 9, 33
Rosinski, Maj. Żygmunt 4
Rosyjskie Towarzystwo Dobroczynnosci 19
roundups, ambushes (*Lapanki*, *Oblawy*) 54, 94
Rova Farms, N.J. 187
Rowno, Poland 30
Ruda (estate near Brest) 20
Russian Church Cemetery, Jackson, N.J. 229
Russian Cossacks (ambush) 125
Russian Good Deeds Society 19
Rys-Trojanowski, Gen. Mieczyslaw 33

Sadowski, Capt. 19
Sales, Molly 213–215
San Remo, Italy 230
Scardemalia, Maj. 230
Shaitaroff, Mrs. 193, 198
Shaitaroff, Yakov ("Yasha") 188, 198
Shchukin steel foundry, Vyazma 14, 15
Shebalin, Emilia Andreyevna 199, 200
Shebalin, Natalia ("Natasha") Sergeyevna 200, 240
Shebalin, Sergey Konstantinovich 191, 200
Shkurin, Gen. 125
Shlykov (Charynskaya), Aleksandra Georgiyevna 22
Shlykov (Trojanowska), Anna ("Hanka") 27
Shlykov, Igor ("Guga") Mikhailovich 18, *26*, *37*, 39, *40*, 53, 71, 72, 74, 96, *97*, *99*, 175
Shlykov (Raubel), Irina 27
Shlykov, Ivan Vasil'yevich 20, 23, 27, *29*, 53, 175
Shlykov (Lobachev), Ludmilla 24
Shlykov, Marta 23, 24
Shlykov, Michael (Mikhail, "Misha") Vasil'yevich 1, 7, 9, 18, 20, 22, 29, 36, 39, *40*, *41*, *49*, 53, *68*, *71*, 99, *142*, 175
Shlykov, Sophia ("Sonya") Nikitichna 18, 20, 22, *26*, *34*, *37*, 39, *40*, 53, 175
Shlykov, Vasiliy Filipovich 22
Shlykov (Mentelhof), Vera Vasil'yevna 20, 22, 24, *26*
Shlykov, Vladimir Vasil'yevich 20, 22, 175
Shlykov, Yevgeniya Vsil'yevna 20, 22
Shmurlo, Lt. Col. Leonard 18
Shock, Capt. Edward 149, 173
Sierpc, Poland 30
Sologub 72
Sosnowska (Korol), Janina 20
Spooner (Radlo), Bridget ("Bertha") 225
Spooner, Mary Jane 225

Starikov, Rev. M. 140
Starikov, Rt. Rev. M. 140
Stroop, Jurgen (SS commander) 57
Szamatuly 30
Szkola im. Gorskiej, Brest 45, 46
Szmugiel (Smuggling) 57, 58
Szyszkowska, Boguslawa ("Bogunia") 64
Szyszkowska, Emilia ("Mila") 58, 61–67
Szyszkowska, Franciszka 61, 62, 64
Szyszkowska, Izabella 58, *59*–61, 64, 65
Szyszkowski, Hipolit 61, 63, 64
Szyszkowski, Kazimierz 60
Szyszkowski, Leon 61, 62

Taquey 188, 189, 193
Terespol (Terespol nad Bugiem), Poland 5,
    58–60
Tloczko ("Dusia") *see* Rosinska, "Dusia"
Tloczko, Janina 4
Tokarev 251
Tomann 191
Tomaszow Mazowiecki 30
Treaty of Brest-Litovsk 16
Treaty of Riga 18
Treaty of Yalta and Teheran 125
Turn-und-Taxis 118
Tyszkiewicz, Count Benedykt Henryk,
    Count 7

Ubezpieczalnia Spoleczna, Sierpc 30;
    Hajnowka 28; Kalisz 89; Kutno 30;
    Miedzychod nad Warta 30; Rowno 30;
    Szamotuly 30; Tomaszow Mazowiecki 30
Ugrinowicz (Lapczynska), Yelena Ivanovna
    14, 112
Ulbrich, Aleksey Vasil'yevich ("Alex") 150,
    153, 159
Ulbrich, Olga Vasil'yevna 150

Vakul'chik, Georgiy ("Zhorzh") 3, 7, 11, *37*,
    41, *44*
Vakul'chik, Mikhail Georgiyevich 11
Vakul'chik (Romenko-Kovenko), Olga
    Nikitichna 8, 10, 11, 14–16, 18, 29, 37, *44*,
    53
Vakul'chik, Yuriy Georgievich 6
Vasiliy, Father (Rev.) 140, *142*
Vienna (arrival at) 117
Volkman (*Lagerfuhrer*) 112, 117
Von Brevern, Dmitriy 2, 53, 69–71, 99, 102

Von Brevern, Mariya ("Marusya") 53, 69
Von Brevern, Wanda 53, 69, *70*
Vyazma, Russia 14
Vydacha Kazakov (*Surrendering the Cossacks*)
    125

Walek, Antoni 225
Walek, Francis 225
Walek, Genevieve 225
Walek, Ignacy 225
Walek, John 225
Walek, Joseph "Joe" 225
Walek, Julia 225
Walek, Marija 225
Walek, Mary 225
Walek, Michal 225
Walek, Raymond "Ray" 225
Walek, Stefania 225
Walek, Valerie 225
Walek, Wojciech 225
Walek, Zofia 225
Walhalla (Valhalla) 150
Wanatowicz, Aldona 162
Wansee Conference 91
Warsaw Uprising 57, 66, 67, 69, 104–110
West Point, N.Y. 240
White Russians 72
Wieniawa-Dlugoszewski, Gen. Boleslaw 35
Wojda, Zygmunt 161
Wojewodzka, Cecylia ("Lusia") 76
Wolf, Eugenia ("Gena") 143, 157, 158, 165
Wolf, "Kristl" 143, 157, *167*
Wolf, Walter 143, 153, 162, 176
Woodberry, Capt. 157, 158, 173
Woodlawn Cemetery, Lakewood, N.J. 91

Zabolotny *142*, 173
Zajac, Celia 225
Zajac, Josephine 225
Zajac, Mary 225
Zajac, Michaline 225
Zajac, Stella 225
Zajac, Wanda 225
Zaslawski, Count 231
Zhgun, Mariya Gavrilovna 124
Zhgun, Tamara 124
Zhgun, Timofey Ivanovich 124
Zigeunerlager-Litzmannstadt 55
Znosko, Rt. Rev. 99, 231
Zylberszteyn 51